EDUCATION IN
METROPOLITAN
AREAS

EDUCATION IN
METROPOLITAN
AREAS

❧ Robert J. Havighurst, *1900–*

Professor of Education
University of Chicago and
University of Missouri

❧ Allyn and Bacon, Inc.
Boston

FIRST PRINTING . . . AUGUST, 1966
SECOND PRINTING . . . JUNE, 1966

PRINTED IN THE UNITED STATES OF AMERICA
LIBRARY OF CONGRESS CATALOG CARD NO. 66–23955

❧ Preface

This book is about metropolitanism—not about urbanism or suburbanism. It looks at education from the point of view of the metropolitan area as a whole.

The standard metropolitan statistical area, as defined by the Census Bureau, is a city of 50,000 or more including its surrounding county and any contiguous counties that are functionally bound to the major city.

Metropolitanism is the result of a process of redistribution of people and jobs which has taken place during the present century. This process has brought people from rural areas into the city, and then caused them to overflow the city limits and to build up suburbs. Like urbanism, it is becoming a way of life, made up of habits and attitudes and expectations. Unlike urbanism, this way of life is not confined to a city and to city life.

Thus, the metropolitan area came into existence at first as a simple geographical area occupied by people who had some of their business in common. But the metropolitan area was more complex than the city in its governmental and economic and social structure. Problems were created by this complexity. Municipal boundaries had to be adjusted. Many people did not live in the municipalities where they worked. To what unit should they pay taxes? The metropolitan area was fragmented into cities, towns, and unincorporated areas; into a variety of school districts; into park districts, water districts, and sewage disposal districts. Something had to take the place of the city, something with unity, to bring order out of the chaos.

The metropolitan area is taking the place of the city. People of all kinds increasingly think of the metropolitan area as their community. Educators, government officials and businessmen are developing a theory and a practice of the relations of the physical environment to human satisfactions in the metropolitan area. The attention of educators will be increasingly fixed on the development of the metropolitan area rather than the growth or decline of a city, or the proliferation of suburbs.

Metropolitanism is at one and the same time a set of *events* occurring in contemporary society and a set of *goals* or *tasks* which society should achieve if it is to become a better society.

These two aspects of metropolitanism will be treated in this book. They will be kept separate, as far as possible. The facts of metropolitan development will be presented with special reference to the schools. The ways of improving the schools through metropolitan area cooperation will be discussed as part of the general task of improving the conditions of life in the United States.

The first half of the book is a systematic description of metropolitan social structure and the evolution of the contemporary metropolitan area. Its aim is to help the student understand the society in which he lives and the way the school system functions in this society.

The second half of the book deals with the sharp changes that are taking place during the present decade, as men try to do something about the problems of metropolitan growth, complexity, and stratification. Urban renewal is the key concept of one chapter, and social integration the topic of another. Teachers must understand the situation and must learn new tasks. Consequently, a chapter is devoted to the teacher in the metropolitan school system.

The book closes with a general analysis of the social systems of a metropolitan area, showing how the school system is related to other systems, such as the local government, the private school system, the cultural agencies, the welfare agencies. The school must cooperate both in planning for the future and in doing its present job with these other social systems. As it adopts new functions, teachers and administrators must adapt their roles to the new demands.

❧ Acknowledgments

This book is an outgrowth of an interest the author began to develop in 1960, when he started to teach a course on "Education in the Big City." As a consequence, he wrote a chapter on "Metropolitan Problems and Education" for the book *Society and Education,* which he and Professor Bernice Neugarten were revising in 1962. Then the writer expanded the earlier material and brought it up to date to include the discussion of recent metropolitan developments.

In writing the present version the author has had the advice of Professor Neugarten. Also the author has been stimulated by conversations with Professor Alan Campbell of Syracuse University, whose comprehensive view of metropolitanization makes him one of the frontier workers in this new area.

The author is especially grateful to his wife, Edythe Havighurst, who has typewritten the manuscript, sometimes in several versions, and has looked after some of the laborious details that go into the making of a book.

ℛ Table of Contents

ix

1 ❧ Metropolitan Schools and Social Structure

Three Schools of the Metropolis

Mrs. James walked into the Whittier School at 8:15, smiled at the school clerk who had just opened the door of the principal's office, and went up to her second floor classroom, which had the number 212 and the name Fifth Grade stenciled in black paint above the door. She opened a window to let in the spring air, and looked out a moment at the children as they sauntered into the playground.

Whittier was a good place to work, in a good area to live. She was glad she could live within walking distance of school, and could go home for lunch; or bring a sandwich to eat when she wanted to be sociable with the other teachers, most of whom lived farther away. She had been teaching at Whittier for 15 years; she had gone back to teaching after her children were grown.

By this time some of the children were entering the room, in couples or small groups. Sidney came in with his friend Jim, whose father was a bus driver. Sidney's father had a drug store in the neighborhood. He was a smart Jewish youngster who knew he was going to be a doctor when he grew up. Jim was new this year. His family had moved into a six-flat apartment on the edge of the district where rents were low, and not far from a public housing project that had some real "trash" living in it, Mrs. James thought. Jim was a kind of rough diamond, and would make good in school, she was sure. She was glad to see him chumming with Sidney, because she thought Sidney would stir up Jim's good mind, which didn't get much stimulation at home—though she liked Jim's mother whom she had met at the PTA meeting and who seemed a quiet, timid woman.

She was glad that she had nobody in her class from the housing project. They were mostly younger children, several of them Puerto Rican, who were not doing well in school. She was sure these new-comers would lower the standards of Whittier, but she thought Whittier could do something for them, if there were not too many of them. Perhaps the new school social worker would help these children get a good start in school. Whittier was lucky to have a social worker half-time on the staff, she thought. The pupils and their families were becoming so varied, with so many different kinds of people, that she was sure the school needed someone to help the families that were not accustomed to a good standard school, as Whittier had always been.

Elizabeth arrived with her friend, Alice. Both were dressed carefully, with neat cases for books, pencils and pens. Mrs. James knew their mothers in the Congregational Church. Elizabeth's father was a lawyer and Alice's father was a doctor. There was a little talk of the two families leaving the area to move to a suburb, but Mrs. James hoped this would not happen. Alice's father had his office in the down-town district, as did Elizabeth's father, and there was really nothing to keep them in the Whittier district except their friendships and their comfortable large homes.

It was now time to start the first lesson, but Mrs. James waited to see whether Bonnie would come dashing in at the last moment, making a big noise and attracting everybody's attention. This is just what happened. Bonnie was an eleven-year-old, already showing the signs of puberty, and she had a provocative way that irritated Mrs. James and made her think of the attraction this girl would be to the bigger boys in the school pretty soon. Bonnie's family was new to the community. Nobody knew her parents, but it was said that her father was not living with the family. Mrs. James had to admit to herself that she was irritated by this girl's manner. She was so different from Alice and Elizabeth. Perhaps she would be influenced by those girls, but so far there was no sign that she was interested in their friendship. Instead, she chummed with a couple of sixth-grade girls who were already causing some trouble by their interest in boys.

As the class settled down to the arithmetic lesson, Mrs. James let her mind stray to the thoughts that came more and more frequently. Might it not be just as well to quit teaching? There was plenty of work to do at home, and in the church, and soon there would be some grandchildren to visit. She could quit now and draw a small pension as soon as she was sixty. And her husband's income was ample, anyway.

There was something about the school, and about the community, that upset her sometimes now. There were changes. New kinds of children in the school. New kinds of families in the neighborhood. It seemed as though she was having to work harder to teach the children, and she was paying more attention now than formerly to where her class stood on the city-wide achievement tests.

• • •

Miss Clarabelle Nelson stood at the girls' entrance to the big old red brick school making sure that the girls formed an orderly line ready to march inside when the buzzer sounded. A big eighth-grade girl said to her, "Miss Nelson, can I talk to you after school this noon?" "Of course, Eleanor," Miss Nelson said. "Just come to my room." She knew what it was about. Eleanor wanted to ask what she should do about the two boys who were asking her to go to the movies. How much necking should she permit them? Should she pick one of them to go steady, or should she keep them both? Eleanor needed help to make up her mind, but there weren't any easy answers. What would have been a good answer for her, Clarabelle Nelson, might not work for Eleanor, whose mother was receiving Aid for Dependent Children, and who did not know her father.

It was a noisy line, waiting for the buzzer to sound, but Miss Nelson was no longer bothered by the noise, as long as it was good natured. She had learned to control the fighting that at first had frightened her. She learned the names of the girls most likely to start fights, and gained some control over them just by telling them that she would not permit fighting within school grounds. Then she reported two of them to the principal, who gave them a good talking-to in her presence, and told them that he and Miss Nelson would not stand for this kind of behavior.

Miss Nelson followed the line into the school and then climbed the stairs to the third floor where her class was making a good deal of noise. She smiled as she walked into the room and said "Good morning, boys and girls."

"Good morning, Miss Nelson," several of them said, and smiled back at her.

A big boy in the back now went over and raised a window. She had taught him to do this, and to keep an eye on the thermometer, so as to keep the room close to 70 degrees. "At least he'll make a better janitor than most of them," she thought, "because he has a sense for comfortable temperatures."

Thirty-five boys and girls stood beside their desks in five rows and, placing their hands on their hearts, they repeated the pledge of allegiance to the flag. Miss Nelson had grown to enjoy this ceremony. It was not so much the idea of patriotism, because she thought there were better ways of teaching patriotism, but it was the idea of all being together and doing the same thing equally well that she liked. There were a great many differences among pupils in this class, and it was her business to understand the differences, but she liked the idea that they were all equal in this one thing.

They were all equal, also, in the fact that they were all Negroes, though some were dark and some were light, and she had long since given up the idea that their skin color made them equal to one another or to her. When she stopped to think of it, she would have preferred a mixed class, which was what she had been used to as a child. She had never been in an all-Negro class until she came to teach in the Carver elementary school.

Growing up in a northern city of fifty thousand where there were not many Negroes, she had been one of a few colored pupils in elementary school and even fewer in high school. She knew something of segregation, because her father was the pastor of a Negro church, but she had never seen an all-Negro school until that September day, three years ago when she started her first teaching job at Carver elementary school.

It was hard for her. She hated the idea of segregation, even if it was only due to segregated housing in the city, and was not a part of a general pattern of racial segregation. What made it harder was the fact that her pupils were all slum children—children of poorly educated and low-paid people. She could hardly understand their dialects, which were different from anything she had heard among her own friends. Only a half dozen of her 36 pupils spoke English with the kind of accent and grammar to which she was accustomed. Frequently she found herself using an hour a day to coach her pupils on how to speak English—getting them to read aloud, and correcting them again and again. If only half of them had spoken clearly, she would have had an easier time. But she and a handful of pupils were in the minority, and she wondered how the minority could correct the majority. Last year she had gotten a cheap tape recorder and taught the children to record their own speech and listen to it. Some of them would stay after school to play with the tape recorder and she encouraged this.

Clarabelle Nelson had a good fifth-grade class, and she and her class were proud of it. She let them know where they stood on the arithmetic and reading tests that were given to all schools in the city. While they never ranked very high, they led the other fifth-graders at Carver, and they always made more than a year's gain when they were in her class.

They were working now, on their arithmetic, and she looked them over. Several of them were really quite good in arithmetic, and she had several special books for them with some extra material about numbers—some of the "new arithmetic" that was being developed experimentally by mathematicians trying to teach children to "think like mathematicians." But the majority were not very good, and the average of the class was in the fourth-grade level. For one thing, they did not do homework, as a rule. Very few of the children had any place to study at home, and no teacher could count on a class doing homework. In fact, few teachers even permitted children to take school books home, because they lost so many of them. Miss Nelson had some special books that she let children take home, after she got to know them well. About a third of her class could be counted on to use books at home and to bring them back in good condition.

Miss Nelson thought about that first year of teaching—that horrible first year. She couldn't understand her pupils when they talked. She couldn't stand the language she heard on the playground and in the hall, what she could understand of it. She couldn't control the pupils in class. They talked and laughed and every now and then they fought. If it had not been for the principal she would have given up after a month of it. He was an elderly white man, patient, firm with pupils, and he reminded her in some ways of her own father. He came to her room sometimes and helped her quiet the children. He helped her to find out the ones she could trust to work quietly. He worked with her at disciplining the unruly ones. And he was always optimistic about the Carver School. "This is the best thing in the lives of many of them," he said, again and again. "Some of them have good homes and they make good use of the school. Others have very poor homes, and the school is the best thing there is for them. Just to watch some of the children grow up is a joy."

Then Clarabelle had registered for an evening course at the local university, during the second semester. The course was in sociology, a subject she had never studied in teachers' college. There she learned about "culture shock," the experience of a middle-class person who comes into close contact with another culture—the culture of the lower-class Negro, in this case. This course helped her to see herself and her job more clearly, and to see how important her job was, if she could do it well.

By the end of her first year, Miss Nelson could come to school in the morning without feeling uncomfortable in her stomach. She decided to stay with it a second year, if only out of loyalty to her principal. During the second year she began to have success with some of her pupils, and she learned to control her class. Then she began to measure the progress her class was making, compared with other classes in similar schools. She and her class became proud of each other.

By the end of her second year, Clarabelle Nelson had enough seniority to be able to apply for a transfer to another school—an all-white school, or one in a mixed neighborhood where more middle-class Negroes lived. But by this time she decided to stay at Carver. She would not spend her life teaching at Carver. She was engaged to be married, and probably she would quit teaching to have a family. But she knew, now, that she liked to teach in a school like Carver, and if they still had such schools when she was middle-aged and might resume teaching, 15 or 20 years from now, she would choose Carver again.

• • •

Miss Bond was seated at her desk in a corner of the room as her fifth-graders came in from the schoolgrounds. They went first to the coatroom to hang up their coats and then to their seats. A few gathered in little groups, talking to one another. School would not start for another two or three minutes. Looking out the window Miss Bond could see other children arriving, many of them in automobiles driven by their mothers, with a child occasionally coming in a long black Cadillac driven by a chauffeur wearing a dark cap. Other children walked from nearby houses.

She rose to pull the drapery across one window where the morning sun bore in too directly. Outside, she could see the sloping curve of the grounds landscaped with dark firs and spruces. The children played in the large field on the other side of the building. Now the last boy sauntered in, and the class was slowly getting to work, most of them at their desks grouped in one half of the room, while a few were sitting at worktables using reference books. It was a large, light, airy room, with green blackboards and green-colored bulletin boards on which brightly colored posters were mounted. The fluorescent lights were not needed this morning, but it was cool, and the floor was comfortably warmed by inlaid heating coils.

Forest Park School was a show place, and Miss Bond felt fortunate to be able to work in such a fine building, in the finest suburb of the metropolis. For five years now she had taught in this school, after ten years at Homeville. She was an excellent teacher, for the best of teachers were employed at Forest Park and then only after they had shown quality elsewhere. She had fewer pupils than she had had in Homeville, and the school had much better equipment with which to work.

The children were all engrossed in work now, most of them on arithmetic, though one small group worked at a table getting together a report about the first Thanksgiving. They were a good-looking lot, clean and sweet-smelling, as though, Miss Bond thought, they had come out of lavender-scented bedclothes. There was Estelle Woodford, taking charge of the committee, acting just like her mother who was president of the Garden Club and who had been PTA president last year. Tommy Beauregard raised his hand to ask for help. He was a plodder, certainly not one of the stars in the class, but he kept at his work. She knew that he would work hard through high school and then through Princeton, and then probably work up into the management of the industrial machinery company of which his father was president and principal stockholder.

Helen Fischer sat in a corner, studying from a sixth-grade arithmetic book. She had finished the fifth-grade book and was going ahead on her own. The girl was too much on her own, thought Miss Bond, as she looked at Helen's slender back and black hair. Dr. Fischer was a psychiatrist who had just bought a big house and moved his family out from the city. Neither the girl nor her mother seemed to have made friends yet, as far as Miss Bond could tell from her observations of the children at play and the mothers at PTA meetings. She would like to help Helen get on more friendly terms with the other children but she hardly knew how to go about it. If this had been Homeville, she would have spoken to some of the mothers and suggested that they invite Helen to their daughters' parties. But in Forest Park she did not know how to do this. She supposed the little girls had parties, but she knew nothing about them. She had thought of speaking to Mrs. Fairbairn, her PTA room mother, but Mrs. Fairbairn seemed so occupied with her own plans for the year's activities and so sure of how

Miss Bond should fit into them that the teacher felt there was no room for her to make suggestions about the welfare of Helen Fischer.

There was only one pupil who reminded her even faintly of her own childhood. That was Anna Metzger, whose father had a bakery shop in the small shopping center of the town and who lived with his family in a flat above the store. Miss Bond's father had owned a small grocery store in a small town. Anna was indeed as much of a teacher's pet as Miss Bond would ever allow herself, and the teacher was pleased when the girl showed attachment to her by bringing little gifts and occasionally something good to eat from the bakery. Anna had friends among the children, for she was good-natured and friendly and quick at games. But Miss Bond wondered whether Anna would be accepted into the clubs and the social life of the younger set of Forest Park when she reached high-school age.

In any case, Anna would be an acceptable student and would certainly finish the Forest Park high school and go to college—the first one of her family to accomplish that much in the field of education. Nobody could attend school in Forest Park and make average or better grades without feeling the pressure of the expectation to go to college. Anna's family might not press her to go to college, but her schoolmates and her teachers would do so, and consequently Anna would do better school work and more of it than she would have done if she had lived in Homeville, where the average student finished high school and then went to work.

Miss Bond wondered whether Anna would be as happy in Forest Park as she would have been, growing up in an average town like Homeville. In fact, Miss Bond wondered whether she herself was as happy living and working in Forest Park as she had been in Homeville. While she knew that she was respected and liked as a teacher in Forest Park, she was not nearly as comfortable in the church as she had been in Homeville and she had fewer close friends—only a small group of teachers and a larger group from other suburbs and from the central city whom she saw at meetings of the State Teachers Association or at conferences at the University. Occasionally she went to the home of one of the parents as a representative of the PTA to help plan a school program. On these occasions she felt uncertain as to what kind of clothes to wear and whether to wear gloves. The women spoke of the eastern colleges they had attended and Miss Bond was afraid they would ask her where she had gone to college. Suddenly the state college which had meant so much to her was something to keep quiet about.

The Social Structure of a Metropolitan Area

These three schools are all in one small piece of the United States, known as a metropolitan area. A metropolitan area is a natural unit of the national society. It is an area inhabited by a group of people who support each other by their work, and who are numerous enough to enjoy almost all of the complexities of American life. It contains industry, wholesale and retail trade, banking, a whole range of schools reaching generally up to the college level, a variety of churches, a number of local governments, social and fraternal clubs, and welfare organizations.

Metropolitan areas vary in size from New York, with 10,700,000 inhabitants, to Meriden, Connecticut, a county seat and its countryside with 52,000 population.

A metropolitan area has a social structure made up of groups. People fall into groups. They work in groups and play in groups. They worship in groups, and they tend to live in group neighborhoods. The community's physical structure reflects these groups. It is cut up by expressways, railroad tracks, and factory and business areas. The people living in one district may be different from those living in another district.

The various social groups have cultural differences. A culture is a common and standardized set of ways of behaving and believing. The different social groups in America have different sub-cultures, while they all share a common culture, which consists of such things as speaking English, using a decimal money system, a British system of weights and measures, a liking for ice cream, and a knowledge of the game of baseball.

One type of social group that is especially important for educators to understand is the *social class*. A social class is a group of people who have similar manners, feel "at home" when they are together socially, tend to belong to the same social organizations and tend to intermarry. They have rather similar amounts of education, types of homes, incomes and tastes in leisure activity.

The social classes are arranged in a hierarchy of power and prestige. The people living in a society determine by common consent who are in the higher and who are in the lower status positions, and the social scientist discovers the social classes by asking people in a community where they would place their neighbors and acquaintances on a scale of social status. When a social scientist studies a community in this way, he finds that the people in a community recognize and describe a number of social classes. There is no set number of such classes, since it is possible for people to define as many as nine or ten social classes in a large community, while this number can be reduced by making wider definitions of a social class. For the purposes of educational research, a set of five social classes is useful, as follows:

	Percent of population
Upper	1–3
Upper middle	7–12
Lower middle	20–35
Upper-working class	25–40
Lower-working class	15–25

The percent of the population in a given social class varies from one kind of community to another. In metropolitan areas of 100,000 or more, the proportions in the various classes are much the same.

A method frequently used to measure social status and to identify social classes is to use an *index of socio-economic characteristics*. This method uses information on a person's occupation, education, house-type, residential area, source of income, club or association memberships as a basis for ratings on the various social characteristics. These ratings can then be combined into a single score that represents his social status. The most important single fact is occupation, but this is usually supplemented by at least one other fact, such as amount of education or type of house, because certain occupations have a broad range of social status. The occupation of salesman, or of business owner, or of lawyer, can be held by people within a wide range of social status.

Another objective way to define social status is to describe the "style of life" or the culture of a social group who are recognized in the community as having the same general social position. This *description of a sub-culture* contains information about the attitudes of the people toward education, religion, politics, family, property, etc.; about the ways they use their leisure time; about their choice of furniture and house styles; and other visible signs of a way of life.

The differences between classes are expressed in two ways. Sometimes a class is described as though all of its members were like a typical person right at the middle of that class. The upper-middle-class person is described as though he must be a college graduate with an income of ten thousand dollars, because many upper-middle-class people are like that. Yet there will be some who have barely graduated from high school, who make five thousand dollars a year, but have other characteristics which are definitely those of the upper-middle class.

The lower-middle-class person is described as though he must be a high-school graduate who makes seven thousand dollars a year. Yet there will be some lower-middle-class people who are college graduates and make ten thousand dollars a year, but have other characteristics which are definitely those of the lower-middle class. Thus it is misleading to describe a social class as though all its members were alike in every respect.

Another way of describing the differences between social classes is to do it in statistical terms. The upper-middle and the lower-middle classes differ by a certain number of years of education, *on the average;* by a certain number of dollars of income, *on the average;* and by a certain number of points on a scale of occupational status, *on the average.* Yet, being contiguous classes, they overlap slightly on all three variables.

Thus the concept of social class is a statistical one. Most people have an extremely high probability of being in a certain class, while others have a 50–50 chance of being in one or the other of two contiguous classes.

This fuzziness of the boundaries between classes is essential in an open class system, the kind that is always found in a democratic society. A modern democratic society always has social classes, but people have opportunity to move from one class to another on the basis of their ability and effort.

The Usefulness of the Social Class Concept

Any concept of group membership is useful in education if it predicts with a fairly high degree of accuracy some important things about its members. Among the various social group concepts, social class probably has the greatest usefulness. It has more predictive value for educational purposes than religion, race, nationality background, region of the country, and every other common social group identification. Knowing the social class composition of a school or a class enables a teacher to plan with a better understanding of such important items as the following:

The general level of educational achievement of the group.

The educational aspirations and plans of the group. Will the majority be interested in job-training, or in college entrance, for example?

The values of the group in certain areas of life that are important for education—such as the drive for achievement, and the willingness to postpone gratification (to do things that are difficult or uncomfortable in the expectation that they will bring a gain in the future).

Above all, social class is the main group determiner for the *family factor* in children's mental development, which will be described in Chapter 6.

The three teachers in our illustration teach in very different kinds of schools though they all teach in one metropolitan area. Mrs. James teaches in a school that has a kind of cross-section of the child population of the city. There are children of professional men and children of bus drivers. Miss Bond in her exclusive suburb has, by comparison, a homogeneous group. Almost all her pupils come from "good" homes where great importance is placed upon the quality of education and preparation for college. Miss Nelson, teaching in what is often called a "slum" school, also has a fairly homogeneous group in terms of socio-economic characteristics, although it is at the other end of the social scale from Miss Bond's.

Culture Shock and the Teacher

In describing Miss Clarabelle Nelson and her school, reference was made to her experience of "culture shock." This referred to the fact that when she began to teach in the Carver school she came for the first time into direct contact with children of the lower working-class. She had been raised in the middle class. She went to school as a child with middle-class children. Her family associated closely with middle-class people, although there were some working-class people in her father's church. These people, however, were from the upper part of the working-class, and they did not seem particularly different from others in the church, partly because they shared the church with her and other middle-class people, but did not share other aspects of life.

When Clarabelle Nelson first came into contact with lower working-class children she felt a kind of physical revulsion. They looked dirty. They smelled dirty. They talked dirty. They seemed to come from a different social world, and a lower world. She had not realized that people like that existed—or at least existed in such numbers that they could populate whole schools in the city.

To a more limited extent Miss Bond experienced culture shock when she went to teach in Forest Park. She was most at home with lower-middle-class people, and in Forest Park she met an upper-middle-class group with some upper-class members. Their ways of speaking and their social events frightened her a little. She was not sure that she could "hold her own" in their social circles. She felt more comfortable with her teacher friends from other suburbs, who were more like her. But in her class she had no experience of culture shock. The children were well-behaved by her standards. They talked the standard midwestern American-English that she knew and spoke, and their their educational attitudes were like her own.

Studies of Social Structure

The sociologists have studied social structure in a number of American communities—generally small cities of 5,000 to 20,000 population. The usual procedure is for a social scientist to choose a community for study, and to live there for a time, visiting and conversing with people and observing the social scene. Thus he discovers the social groups that exist in the community and he begins to learn how they are related to one another. He learns who associates with whom, who are considered the "top" people and who are considered to be at the "bottom" and why. Gradually he pieces together a picture of the social structure of the community as it is viewed by its members. This picture shows groups of people arranged on a social scale from top to bottom.

The various studies of this sort all report a rather similar structure for small cities—a structure with five or six social classes.

Until recently no metropolitan area had been seriously studied with reference to its social structure. There was difficulty in adapting the methods of studying a small city to the study of a large population spread over a wide area.

In the 1950 decade a study was made of the social structure of the Kansas City metropolitan area, which represents the first study of this sort. The Kansas City area contains not only the city of Kansas

City, Missouri, but also the city of Kansas City, Kansas, and several smaller cities, together with parts of six counties located in two states. The population when the study was made consisted of about 850,000 people.

Early in the study it became clear that the social structure of no one city in the area was truly representative of the whole area. For example, Kansas City, Kansas, has relatively few upper-middle and upper-class people. Johnson County, Kansas, contains the "best" suburbs, and is largely upper-middle class. The upper class live generally in one section of Kansas City, Missouri, but this city is losing some of its middle-class population to the growing suburbs.

The social classes of the Kansas City area have been studied by the socio-economic indices already mentioned—occupation, area of residence, house-type, source of income, amount of education. They show percentages of people in the total metropolitan area which correspond to the figures already cited, although no one community or city in the area has exactly this structure. (Coleman, 1959.)

The Negro in the Social Structure

In so far as Negroes have a separate social existence as a group from other groups in the United States, it is possible to ask about the place of the Negro in the social structure. Although there is very little evidence that the Negroes have a separate sub-culture, they have been considered a separate group for so long that it is necessary to consider them separately in order to understand the social structure of the United States and also to understand the place of Negroes in the social structure of a metropolitan area.

Caste and Caste-like Groups

When one group of people is separated from other groups by a rigid barrier that prevents movement from one to the other, when the society prevents or punishes intermarriage, and when it passes this status from parent to child, the group may be called a caste.

The Negroes and the whites of the United States are castes or at least caste-like groups. There is a barrier of both law and custom against movement from one group to another in many states of the United States, and a barrier of custom in all other states. However, the barrier is less effective now than it was earlier in the twentieth century, and consequently it is well to speak of the Negroes as being a caste-like group rather than a caste in the strict sense. In recent years the earlier practices of segregation of Negroes in schools, colleges, churches, railroad cars, restaurants, hotels, and theaters have been reduced and even abolished in most states. Furthermore, the former bars against Negroes in certain professions and trades have been lowered. Still, largely by reason of the difference in skin color between Negroes and whites, some of the elements of caste-like status are present.

While it is not necessarily inherent in a caste system that one caste has higher rank and social esteem than the other, generally there is a distinction in status between castes, as there has been in America where Negroes occupy the lower position.

There are other caste-like groups in the United States such as the Mexican-Americans, the Filipino-, Hawaiian-, Japanese-, and Chinese-Americans, and the American Indians. However, these groups have less of a caste-like status than the Negroes, because there is less of a bar to intermarriage between these groups and others. The single best test of whether or not caste difference exists between two groups is the test of intermarriage. If intermarriage is strictly forbidden, and if the children of mixed unions are always relegated to the lower caste, then we can say that caste does exist.

Social Structure in the Negro Group

Within a caste-like group there is likely to be a social class structure if the group is large enough, and if it has a degree of economic opportunity great enough to enable some members to secure property or occupations that confer leadership and prestige. This has happened in the Negro group.

There is a social class system among Negroes similar to that existing among whites. The main difference is that relatively more Negroes are in the lower classes. For example, in the "Georgia Town" study, the proportions of Negroes in the five social classes were 0.3, 2, 9, 26, and 63 percent respectively, as compared with corresponding proportions of 4, 21, 36, 29, and 10 among the whites. (Hill and McCall, 1950.)

In the metropolitan area of Kansas City, in the early 1950's, it was estimated that 2 percent of the Negro population was upper-middle; 8 percent, lower-middle; 40 percent, upper-lower; and 50 percent, lower-lower. (Coleman, 1959.) The smaller proportion at the lowest social level, as compared with Georgia Town, reflects both geographical and urban-rural differences. By and large, economic opportunities are greater for Negroes in large cities and in areas other than the Deep South.

The socio-economic distribution of nonwhites in the United States was compared with that of whites by Nam and Powers (1965) by using the 1960 Census data and computing for each head of a family a socio-economic status score based on occupation, education, and family income. These scores ranged from zero to 100. Figure 1 shows the percentage distribution of whites and nonwhites in the central cities of the metropolitan areas of the country, in the urbanized areas around the central cities, and in the remainder of the country which lies outside of urbanized metropolitan territory. There are Negroes at all socio-economic levels in this Table, but the proportions of Negroes in the upper half of each graph is substantially smaller than the proportions of whites. This type of difference reflects an earlier, more rigid caste structure in which Negroes were systematically subordinated. If present trends continue for another hundred years, it is probable that the social class distribution in the Negro part of the society will become similar to that of the white group. In the South, with a relatively strict caste line, only small Negro upper and upper-middle classes have developed. In northern industrial cities, on the other hand, there recently has been a striking increase in the size of the Negro middle class.

The increasing size of the Negro middle class in the big cities has enormous importance for the system of public education in metropolitan areas. The time has already come in several cities—Washington, Manhattan (New York), Philadelphia, Chicago, Detroit—where there are large numbers of middle-class Negro students in the public high schools and in the public junior colleges, and teachers colleges.

Social Mobility

One essential characteristic of a complex democratic society is that a considerable degree of movement from one social class to another is

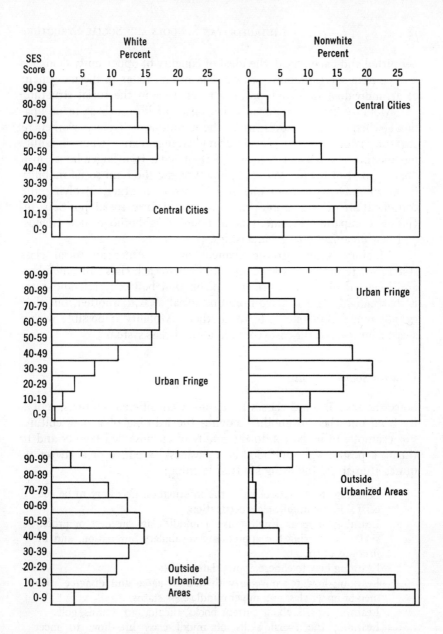

Figure 1.1 *Socio-economic Status of Family Heads by Race and Residence in the U.S.A.: 1960.* The higher the score, the higher the status. The sum of percentage distributions is 100 for the whites and for the nonwhites in each type of census unit. Source: Nam and Powers, 1965.

permitted and encouraged; the ideal of equality of opportunity demands it. The term social mobility—as we shall use it—refers to the movement of an individual from one position to another in the social structure.

Mobility may occur in only one phase of life, such as in occupation (when a man moves from the position of factory worker to that of factory foreman) or in living arrangements (when a family moves from a small house in one part of town to a larger house in a "better" part of town). We shall, however, use the term social mobility to mean movement from one social class to another, involving the consolidation of the various elements of the new social position, including occupation, income, type of house, neighborhood, new friends, and new organizational memberships.

Mobility is an intrinsic element of the American social class system where social classes are open and where each class gains members and loses members. The principal distinction between class and caste is that individuals can move from one social class to another, but they cannot move from one caste to another. (Mobility is possible *within* a caste, however, if the caste contains a social class system.)

Upward Social Mobility

Since the several social classes have somewhat different cultures, mobility from one class to another requires the learning of a new culture. For example, to be born into the family of an unskilled laborer and to rise to a position in adulthood as a business executive or a lawyer requires at least the following kinds of learning:

1. Learning the techniques and the information necessary to be successful in the middle-class occupation.
2. Learning to speak English like a middle-class business or professional man, using the appropriate vocabulary, intonation, and inflections of speech.
3. Learning how to choose appropriate clothes.
4. Learning how to converse with and to agree and disagree with men of upper-class and upper-middle-class status.
5. Learning to talk about current books, theater, art, tennis, golf.
6. Learning the social skills of middle-class life—how to meet strangers and introduce them to one's friends, how to converse with women, how to take a room at a first-class hotel, how to check one's coat and hat, order a meal, and tip the waiter at a first-class restaurant or club.

There are several contemporary examples of inter-system cooperation in which the public schools are cooperating with welfare systems to develop a new function. One of them is the use of social workers by the school system. Although some big city systems have had school social workers or "visiting teachers" for years, others have not used social workers but have counted on social service agencies to help families whose children are maladjusted to school. The proportion of such children in an inner-city school has grown so large that some kind of school-home coordinator has been seen by school administrators as essential. Currently there is a good deal of experimentation with home-school coordinators, who are people with social work training and located on the staff of the school.

Another example of inter-system cooperation is found in the joint operation by school systems and welfare systems of pre-school classes for socially disadvantaged children. In the past this work has been the function of welfare systems such as nursery schools and child-care agencies, but the current emphasis on a massive program of compensatory education with the aim of achieving readiness for reading has brought the schools into the field. If the pre-school classes prove to be successful, the schools in the big cities will probably develop sub-systems of their own.

It has long been a basic principle among school administrators that the school system should be protected from invasion by other social systems. Professor Strayer of Columbia University, the most influential leader among school administrators during the period from 1920 to about 1945 said frequently what he wrote in his report on the Chicago School Survey in 1932, "It is always a mistake for the schools to be organized so that agencies other than a board of education are responsible for the administration of vital and indispensable services in the schools." (Strayer, 1932, Vol. 3, p. 145.)

This principle of school administration may be interpreted broadly to mean that the schools should control the administration of all services they perform—even the new and marginal ones such as the school lunch program, recreation services in city parks, job placement of students taking part in work-experience programs, delinquency-prevention programs, transportation of pupils. In these and other programs, other social systems have an interest and may not cooperate if the school system is too aggressive or too uncooperative, as they see it. Thus in the present decade there are problems of cooperation between school systems and social welfare agencies, recreation agencies, police and youth-serving agencies, and transportation systems.

Frequently the local city government is responsible for social systems which might cooperate with a school system. But such city government agencies as the police department, public housing authority, department of human relations, park department, are often seen by the school administrator as sources of trouble for him. He feels that cooperation with them will involve him in "local politics." Yet city government is increasingly responsible for a program of *positive welfare of the city* which brings it very close to the activities of the school system. The mayor or the city manager wishes to cooperate with the superintendent of schools.

This striving for cooperation between city government and school government has become more pronounced since about 1950, with the advent of urban renewal legislation and funds. Civic improvement, under the conditions of the 1950's and 1960's, was obviously tied up with improvement in the city schools, which were suffering generally from aging buildings, crowded by the post-war population boom, and were losing many of their best pupils and teachers to the growing suburbs.

Then the federal government stepped in, early in the 1960's, with substantial funds aimed at improving the quality of the city's population as workers, parents, and citizens. There was the Manpower Development and Training Act, the Vocational Education Act of 1963, the Economic Opportunity Act, and the Elementary and Secondary Education Act of 1965, all of which pumped money from Washington into the city school systems, and all aimed at improving the quality of city life. These funds stretched the functions of the school system into forms of more direct service to the city. Education was seen increasingly by civic leaders as serving to improve the city, not only through its effects on the mind and character of the pupil, but also through its effects on the economic system and the social structure of the city. The school system became an instrument for attracting and holding desirable population elements in the central city, for stabilizing racially integrated neighborhoods, and for solving or holding in check the problems of an alienated and economically marginal minority of slum dwellers.

It appears probable that local government and the public school system will find more ways of effective cooperation in the immediate future.

Optimal Relations Among Educational Systems in the Metropolitan Area

The educational sub-systems of a metropolitan area consist of the various public school districts in the area; the system of Roman Catholic schools, the system of Lutheran schools, other church-related school systems such as the Christian Schools, the Seventh-Day Adventist Schools, and other church-supported schools; and the independent private schools.

These sub-systems have a tradition of working separately, and no doubt will continue to do so in large part. However, there are many possibilities and needs for cooperation, among the public school districts, on the one hand, and between public and private schools on the other hand.

Among public school districts there are a variety of shared educational projects, including television, special schools for handicapped children, junior colleges, and in-service teacher training programs. A good example is the program of the Educational Research and Development Council of the Twin Cities (Minneapolis-St. Paul), which was described in Chapter 5.

Cooperation between the public school and some church school systems has been talked about a great deal and tried out to a small degree. Since there are laws against public support of church-operated schools in this country, the several church school systems have tended to operate in isolation from the public schools as well as from each other. However, the trend of social forces is pushing the public and church school systems closer together. Some "shared-time" or "dual enrollment" arrangements have been working, apparently with general satisfaction. The new federal Elementary and Secondary Education Act of 1965 provides funds for "Supplementary Educational Centers" which serve children regardless of their school affiliations. This will require cooperation between public and church school systems.

Cooperative Planning by Social Systems

In a time of social change there is a premium on planning for the future. Innovation is necessary, and planned innovation gives better results than haphazard innovation. The planning that is needed depends, of course, on the particular social system. With changes in the numbers of people living in the different parts of a metropolitan area, there is need for planning of new school buildings, churches, libraries, shopping centers, sewer lines, water pipes, and expressways. With changes in the numbers of people in various occupations there is need for planning of occupational training programs and of employment services.

The opportunities and the needs for planning are greater than they have been in the past for two reasons. First, the pace and depth of social change are so great now that failure to plan is tantamount to failure of a system to function. Second, vast amounts of federal government money are being used in ways that are largely determined at the local and metropolitan area levels. This money goes into urban renewal, public housing, education, manpower training, highways, health and retirement insurance and cultural activities.

The federal government is itself putting a premium on planning by requiring a plan before releasing money to local goverment systems for certain purposes. For instance, recent additions to the Federal Highway Act required every population area of 50,000 or more to produce a transportation plan by July 1, 1965, in order to be eligible for federal highway money. The government is also making "planning grants" under the Economic Opportunity Act and other acts to enable local and metropolitan units to plan programs before asking for funds to support them.

Intra-system Functioning

The school system performs its functions through roles and constellations of roles filled by people. The roles which make up a school system are the following: administrator, teacher, non-professional personnel, student, board of education member, parents organization member, civic organization member.

Each of these names stands for a pattern of behavior which in the case of a successful school system is fitted into the other roles with the result that the school system performs its functions and the people filling the roles feel satisfaction.

These roles are now undergoing considerable change in a city school system. The social changes which have disarranged the functions those accounting courses because it came at the same time. I guess I'll go into personnel management or, bad as it sounds, sales work."

Paul is not an impulsive sort of fellow; he likes to plan. He recently became engaged to a girl who will be a junior at his college this fall, but they have no definite plans for marriage at this time. He thought they would wait until he had at least finished his military service. He said that he would just as soon not have his wife work when they do get settled.

Paul will undoubtedly succeed in business, and will be mobile from upper-working class and upper-middle class. His social effectiveness is his strong point.

3. AMBITION AND DRIVE. Often a person with only average intellectual ability and social effectiveness succeeds in becoming upward mobile through industrious effort. This is likely to happen to working-class youth who move up into lower-middle-class positions. Education is not so important to this kind of person, though he generally completes high school. An example is Robert.

Robert. Robert came from a stable working-class family. He had average ability and made average grades in school. He was a mild and pleasant-mannered youth with a good number of friends. As a young adult he is still a rather quiet person, has a youthful appearance, and speaks with a soft voice. He has an initial adult status of lower-middle class.

Robert and his wife now have three young daughters and live in a small two-story bungalow that is situated right along the sidewalk in an old section of town. The building is well maintained. The rooms are small but they are reasonably well furnished even though things are a bit crowded because of the small size.

He was in a distributive education program in his senior year in high school. "I realize I should have studied harder and taken more subjects than I did. I just took average classes. I guess I should have taken more difficult classes like science and mathematics."

Since leaving high school he has worked only in supermarkets, where he was trained on the job. He worked for a local market and then his firm transferred him to a town in another state where he was an assistant manager. He quit that job to come back to his home city about a year ago. "The main reason I quit was that I was putting in an extra amount of hours for what I was getting paid. It got so I couldn't see my family at all. It was strictly voluntary work, but the work was there and it had to be done and somebody had to do it. When we came back here I got a job as a stock clerk in another store and I made as much at that as I did as assistant manager before. About a month ago I became assistant manager of this store. Actually, this is part of a training program. If I am good enough to stay in the program I will then go into a co-manager position, probably in another town and then from that into a store as manager. This will probably take about six or seven years, but I can wait. I don't want it before I really think I can handle it because it is a job I would want to stay with a long time when I get it."

Robert's wife worked for a while when they were first married but she does not work now. They are members of a church but they do not belong to any kind of social group. "We go to shows a lot and we go with my folks. They have a boat and we go up the river and ski and swim. I guess we don't do things separately much; most things we like to do together."

The interviewer asked Robert how he felt about early marriages. "Well, we were married the year after I got out of school. I guess it all depends upon the person. For myself I think it worked fine. I know if I had it to do over I would get married at the same time." Robert was asked if he was pretty well satisfied with the way things had gone since he left school. "Well, yes; but I am not really satisfied. We want more; we want to advance but so far I think it has worked out all right."

These cases illustrate the fact that educational opportunity is essential for much individual upward mobility in the United States, especially among boys. If the schools of the big cities which serve a growing proportion of working-class youth are inferior and do not effectively provide educational opportunity, then the society of today is in serious danger. For the quality of the young people who move up the social scale tends to determine the quality of our society, and this quality is increasingly dependent on the schools of the big cities.

Exercises

1. On the basis of your experience, describe the social class composition of the elementary school that you attended for the longest period. Can you describe some children who deviated from the typical social class composition of that school?

2. Draw a crude map of the town or city in which you live, or obtain a simple map with the principal streets and the main features on it. On this map, mark out a set of residential areas that you know something about, and label them from 1 to 5, in order of their social status. Then locate a number of schools on the map, and comment on the nature of these schools.

3. Write a brief sketch of someone you know fairly well who has been upward mobile. Describe this person's family background in socio-

economic terms and tell what part his or her schooling had in making him a mobile person.

Suggestions for Further Reading

1. For a more detailed treatment of social classes and social mobility and their relation to the school system, read Chapters 1 and 2 of *Society and Education* by Havighurst and Neugarten. A more technical treatment may be read in *Social Class in America*, by Warner, Meeker and Eells.

2. An interesting description of the various social classes is given by Harold Hodges in his chapter entitled "Peninsula People," in the book of readings, *Education and Society*, edited by Kallenbach and Hodges. Hodges studied people in the Peninsula area, south of San Francisco.

3. For a description of the social structure of a small city, see the first chapter of *Growing Up in River City*, by Havighurst, Bowman, *et al*.

2 ❧ Urban and Metropolitan Development

Great cities are relatively new as the habitation of large sections of the human race. Jerusalem was a city of 25,000 in the time of King Solomon, and this was a big city. Babylon at her height was somewhat larger, and Athens may have had 150,000 inhabitants in the fifth century B.C. Rome may have reached a million at her height, but her population declined to 20,000 in the Dark Ages. Constantinople was the largest city in the western world in 1500. Paris was the largest in 1600 when according to Lewis Mumford (1961) she had about 180,000 inhabitants. London was the largest city in the world in 1800. There were only 21 cities of 100,000 or over in Europe in 1800, and none with a million.

During the nineteenth and twentieth centuries the cities have grown. By 1950 there were 46 cities of a million or more and 700 with a population between 100 thousand and a million. Europe and North America each had 15 cities with over a million, Asia had ten, South America had three, Australia had two, and Africa had one.

The first large cities grew up before the advent of modern technology, which brought large numbers of industrial workers together to create the modern urban center. Before that, the great cities were the centers of political and military power, great trading posts where landways and waterways came together, and brilliant collections of palaces and temples where the powerful people lived and worked.

Until 1800, the large cities were still close to the field and the pasture, and the people were spiritually close to land and sea. Even when Paris was the biggest city in the world, in the seventeenth century, its citizens when out for a walk could see the windmills of Montmartre and drink goat's milk on the Champs Elysées.

Table 2.1 shows the locations of the cities over 100,000 by continent in 1960. This table also shows the proportions of the total population living in metropolitan areas of 100,000 and over.

Table 2.1   *Great Cities in 1960*

CONTINENT	AREAS WITH OVER 100,000 POPULATION	% OF TOTAL CONTINENTAL POPULATION IN METROPOLITAN AREAS:	
		1,000,000 & over	*100,000 & over*
North America	153	27.2	49.7
Latin America	68	14.7	27.4
Europe (inclusive of Russia)	435	12.5	29.6
Asia (exclusive of Russia)	435	6.2	12.3
Africa	64	2.6	8.1
Australia-Oceania	11	23.6	43.3
TOTAL	1,166	9.6	19.9

Sources: United Nations Statistical Office, Department of Economic and Social Affairs, *Demographic Yearbook*, 1960. New York: 1960.

Homer Hoyt, *World Urbanization*. Technical Bulletin No. 43. Washington, D.C. Urban Land Institute, 1962.

The City in an Essentially Rural Society

Until 1800 the people of even the most powerful and up-to-date societies were mainly engaged in getting food and water from sea and land—some 80 percent of the population were tillers of the soil, or sheep and cattle tenders, or fishermen or foresters. Then the growing productivity of agriculture and extractive industry enabled fewer people to produce more food and mineral and forest products, and the excess population of the rural areas moved toward the cities. From 1800 to 1960 the proportion of people in the United States living in urban places (2500 population and over) rose from 6 to 70 percent.

In the pre-industrial millennia there were empires which required military and political organization, and these produced large cities to serve as their administrative headquarters. Babylon, Rome, and Constantinople are examples.

As the rural population raised itself above a subsistence level and produced a surplus, trade became important and trading centers came into existence. The major trading centers were located at the intersections of busy land routes or at places where land and water routes met. Paris and Moscow represent the first type, and Hamburg, New York and Buenos Aires the second. The great European colonial empires of the nineteenth and early twentieth centuries developed cities as trading centers. Examples are Calcutta and Bombay in India, Singapore, Hong Kong, Saigon, Rangoon, Manila, and Cape Town.

After 1800, as industry developed, some industrial cities grew to serve as the centers of industrial complexes. Melbourne served this purpose in Australia, São Paulo in Brazil, Pittsburgh in the United States and the Ruhr complex of Duisburg-Dortmund-Essen in Germany.

The City in an Industrial Society

Industrialization and urbanization have gone together. The urbanization of the United States (proceeding from 6 to 70 percent between 1800 and 1960) was paralleled by a reduction in the proportion of the labor force engaged in agriculture from 80 percent to eight percent during the same period. It was not until 1820 that any American city reached 100,000.

For the world as a whole, Kingsley Davis (1955) estimates that in 1800, some 1.7 percent of the world's population were living in cities of 100,000 or over, and this figure had increased to 20 percent in 1960. Even basically rural countries such as Mexico and Brazil have their urban population increasing three times as fast as their rural population.

It sounds paradoxical, but it is true that poverty stricken people go to the big cities because they are better off there. The rural poor are not so visible, and perhaps they do not feel poverty as much as the city poor. But the big city has a magnetic attraction for poor people. Thus nearly every big city has slums which are eyesores. They are more picturesque in some cities than in others. When seen from a distance they are almost beautiful in Rio de Janeiro where they are perched on the steep hillsides. But they are ugly in São Paulo, and Buenos Aires and Santiago de Chile, and Lima, just as they are ugly in Johannesburg, London, Milan, and Chicago. Only a few medium-large cities in North Europe seem to have conquered the problem of urban poverty.

Types of Urbanization

In the modern world the big cities and the big urban agglomerations dominate practically all countries. But some of these countries are not really urbanized. To be urbanized a country needs more than a few large cities. It is useful to make a distinction between *sporadic* and *systematic* *urbanization.*

Sporadic Urbanization—Big Cities in Rural Countries

Countries which have the majority of their population engaged in agriculture need a few large cities to serve as trading and manufacturing centers. Australia is a striking example of sporadic urbanization. Though its economy is essentially rural, over 50 percent of its inhabitants live in a few provincial capitals, with Sydney and Melbourne each having over a million inhabitants.

Looking at Table 2.2, which reports the metropolitan areas with three million or more population, one sees examples of this type of urbanization in São Paulo and Rio de Janeiro in Brazil, Buenos Aires in Argentina, Mexico City in Mexico, Cairo in Egypt, Calcutta and Bombay in India, and Seoul in Korea. Also, the big Chinese centers, five of them, serve an enormous country whose population is 85 percent rural.

Other examples of sporadic urbanization are the cities that grew up in the colonies of European powers of the nineteenth century to serve as centers of colonial trade and government. During the twentieth century there was rapid growth of important cities in the African colonies which continued after they became independent. Examples of cities over 200,000 which hardly existed in Africa in 1900 are: Elizabethville, Leopoldville, Abidjan, Accra, Lagos, and Nairobi.

Systematic Urbanization

An urbanized country is one with a relatively large urban population which is engaged in maufacturing and trade. Western Europe began to become urbanized in the sixteenth century. After 1600 a number of large European towns became substantial cities. Paris, London, Naples, and Milan had over 200,000 inhabitants; while Palermo, Rome, Seville, Lisbon, Antwerp, and Amsterdam exceeded 100,000. Subordinate to them grew a large number of medium-sized or small cities.

The United States went through this process of urbanization rapidly after 1850, as can be seen in Table 2.3 The systematic nature of

Table 2.2 *The World's Largest Metropolitan Areas: 1960–1965*

RANK	CITY AND COUNTRY	POPULATION
1	New York City, U.S.A.	14,759,000
2	Tokyo-Yokohama, Japan	14,085,000
3	London, England	10,975,000
4	Shanghai, China	10,000,000
5	Moscow, Russia	8,350,000
6	Osaka-Kobe, Japan	8,050,000
7	Paris, France	7,750,000
8	Buenos Aires, Argentina	6,975,000
9	Chicago, U.S.A.	6,794,000
10	Calcutta, India	6,350,000
11	Peking, China	6,100,000
12	Los Angeles-Long Beach, U.S.A.	6,039,000
13	Mexico City, Mexico	5,215,000
14	Essen-Dortmund-Duisburg, Germany (West)	4,800,000
15	Rio de Janeiro, Brazil	4,700,000
16	São Paulo, Brazil	4,650,000
17	Philadelphia, U.S.A.	4,343,000
18	Bombay, India	4,300,000
19	Chungking, China	4,070,000
20	Berlin, Germany (East and West)	4,000,000
21	Leningrad, Russia	3,950,000
22	Detroit, U.S.A.	3,762,000
23	Cairo, Egypt	3,300,000
24	Tientsin, China	3,278,000
25	Seoul, Korea (South)	3,060,000
26	Talien-Port Arthur, China	3,000,000

Sources: Census of 1960 or later, with estimates for most oriental cities.

See *Today—1966.* p. 155. Chicago: Field Enterprises Educational Corporation.

this process is indicated by the fact that there are many towns and small and medium-sized cities which are distributed in a regular manner related functionally to the large cities. At the same time, the rural or farm population functions efficiently in the economy, producing a surplus of materials for sale and buying manufactured goods and a

Table 2.3   *Growth of Urban Population in the United States*

YEAR	DISTRIBUTION OF URBAN POPULATION (BY PERCENT)		
	Places of 2,500 and over	*Places of 100,000 and over*	*Metropolitan Areas*
1790	5	—	—
1810	7	—	—
1830	9	2	—
1850	15	5	—
1870	26	11	—
1890	35	15	—
1910	46	22	46
1930	56	30	54
1950	64*	29	59
1960	70*	29	63

* Current U.S. Census definition of "urban" adds about 5 percent to number based on pre-1950 definition.

Source: *U.S. Census of Population: 1960, Selected Area Reports. Standard Metropolitan Statistical Areas.* Final Report PC(3)10, p. 1.

variety of services. A country which is systematically urbanized has very few "subsistence farmers," who try to produce all the food and other material they need for a bare subsistence, without selling much of their product or buying much from other parts of the economy.

Most countries of Western Europe are systematically urbanized. The Soviet Union is moving rapidly in that direction, and it is supposed that China is beginning this process.

Metropolitan Development

Modern cities grew in sheer physical size by annexing land around their edges. Sometimes the land was open farmland which was laid out in city blocks with new streets and sidewalks. Other times the newly-annexed area was a town or village which had grown up separately and then was engulfed by the city as an amoeba spreads itself around a foreign object. Cities thus became larger in area as well as in population.

In another form of growth, cities extended their economic and

social nets to take in people who did not live within the geographical
city limits. Many people living outside of the city bought their furniture and clothing in the central city. People from a wide surrounding
area came into the city for theater, concerts, and lectures. Thus the city
was the intellectual and economic capital of an area that extended out
some distance from its physical boundaries.

By the middle of the current century it had become clear that a
new type of community was in existence. The Bureau of the Census
recognized this fact by defining a "standard metropolitan statistical
area," as a city of 50,000 or more with its county and any contiguous
county that is economically and socially integrated with the central
county. A number of SMSAs contain two or more cities, such as Minneapolis-St. Paul, Philadelphia-Camden, and San Francisco-Oakland-
Berkeley-Richmond.

There were 212 metropolitan areas in 1960, with 112 million, or
63 percent of the population. Although metropolitan units gained 24
percent between 1950 and 1960, central cities gained only 8 percent,
while the suburban areas gained 47 percent. In fact, some of the central
cities actually lost population. There were 225 central cities included
in the SMSA's of 1950. Of these, 72 lost population, while 153 gained.
Of the five cities with populations of one million or more, only Los
Angeles gained. Among cities that lost population were Boston, St.
Louis, Detroit, Minneapolis, Washington, Philadelphia, Cleveland,
Chicago, Cincinnati, Baltimore and New York, with losses ranging
from 15 to 3 percent. While the 225 central cities as a group moved
up from 51 million in 1950 to 56 million in 1960, their suburban areas
expanded with almost explosive effect from 36 million to 53 million.

The land area of the 212 SMSAs in 1960 was nine percent of the
country's total, and contained 310 counties, or ten percent of the number of counties in the country. There were 4,142 municipalities in these
212 SMSAs, and 2,575 townships. There was a total of 18,442 government units, including six thousand school districts.

The most populous SMSA was New York, with 10,695,000 inhabitants and the smallest was Meriden, Connecticut, with 52,000.
The median size was 250,000. The distribution of SMSAs by size was:

More than 3,000,000	5
1,000,000 to 3,000,000	19
500,000 to 1,000,000	29
250,000 to 500,000	48
100,000 to 250,000	89
50,000 to 100,000	22

There were only four states without at least one SMSA—Alaska, Idaho, Wyoming, and Vermont.

Most of the metropolitan areas, 133 of them, consist of only one county, but there are eight counties in the New York SMSA, six in the Chicago SMSA, and six in the Kansas City SMSA. When a county without a central city of 50,000 is included in an SMSA, it must satisfy certain criteria of economic integration with the central county in the area. (See Bollens and Schmandt, 1965, p. 7–8.)

This means that very few metropolitan areas contain much rural territory or open land. However, there are a few exceptions to this rule. For instance, San Bernardino County, the largest county in the United States, is the central county of a metropolitan area. It stretches from Los Angeles County on the west almost 200 miles to the Nevada state line, and much of this area is desert.

The number of SMSAs was increased to 216 by the Bureau of the Census in 1963, on the basis of the latest census data. Probably another ten or twelve will be added by the 1970 Census. The United States has become a metropolitan country. Two-thirds of its school children and school teachers are located in metropolitan area schools.

The Evolution of a Metropolitan Area

The growth of a metropolitan area has taken place in five stages. These are described in the following pages.

I. THE BEGINNING.   It all commences with a town which is a small trading center, such as Chicago was in 1840. This center grows over a period of years to be a medium-sized city of 25 to 50 thousand.

By this time the city has a fairly well-defined structure that is related to the incomes and social statuses of the people who live there. One area is where the well-to-do people live. Sometimes it is called the "country club area" because it is close to the country club to which the "upper crust" of society belong. Another part of the city becomes a slum area, with small, old, run-down houses. There is usually one side of town which is spoken of as "on the wrong side of the railroad tracks," where working people live. The houses are generally well-kept and the lawns are neat, but it just is the wrong place for people to live who want to move in "the best social circles."

The schools reflect the socio-economic stratification that is beginning to take place. Probably the oldest school in town will be in the slum area. People who can afford to live where they choose try to avoid living in the district of the "poorer" schools. There are one or two modern schools where most teachers like to work and where the parents most interested in the education of their children try to live.

During this period there is only one public high school, drawing a cross-section of youth in terms of ability, educational motivation, and socio-economic status.

II. THE STRUCTURED CITY. Oscar Handlin in his book *The Newcomers* tells how New York City grew from the first into the second stage. If the city in stage I is located in a strategic place with respect to water and railway transportation, raw materials, or markets, it attracts large numbers of people who come there to work. Soon it develops industries, and grows to be a center of several hundred thousand. By this time the areas near the center of the city become industrialized, or their houses deteriorate and their owners move away from the center of the old town. Slum areas develop, and choice residential areas appear on the edges of the growing city. Sometimes these areas are annexed by the city.

During this period the schools separate out into types with qualities of the areas in which they are located. Some elementary schools become entirely working-class in character; others, middle-class. At the same time a number of high schools are built, generally to serve youth of geographical districts which contain eight or ten elementary schools. The single comprehensive high school that served all kinds of youth in the smaller city is replaced by a variety of schools with contrasting student bodies. Some schools get a reputation for college preparation; others begin to specialize in vocational education.

Even if a city developing out of stage I does not grow to a size of several hundred thousand, it may go through some of the same changes while growing to be a hundred thousand, like Canton, Ohio, or Decatur, Illinois. The city develops a geographical structure related to its social structure and the schools develop accordingly.

III. CENTRAL CITY AND THE SUBURBS. By the end of World War I a number of American cities had gone through stage II and were moving into stage III, while other smaller cities followed them into stage II. The main characteristic of stage III is the appearance of choice residential suburbs at first strung out along the railway lines that lead into the city.

These suburbs are exclusive residential areas, expensive to live in, with gardens around the houses, parks and country clubs and tennis clubs, and with superior schools provided at no greater cost to the taxpayer than in the central city. These suburbs are heavily upper-middle class with a fringe of upper-class and of lower-middle-class residents. Their schools, elementary and secondary, are homogeneous along socioeconomic, racial and ethnic lines.

When these suburbs first came into existence it was almost impossible for a Jewish family to buy or rent a house, and Negroes were unknown except as servants.

The principal reason given by people for moving out from the central city to a suburb was and still is that it is better for their children. The schools are better, there is more play space for children, and the children can find congenial playmates. In addition, many people like the gardening, the golf and tennis, and the other leisure activities that are easily found in the suburbs.

During this phase, which, for cities already in stage II by 1920, lasted from World War I to World War II,[1] some of the suburbs developed well-known public schools along "progressive" lines. Known throughout the educational world were the school systems of Winnetka, Bronxville, Manhasset, Shaker Heights, Clayton, and Pasadena. This was an interesting development in view of the fact that the people in these suburbs were politically conservative. In educational matters they were progressive, and their schools have tended to retain many of their progressive features during the conservative reaction in education that followed World War II.

Since the suburb is a part of the metropolitan complex, the fact that it draws mainly middle- and upper-class people results in an increase in the proportion of lower-class population in the central city. As population in general expands, and as more persons move into metropolitan areas, the working-class areas of the central city expand, with obsolescence and reduced money values of former middle-class residential areas. Slum areas expand. The area of solid middle-class residences becomes smaller and is often cut up into small islands within lower-class areas.

---

[1] There are some metropolitan areas just now in stages II and III, and other small cities are becoming metropolitan areas. Thus, at present, all stages of metropolitan development are visible. The newer metropolitan areas are evolving more rapidly than the older ones, and some may combine stages III and IV, since the automobile has largely replaced the railroad as a means of transportation.

Theories of Urban Evolution

As the growing American cities moved into stage III, the sociologists who were studying city growth thought they saw that all American cities were going through similar changes, and began to look for "laws" of city growth. One very popular theory was that developed by the "Chicago" school of sociology, which centered in the University of Chicago and used the City of Chicago as a kind of social observatory. Professors Park (1952) and Burgess pointed out that as the big city grows, it forms shells or rings growing out from the center.

The first shell, around the business center, consists largely of warehouses and industry and run-down dwellings; yet this area in the early years of the city was generally a choice area for living. The fine dwellings are torn down to make way for warehouses, or they are converted into apartment and rooming houses or funeral parlors. This process can be seen today in many cities of 100 to 200 thousand.

The second shell consists of solid residential areas that housed middle-class people for a couple of generations. The houses became obsolete, and the middle-class people moved further out to a new shell, leaving their houses to be sold or rented to the growing number of workers, often immigrants, who were moving into the growing city. New shells were formed as the city grew. The outer shells tended to be the most desirable, from the point of view of social status.

Thus a shell stretching from five to seven miles from the center of the city would have certain characteristics of income level, occupation, types of churches and schools, no matter whether it was north or south or east or west of the city center. Of course this structure was modified by the physical geography of the city. Chicago had Lake Michigan to prevent eastward growth, Detroit had the Detroit River; New York City had various bodies of water; San Francisco had a bay on three sides which distorted its growth.

The general sequence of obsolescence of dwellings, conversion to other uses or to slum dwellings, and outward growth of the city with the working-class population closer to the center than the middle class was a familiar North American phenomenon.

Another theory of city growth sees cities as growing out from the center by sectors. In one direction from the center are the houses of the wealthy people, while the houses of poor people extend out in another direction. These sectors tend to grow outward—the children of the wealthy people build their houses farther out along the same avenues. The middle income people fill up the sectors in between. A growing Negro population tends to move out from the center in one or two sectors.

This theory is linked to the development of suburbs, which grow outward from the central city along railways and later along major highways. Thus the suburbs extend out along what look like the spokes of an expanding wheel. Along these spokes of the wheel were located small towns 5, 10, 15, and 20 miles from the city when it was in stage II. People move out to these towns and turn them into suburbs. Some completely new suburbs come into existence. By 1940 the major cities all had this kind of structure. The spaces between the spokes of the wheel were open country, often used for market gardening. Then gradually industrial plants came into these areas, with branch railway lines built to connect them with the main lines.

The coming of the automobile, the motor truck, and the super-highway changed this picture after World War II. But the concentric shells and spokes of a wheel structure continue to control and condition the life of the contemporary city. Schools and residential areas reflect the structure. Much of modern city planning for urban renewal is an effort to break out of this pre-war structure.

Still another view of urban development sees it as taking place around a number of nuclei. Business gets located in one place, and develops. Industry is located in certain areas where transportation is good, land is cheap, and there are no wealthy people living nearby. An immigrant group settles in a certain area and expands outward from this nucleus. An upper-class group build their homes around a small lake and golf course. The city consists of this collection of nuclei and their subsequent growths.

The American City Is Not Like Cities in Other Countries

The big cities in other parts of the world are generally quite different from the North American model. They generally did not develop such a marked concentric shell structure, though the spokes-of-a-wheel structure was evident. Generally, the big cities retained areas of upper- and upper-middle-class residence close to the city center on an arc of 90 to 180 degrees, while working-class sections stretched out in other directions. Thus Paris had the fashionable area west of the Arch of Triumph,

Berlin had the Tiergarten and Kurfuerstendamm to the west and south of the city center. London had Hyde Park, Regents Park and the area north and west of the center. Buenos Aires had the area north of the city center, out from the Opera House. Mexico had the Reforma area stretching northwest to Chapultepec.

One reason why the big cities of the United States had their own peculiar structure is that they were built at first largely of wood which does not last as well as the stone and brick of the European and South American cities. A wooden house deteriorated in 30 to 40 years unless it was repaired frequently, and its owner generally moved to another area rather than rebuild or recondition the old house. In contrast, Paris has fine stone houses two or three hundred years old. Furthermore, the very rapid growth of the American cities put a premium on selling an old house and buying or building a new one. With new people crowding in and renting or buying the older houses, an owner in one of the older districts would find himself living among people he did not know and did not want to know, while his former friends had moved farther out to new houses. Hence he sold and moved out.

IV. APPEARANCE OF THE METROPOLITAN COMPLEX. Up to the close of World War II, the big city appeared to be growing in a rational manner which served fairly well the interests of the diverse groups who lived and worked in the metropolitan area. However, in the 15 years after World War II, a new stage of metropolitan development began to threaten the well-being of urban society. As the society became a metropolitan one, it discovered a set of problems which seriously threatened its democratic existence.

Rapid growth of suburbs was the obvious characteristic of this phase of development. Table 2.4 shows how the distribution of metropolitan area population changed from a 66–34 ratio of central city to suburban numbers in 1920 to a 50–50 ratio in 1963. The period of most rapid change was the 1950–60 decade. During this decade suburbs of the five largest SMSAs increased about 70 percent while four of the central cities actually lost population.

Two things combined to give the suburbs their rapid growth. First, the pre-war pattern of migration of middle-income people from the central city to the suburbs intensified. The most frequent reason given by the people for moving out to the suburbs was that it was better for children. Thus, in one study of recent migrants to suburbia, 83 percent said they had moved to the suburbs, for such reasons as "better schools,"

Table 2.4   *Division of Metropolitan Area Population between Central Cities and Outside Central Cities: 1900–1960*

YEAR	TOTAL SMSA POPULATION (000)	PERCENT OF SMSA POPULATION WITHIN CENTRAL CITIES	PERCENT OF SMSA POPULATION OUTSIDE CENTRAL CITIES
1900	31,895	62.2	37.8
1910	42,094	64.6	35.4
1920	52,631	66.0	34.0
1930	66,915	64.6	35.4
1940	72,834	62.7	37.3
1950	89,317	58.7	41.3
1960	112,895	51.4	48.6
1963	118,761	50.0	50.0

Source: U.S. Bureau of the Census. *U.S. Census of Population: 1960. Selected Area Reports. Standard Metropolitan Statistical Areas.* Final Report (PC(3)–1D).

"nicer children for playmates," and "more healthy for children." (Dobriner, 1958.)

The second cause of rapid suburban growth was the decentralization of industry. Formerly there had been a few small industrial cities around the fringe of the big cities, such as Chicago Heights, Harvey, Whiting, and Gary—south of Chicago; Passaic and Elizabeth—outside of New York; and Alameda and Richmond—outside of San Francisco. After the war, there were various economic factors, as described by Vernon (1959) that led to decentralization of industry. "Light industry" manufacturing electronic equipment, plastics, pharmaceuticals, airplanes and airplane parts became established in suburban areas. This in turn pulled workers out from the central city into new working-class suburbs. Here the people were mainly upper-lower and lower-middle class, with relatively high incomes and with automobiles that enabled them to travel to work independent of railways and electric lines. Examples of this type of development are seen in the new suburbs northwest of Chicago, in North Kansas City, in Edwardsville and other suburbs across the Mississippi from St. Louis, in some of the new suburbs in central Long Island, and in the northern and southern suburbs of Los Angeles.

Express highways leading into the central city and going around the city from one suburb to another permit new suburbs to grow up in the open spaces between the older suburbs.

At the same time, if there is a substantial Negro population, as in Chicago and Detroit, a few Negro working-class suburbs come into existence. With a large Negro slum area developing in the central city, Negro middle-class people find their way into mixed Negro and white middle-class residential areas in the central city, and into middle-class suburbs.

Workers tended to follow industry as it decentralized, and therefore to move out of the central city, though in smaller numbers than the numbers of middle-class people. This was part of a long-term process which is illustrated in Table A–1. This Table shows that the proportion of production workers in manufacturing plants who lived in the central cities and worked in the metropolitan area has been decreasing since 1899. For the 48 largest metropolitan areas, Vernon (1959) found that the proportion of manufacturing production workers living in the central cities decreased from 67 percent in 1929 to 38 percent in 1954.

The net effect of this differential growth of suburbs and central city was to impoverish the central city. The poorest people remained in the central city, or migrated from rural areas to the central city, while those with means moved out to the suburbs. Data from the Detroit area illustrate this generalization, which applies also to most, if not all, of the other great cities.

According to a study of incomes of families in Detroit and its suburbs, conducted as part of the Detroit Area Study of the University of Michigan (1960), the median income per family in the Detroit metropolitan area was related to the distance the family lived from the central business district. For families living within six miles of the central business district, the median income rose three percent between 1951 and 1959, to a total of $3800; but the cost of living rose 12 percent. Thus in 1959 the median family in this area had less "real income" than the median family who had occupied this area eight years earlier. Families living further out, between the six-mile radius and the city limits, gained 18 percent in median income and reached $6,000, which gave them a small gain in real income. Meanwhile, families living in the Detroit suburban area gained 47 percent in median income, reaching $7,200.

Thus the central part of the city grew poorer during this decade, while the suburbs grew richer. Or, in other words, the central part of the city became more solidly working class in composition while the suburbs became more middle class. This was due to the movement of middle-class people out of the central city.

Some of the effects of this process on schools can be seen by looking at what happened in a particular elementary school in a northern industrial city between 1955 and 1960.

Leibnitz School in 1955 was attended by 1,250 pupils coming mainly from lower-middle- and upper-middle-class families of German, Dutch, and Swedish origin. The district was situated about seven miles from the city center, and close to transportation lines. Parents of some of the pupils had attended the same school.

Then came a period of rapid change. Some of the three-story apartment buildings were cut up into smaller units and rented to southern white and Negro families who were moving into the city in large numbers. By 1960 the school enrollment was 2,400. The school was running on a double-shift schedule, with one group of children coming in the morning to one shift of teachers, and another group coming in the afternoon to a new shift of teachers.

The campus of Leibnitz School was at one time beautifully landscaped, but it has now been filled with gravel to accommodate the hundreds of pupils who arrive at noon and mill around while waiting for their shift to begin.

Transiency at the Leibnitz School is calculated at 70 percent, which means that 1,900 pupils transferred in or out of the school during the year from September, 1960, to June, 1961. At times of heavy turnover the children waiting to transfer in or out are seated in the auditorium, in some cases with their parents; in some cases, without. One clerk sits at a desk on the stage and processes transfers and records from incoming children; another clerk sits on the opposite side of the stage and processes papers for the outgoing children.

The records of transfers out during the past several years show that most of the children leaving the school have transferred to schools farther out from the city center, or to the suburbs.

The influence of transportation methods on the development of the contemporary metropolitan complex is illustrated by Table 2.5, which shows the changes in railway and motor transport since 1900. As motor highways and automobiles and motor trucks have increased, the metropolitan area has grown larger and more complex, though during this period transportation has become a major metropolitan problem.

Table 2.5   *Development of Transport in the Twentieth Century: U.S.A.*

YEAR	MILES OF RAILROAD TRACKS	RAILWAY LOCOMOTIVES	MILES OF SURFACED HIGHWAYS	MOTOR VEHICLES
1900	193,348	37,663	128,500	8,000
1910	240,293	60,019	204,000	468,500
1920	252,845	68,942	369,000	9,239,000
1930	249,052	60,189	694,000	26,532,000
1940	223,670	44,333	1,367,000	32,035,000
1950	223,729	42,951	1,714,000	48,567,000

Metropolitan Area Problems

The metropolitan complex which had come into existence by 1960 brought with it a host of problems for which the society was ill-prepared. As the suburban population increased, and the central city population became relatively impoverished, there was growing difficulty for the government and the school systems of the central city. The suburbs, in turn, found themselves facing unexpected difficulties during the mid-sixties.

The large suburban cities closest to the central city became increasingly like the central city during stage IV. Their growth slowed down as they reached their geographical limit, their houses aged and some became run-down or obsolescent. Slums grew up, and there was an interchange of Negro for white population. This happened in Mount Vernon, next to New York; in Oakland, across the Bay from San Francisco; in University City, next to St. Louis; in Highland Park, next to Detroit.

In the Chicago area, seven close-in suburbs suffered a net out-migration between 1950 and 1960, and continued to grow only because of the natural increase of their residents. Berwyn, Blue Island, Cicero, Evanston, Forest Park, Oak Park, and Maywood had a total net gain in population of 9,300 (three of them actually lost population) and an out-migration during the decade of 22,300.

It is likely that the volume of out-migration from such suburbs will grow larger, unless they develop urban renewal programs that hold people and attract new middle-class residents. Meanwhile, the suburbs further out exert a strong pull on the inner suburbs as well as the central city.

Thus, stage IV has produced a metropolitan complex in which the earlier simple distinctions between central city and suburbs are losing their validity. As the problems of the metropolitan area increased during this stage, the movement of urban renewal gathered momentum in preparation for the next stage, the one in which the major cities are now involved.

Metropolitan growth has produced a set of problems in the mid-sixties which are partly to be solved by improvement in local government, and partly by the efforts of school systems, welfare agencies, church groups, and business groups.

Central cities are faced with growing slums, overcrowded schools, increased juvenile delinquency, heavy unemployment and welfare burdens, and the breakdown of local transit systems. At the same time, the tax base threatens to decrease.

Suburbs are faced with chaotic intergovernmental relations, inadequate public services such as water supply, sewage disposal, police and fire protection.

These problems which have arisen out of metropolitan growth and complexity are the setting for a type of action called *urban renewal*, which is the fifth stage of metropolitan development.

V. URBAN RENEWAL. Urban renewal had its official start with the Federal Housing Act of 1949, which authorized federal grants to cities to acquire and clear blight areas which could be used for subsidized public housing or for sale to private land developers. The clearance of obsolete buildings and redevelopment of the area was the main goal of urban renewal until about 1965, when the goals of *social urban renewal* came into some prominence.

Urban renewal has had two aims—to make living conditions for poor people better in the central cities, and to make the central city more attractive as a place to work and to live for all kinds of people. As we shall see in Chapter 5, the broader aim is coming more and more to dominate this stage of metropolitan development, and the concept of urban renewal is being applied to the entire metropolitan area—to the suburbs as well as the central city.

At its minimum, urban renewal consists of tearing down the worst of the slums and building large blocks of public housing for low-income families. Beyond that minimum, urban renewal consists of planning the growth of the metropolitan area from the center out to the suburbs, with parks, shopping centers, libraries, churches, and schools organized to serve people near where they live; and with industry, the central business district, and the centers of residence linked by fast, comfortable transportation, public and private. Billions of dollars are being spent on bold new physical structures of shopping plazas, garden villages, high-rise apartment housing, and expressways.

Since more than three-fifths of American children go to school in metropolitan areas, and three-fifths of all teachers work in these schools, the schools can hardly be insulated from these momentous events. In fact, organization of school systems and the programs of schools are likely to be determining factors in the forms which urban renewal will eventually take.

This stage of metropolitan development overlaps stage IV and even stage III of some of the smaller cities. Urban renewal funds are available to small and medium-sized cities which do not have much metropolitan complexity, but do have obsolescent housing.

The Emerging Metropolitan Era

As late as 1900, the burgeoning cities of the United States seemed foreign both in spirit and in composition to the land of vast open spaces and expanding frontiers. The cities of those decades were fed by streams of European immigrants. Chicago in 1890 seemed as much foreign as American. There were only two German cities (Berlin and Hamburg) with greater German populations than Chicago; only Christiania and Bergen had more Norwegians than Chicago; and only Stockholm and Goteborg had more Swedes. New York City had half as many Italians as Naples; twice as many Irish as Dublin, as many Germans as Hamburg; and one half as many Jews as Warsaw. (Martindale end Neuwirth, 1958.)

The cities of the late nineteenth century had many problems. They had inadequate roads; the majority of streets were unpaved and became seas of mud in rainy weather. Horse cars and cabs were not adequate for urban traffic needs, and electric trolley lines were just coming into use in 1890. Josiah Strong, writing in a prophetic vein in 1898 about the "Twentieth Century City" said, "We must face the inevitable. The new civilization is certain to be urban; and the problem of the twentieth century will be the city." (Strong, 1898, p. 53.)

The city has supplied its share of social problems, but it has put its stamp upon the twentieth century. One of the great American sociologists, Robert Park, wrote a famous essay which commented on the city as follows:

The city . . . is something more than a congeries of individual men and of social conveniences—streets, buildings, electric lights, tramways, and telephones, etc.; something more than a mere constellation of institutions ̄d administrative devices—courts, hospitals, schools, police, and civil functionaries of various sorts. The city is, rather, a state of mind, a body of customs and traditions, and of organized attitudes and sentiments. . . . The city has, as Oswald Spengler has recently pointed out, its own culture: "What his house is to the peasant, the city is to civilized man. As the house has its household gods, so has the city its protecting Deity, its local saint. The city also, like the peasant's hut, has its roots in the soil." (Martindale and Neuwirth, 1958, p. 34.)

Not only did the city produce an urban type of man. It produced urban fauna and flora: insects such as the bedbug, cockroach, carpet beetle and silver-fish; animals such as rats and alley cats; birds—the English sparrow, pigeon, and starling; plants—ragweed and tree of heaven. The city blotted out the stars with its smoke and created a new atmospheric phenomenon—smog.

The city was always changing. Some of the characteristics referred to above were true fifty years ago, but they seem quaint and archaic to modern city dwellers. Cities are no longer full of foreigners, though ethnic groups still are strong political and religious elements. Cities now recruit their newest members from rural America.

What the students of the city in 1900 did not foresee was the coming of the metropolitan area as the unit of human social living. The metropolitan area is taking the place of the city as the most useful geographical unit for thinking about the coordination and the organization of educational, governmental and other social systems. Educators and government officials and businessmen are developing a theory and a practice of the relations of the physical environment to human satisfactions in the metropolitan area. The attention of educators will be increasingly fixed on the development of the metropolitan area rather than the growth or decline of a city, or the proliferation of suburbs.

The growth of population in the United States since 1900 has taken place largely in metropolitan areas, as is shown in Table 2.6, and

Table 2.6   Population Growth in Metropolitan and Non-Metropolitan Areas: 1900–1960

YEAR	UNITED STATES		SMSA		NON-SMSA		
	Population U.S. (000)	Percent Increase by Decade	Population (000)	Percent Increase by Decade	Population (000)	Percent Increase by Decade	SMSA Population as Percent of Total Population
1900	75,995	—	31,836	—	44,159	—	41.9
1910	91,972	21.0	42,012	32.0	49,960	13.1	45.7
1920	105,711	14.9	52,508	25.0	53,203	6.5	49.7
1930	122,775	16.1	66,712	27.1	56,063	5.4	54.3
1940	131,669	7.2	72,576	8.8	59,093	5.4	55.1
1950	150,697	14.5	88,964	22.6	61,733	4.5	59.0
1960	178,464	18.4	112,385	26.3	66,079	7.0	63.0

Source: U.S. Bureau of the Census. U.S. Census of Population: 1960 Selected Area Reports. Standard Metropolitan Statistical Areas. Final Report PC(3)–10, p. 1.

the growth in metropolitan areas has taken place increasingly in the suburbs, as is shown in Table 2.4. In 1963 the central city was balanced in population by the suburbs. Between 1950 and 1960 the central cities in metropolitan areas increased only 1.5 percent when annexations are not counted, while the areas outside the central cities grew 62 percent.

It is possible that a balance between suburb and central city is now taking place. The economic and racial polarization between them has probably reached its maximum and is already receding. From now on it is likely that the suburbs and central cities will become more like one another, rather than more different from one another.

From now on, suburbs and central cities will increasingly recognize their similarity, and their common interest in cooperation. This will come soon in the more technological aspects and processes of the human enterprise, such as water supply, sewage disposal, streets, and fire protection. It has already come in the area of communication, with newspapers, radio and television serving the entire area.

Cooperation between suburbs and central city will come slowly and with more difficulty in the areas of government and education. These complex social systems are so entrenched in law and custom that they will be hard to change. For instance, the six counties around and including Detroit have more than four million inhabitants and will reach five million before 1970. In this metropolitan "community" there are 214 local governmental units, with 17 special districts and 159 school districts. The Detroit area will soon become one continuous community in the physical urban sense. It is already a community to the newspapers and television stations. How rapidly will it become one community in the governmental sense and the educational sense?

Formation of Megalopolis

In the more populous areas the metropolitan areas stretch out and touch each other, with almost no open farm or forest land between them. To the greatest of these urbanized complexes has been given the name "megalopolis" by Jean Gottmann, the French geographer. Stretching from northeastern Massachusetts through Rhode Island, Connecticut, and along the seaboard and the great bays of New York, New Jersey, Delaware, Pennsylvania, Maryland and Northeast Virginia, this region is given the name "giant city" by Gottmann who says of it:

In this area, then, we must abandon the idea of the city as a tightly settled and organized unit in which people, activities, and riches are crowded into a very small area clearly separated from its nonurban surroundings. Every city in this region spreads out far and wide around its original nucleus; it grows amidst an irregularly colloidal mixture of rural and suburban landscapes; it melts on broad fronts with other mixtures, of somewhat similar though different texture, belonging to the suburban neighborhoods of other cities. (Gottmann, 1961, p. 5.)

This area had 34 SMSAs with 37 million inhabitants in 1960, or one-fifth of the population of the United States. Airplanes shuttle back and forth, and buses and private automobiles traverse the distances between cities on expressways in half the time they needed 30 years ago. On a clear night, jetting in an airplane over this megalopolis, one is never out of sight of the red glow of one or another city.

Other megalopoleis, not yet so large, extend from San Jose through the San Francisco Bay Area to Richmond and Marin County; from San Diego through Los Angeles to Bakersfield; from Milwaukee through Chicago, Gary, South Bend, across southern Michigan to Detroit, Toledo, Cleveland, and over to Pittsburgh; and there is one in the making from Houston to Dallas–Fort Worth.

Planning for Metropolitan Development

These changes and the problems they have created have caught the attention since 1950 of government—local, state, and national—of the business organizations of the country, of the church organizations and of the educational systems. All of these groups through their national and regional organizations have commissions or "task forces" that are actively studying the metropolitan complexity.

This has caused the phrase "urban renewal" to take on a much wider meaning than its original sense of physical slum clearance. It is now a process of planning and developing a rationally-operating metropolitan area, as will be seen in Chapter 5.

Metropolitan areas have most of the people, most of the money, most of the jobs, most of the schools and colleges, theaters and museums. They also have most of the problems—debt, political corruption, racial tension, delinquency, unemployment.

It was inevitable that the national government would pay special attention to metropolitan areas through a cabinet department, and

President Johnson made this clear in his 1965 message to the Congress in which he proposed the new Department of Housing and Urban Development. He redefined the city as "the entire urban area—the central city and its suburbs." He said:

Numbers alone do not make this an urban nation. Finance and culture, commerce and government make their home in the city and draw their vitality from it. Within the borders of our urban centers can be found the most impressive achievements of man's skill and the highest expressions of man's spirit, as well as the worst examples of degradation and cruelty and misery to be found in modern America.

The city is not an assembly of shops and buildings. It is not a collection of goods and services. It is a community for the enrichment of the life of man. It is a place for the satisfaction of man's most urgent needs and his highest aspirations. It is an instrument for the advance of civilization. Our task is to put the highest concerns of our people at the center of urban growth and activity. It is to create and preserve the sense of community with others which gives us significance and security, a sense of belonging and of sharing in the common life.

Aristotle said: "Men come together in cities in order to live. They remain together in order to live the good life."

The modern city can be the most ruthless enemy of the good life, or it can be its servant. The choice is up to this generation of Americans. For this is truly the time of decision for the American city. (Lyndon B. Johnson, 1965, I.)

For the remainder of this century, the greatest domestic social task of the United States is to develop a rationally-operating metropolitan area, with appropriate planning, urban-suburban cooperaton, and political-social reorganization.

Metropolitan Development Around the World

The North American experience with urban and metropolitan development during the current century parallels that of most of the rest of the world. Metropolitan areas exist in every part of the world.

In order to make comparison possible, the International Urban Research group at the University of California at Berkeley has developed a set of criteria to define a metropolitan area as one with 100,000 or more inhabitants, containing at least one city of 50,000 or more. The territory adjacent to the central city must have at least 65 percent of its labor force working at non-agricultural occupations.

Table 2.1 shows the numbers of such urban centers in 1960. According to Gibbs (1961) there were 1,064 of them in 1959. The United Nations' Demographic Yearbook reported 858 in 1950 and 1,166 in 1960.

Among other characteristics, the metropolitan areas of industrialized countries show faster growth in their suburbs than in their central cities.

Growth of metropolitanization is world-wide, in underdeveloped countries as well as in the economically developed countries. Hoyt (1962) estimated that the proportion of the world's population living in metropolitan areas will increase from 20 percent in 1960 to 42 percent in the year 2000.

Exercises

1. Study and report on the development of the metropolitan area in which you live. In what stage of development is it? What were the approximate dates for the preceding stages? What can you predict for the next 20 years?

2. If you live in a metropolitan area of 100,000 to 300,000 try to apply the "concentric ring" theory of urban growth to your area. Make a set of maps to show the structure of the city at various times in its history.

3. If you live in a large metropolitan area, try to apply the theory of "multiple nuclei" to its development. Draw a map showing these nuclei and show how they fit into the total pattern of development.

4. If you live in a city of less than 50,000, study it and its county as an example of conflict between urbanizing and rural styles of life. How do the schools fit in? Do they tend to work toward urbanization?

Suggestions for Further Reading

1. For a good general description of the development of metropolitan areas in the United States, read Chapters 1–6 of *The Metropolis* by Bollens and Schmandt.

2. For studies of the structure of developing cities, read Robert E. Park; *Human Communities,* and Amos H. Hawley, *Human Ecology.*

3. Lewis Mumford's *City in History* gives perspective on the development of cities.

4. Urbanization in the United States and the whole world is described in detail in the fifth edition of *Urban Society*, by Gist and Fava. An excellent set of readings on urban and metropolitan America is found in the book edited by Warren, *Perspectives on the American Community*.

3 ❧ Socio-economic and Racial Stratification in Metropolitan Areas

Metropolitan development is a name for a vast redistribution of people and of jobs which has been going on during the present century and especially since 1920. From the open country and the small towns and cities people have moved toward the larger cities, where the jobs were in a rapidly industrializing society. Then, from the cities they streamed out into the suburbs, to live there, and often to work there in response to the decentralization of industry and business after World War II.

During the process of metropolitan growth, the central cities gained in their proportion of working-class residents and of Negroes, while the suburbs gained in their proportions of middle-class residents. Thus the metropolitan area became stratified along economic and racial lines. The inner shells of the city are populated largely by people with low incomes; the outer shells of the city contain people with middle incomes; and the outer edges of the city and the suburbs have high incomes.

Since the total population of the metropolitan areas has increased, an area that had 500,000 people in 1940 might have 1,000,000 people in 1960. This means that the number of working-class people was doubled, approximately, and the number of middle-class people also doubled. They tended to live in separate and segregated residential areas, which thus grew in size. As a result of this process, children grew up with less contact with children from other types of families than their parents had experienced as children.

In effect, schools became more homogeneous with respect to socio-economic status. From 1920 to 1965, the segregation of children by social class (and by race in northern cities) was increasing. This means that the percent of middle-class children attending schools in which 80 percent or more of the students are middle class has increased since 1920; and the percent of working-class children attending schools in which 80 percent or more of the students are working class has increased since 1920. In the northern cities, the percent of Negro children attending schools in which 80 percent or more of the pupils are Negroes has also increased.

The purpose of this chapter is to explore the phenomenon of increasing stratification in metropolitan areas and to explain its implications for education. To do this we need to use a method of measuring the socio-economic composition of an area, and we do this with the socio-economic ratio (SER).

The Socio-economic Ratio

The socio-economic ratio is essentially a ratio of white-collar to blue-collar workers. It has been slightly refined by the procedure described below, but it is easy to work out with ordinary census data, and can be determined for any city or metropolitan area with a few minutes' work.

The census data on occupations in the male labor force, aged 14 and over, is the base for the SER. The occupations are placed in four categories, as follows:

A. Professional, technical and kindred occupations
   Proprietors, managers and officials
   Farm owners and managers (one fifth of total)
B. Sales and clerical occupations
   Farm owners and managers (two fifths of total)
C. Foremen, craftsmen and kindred occupations
   Operatives and kindred occupations
   Farm owners and managers (two fifths of total)
D. Service workers, including private household workers
   Laborers, including farm laborers

There are some obvious errors in these categories, if a true hierarchy of occupational prestige is wanted. For example, policemen and firemen are included in service workers, but they rank above factory operatives in occupational status. However, the errors tend to neutralize each

other, since semi-skilled workers such as truck drivers are included in
category C but probably should be in category D. In order to test the
SER's, the ratio was computed for the male labor force of the USA
aged 25 to 64 in 1960 more exactly. Farm owners and managers were
distributed between A, B, and C, according to their levels of education.
Men with occupations unreported were distributed between the four
categories according to their incomes. The resultant SER was .80, quite
close to the value of .82 obtained with the cruder method.

The SER is computed by the formula $\dfrac{2A + B}{C + 2D}$

Categories A and D are given a double weighting because they
represent more fully the upper-middle- and lower-working-class characteristics.

This form of the SER could be improved by taking account of the
unemployed, which is a relatively large category in low-income areas of
the city. The unemployed could be added to category D. There are
other refinements which might be made, but the simple form of the
SER is adequate for the purposes of this chapter.

The increasing degree of economic stratification in a metropolitan
area is illustrated in the data of Table 3.1. A socio-economic ratio has
been computed for the years 1940, 1950, and 1960 for the USA, and
for the metropolitan area of Chicago as well as for the suburbs and
the central city of Chicago.

Looking at the SER for the USA, we see that this ratio has been
increasing since 1940, and especially since 1950. This expresses the fact
that the proportion of white-collar jobs in the American economy is
increasing while the proportion of blue-collar jobs is decreasing. The

Table 3.1   *Socio-economic Ratios of the Chicago Area (Based on male
labor force, aged 14+)*

YEAR	USA	CHICAGO SMSA	CHICAGO CITY	CHICAGO SUBURBS	CHICAGO CITY	
					White	*Nonwhite*
1940	.66	.71	.69	.77	.75	.17
1950	.71	.77	.73	.86	.84	.18
1960	.82	.92	.69	1.28	.82	.25

SER for the Chicago Metropolitan Area shows a similar increase, and is higher at all three dates than the SER for the USA as a whole.

In 1940 the city of Chicago was slightly below the average of the metropolitan area. In 1950, the Chicago city SER had increased from .69 to .73, while the total metropolitan area increased from .71 to .77. Clearly, the suburbs were carrying up the metropolitan area total, for they increased from .77 to .86. The city was lagging. The flight of middle-class people to the suburbs was in full course.

But the decade after 1950 saw changes much greater than those which had occurred previously. The city of Chicago decreased in SER from .73 to .69, while the total SMSA increased from .77 to .92, and the suburbs jumped from .86 to 1.28. The central city was decreasing its average socio-economic level in the face of a country-wide increase, as well as a sharp increase in the Chicago area suburbs.

The racial aspect of this phenomenon is also seen in Table 3.1 for the city of Chicago. While the SER of white male workers was going up from .75 to .84 and down to .82 between 1940 and 1960, the SER for nonwhites (almost all Negroes) was increasing very slowly, from .17 to .18 to .25. Since the proportions of nonwhites in Chicago increased from 8.2 percent in 1940 to 22.9 percent in 1960, it was the in-migration of nonwhites with relatively low SER that caused a substantial part of the change in Chicago.

Racial Segregation in Northern Cities

As a part of the increase of socio-economic segregation, there was increased racial segregation in most northern cities. Negro "ghettos" came into being, and the schools reflect this fact. For instance, the 1958 report of New York City's Superintendent of Schools (New York City, 1959) showed a net loss of 15,000 white pupils per year for the preceding five years, pupils who had moved out to the New York suburbs. Negroes formed 20 percent of the school enrollment, and Puerto Ricans, 15 percent. (Because of the heavy immigration of Puerto Ricans into New York City after World War II, data were kept on them as a separate group, though most of them have white skins.) In 1958, of 704 public schools, 455 had 90 percent or more of their pupils of one group, either Negro or white or Puerto Rican (Morrison, 1958). Only one in five schools could be said to be "integrated" in the sense that it had more than ten percent of pupils who did not belong to the majority group for that particular school.

Racial segregation in the schools was a direct result of residential segregation in the cities. Residential segregation grew up after World War I in the northern cities as Negroes migrated to those cities increasingly. Home owners and real estate dealers in the northern cities used the device of the "restrictive covenant" to prevent Negroes from buying homes in areas that were white in composition. The restrictive covenant was written into the deed of ownership of the house, binding the owner not to sell or rent to a colored person. This tended to confine Negroes into areas where the former home owners and the real estate companies by mutual agreement quit enforcing restrictive covenants. But an individual home owner in an all-white area could be brought into court if he sold his house to a Negro in violation of the restrictive covenant in the deed to his house.

Restrictive covenants were declared illegal by the courts toward the close of World War II, and thus it became possible, in theory, for a Negro to acquire a house anywhere in the city, if he could pay the price. Still, most Negroes including the new in-migrants lived in segregated areas due to a general unwillingness of white people in these cities to live in an area that contained substantial numbers of Negroes.

Because of the very rapid increase of Negro population in the northern cities after World War II (see Table 6.3 in Chapter 6) there was a severe pressure for housing, which caused whole city blocks and groups of blocks to "change" within a few months. First a few houses would be sold or rented to Negroes. Then "For Sale" and "For Rent" signs would appear on the other houses. Under the pressure of Negro in-migration, there were always buyers or renters for houses available to Negroes. White people who wished to remain in integrated residential areas were in such a small minority that they were generally powerless to influence enough of their white neighbors to make a stabilized inter-racial neighborhood.

A few areas of middle-class white people resisted the segregation movement by forming local community conservation groups that welcomed Negro neighbors who could afford to buy middle-class housing and would keep up the property, and by insisting on the enforcement of housing codes so as to prevent subdividing of houses and apartments with resultant overcrowding and deterioration.

Also a few housing projects were developed for middle-income apartment dwellers in favorable locations in the central city. An area which had become largely slum would be torn down and new middle-income apartment buildings built, to serve a racially mixed clientele. This proved fairly successful on a small scale in several cities. The people who rented the apartments were generally young married people without children or with small children, or older couples whose children were grown up. Thus these people were not especially concerned with the schools. These middle-class residential islands were too small to populate schools of their own, except occasionally an elementary school. For children of high school age, the nearest high school was often an all-Negro and largely working-class school.

The growth of Negro population (and correlatively, of segregated schools) is illustrated by Table 3.2, which shows the population of whites and nonwhites in the central city and the suburbs of Chicago. From 1940 to 1965 the numbers of white residents of Chicago decreased while the numbers of nonwhite residents increased sharply. Similar population changes took place in all the big northern industrial cities.

Table 3.2   *Population of Chicago and Suburban Area: 1940–1980*

YEAR	CITY OF CHICAGO		SUBURBAN RING	
	White	*Nonwhite*	*White*	*Nonwhite*
1940	3,115,000	282,000	1,148,000	25,000
1950	3,112,000	509,000	1,512,000	45,000
1960	2,713,000	838,000	2,588,000	82,000
1965	2,579,000	980,000	2,980,000	113,000
1970 (est.)	2,427,000	1,173,000	3,525,000	175,000
1980 (est.)	2,234,000	1,540,000	4,499,000	347,000

Source: U.S. Census and *Population Projections for the Chicago Standard Metropolitan Statistical Area and City of Chicago.* Population Research and Training Center, University of Chicago, 1964.

Projections of School-Age Population in Chicago SMSA.

Unless something happens to alter the trends, there will be further stratification along racial and economic lines. Table A–2 shows the projections of school-age population by race for the City of Chicago and its suburban ring. This is based on careful analysis of census data by the Population Research Center of the University of Chicago. It assumes that present trends of birth rates and death rates will continue and that the rate of Negro migration from the South will be reduced while the rate of Negro migration to the suburbs will increase. Even with these assumptions, the school population of Chicago will increase substantially in its Negro population.

There is every reason to expect the same trends in other urban and industrial areas—Philadelphia, Cleveland, Detroit, Cincinnati, St. Louis, Kansas City, Los Angeles, Portland. On the other hand, projections are not facts. Trends can be changed if people work to change them. And the aim of the contemporary movement for social urban renewal is to change these trends, so as to produce a more balanced and mixed metropolitan area population, with all kinds of people in terms of income and color living all over the area.

Stratification Within the Central City—Effects on the Schools

The school achievement of pupils in schools of the central city and the suburbs reflect their socio-economic differences. Studies of school achievement in relation to socio-economic characteristics of the school neighborhood show a clear relationship within the central city. Havighurst (1964) reported this in the Chicago School Survey. Table 3.3 shows how the elementary schools in Chicago's 21 school districts reflect the socio-economic status of their neighborhoods. The median family income and the median level of education of adults in the various districts were combined into a single measure of socio-economic status, and the 21 districts are recorded in Table 3.3 according to this index. The IQ, achievement level at the sixth grade in reading and arithmetic on a standardized achievement test, and the performance of the beginners of Grade 1 on a reading readiness test are related quite closely to the socio-economic rank of the school district.

It will be noted in Table 3.3 that the seven school districts lowest in socio-economic status contain 61 percent to 100 percent Negro elementary school pupils; and that the reading readiness scores indicate that only one of the seven districts has as many as 50 percent of first graders "ready" to learn to read. According to the manual for the Metropolitan Reading Readiness test, a child who does not score average or above average on the readiness test has very little chance of learning to read in the first grade unless he receives a great deal of individual attention from the teacher. In classes with 50 to 65 percent of first graders needing individualized instruction, the ordinary first-grade teacher with 35 pupils can hardly be expected to supply this kind of help unless she has assistance. On the other hand, in the top third of the school districts according to socio-economic status, the number of pupils needing individual help varies from one tenth to one fourth, and the first grade teacher may be able to work with that many.

A study made by Patricia Sexton (1961) in a big northern city shows how the socio-economic characteristics of pupils are related to other factors. She obtained the average incomes of families living in

Table 3.3 *Socio-economic Status, School Achievement, and Race by School Districts in Chicago*

RANK ORDER IN *SE* STATUS DISTRICT NO.	*IQ*	GRADE 6, 1963 ACHIEVEMENT IN READING & ARITH., GRADE LEVEL	GRADE 1, 1963 READING READINESS, % AVERAGE OR ABOVE	OCTOBER 1963 % OF ELEMENTARY PUPILS NEGRO
2	111	7.5	75	0
18	104	6.8	74	37
1	112	7.8	89	0
17	108	7.4	74	7
16	101	6.4	67	77
4	107	7.1	78	1
3	107	6.8	74	0
14[1]	95	5.8	48	85
7[2]	94	5.8	44	48
5	109	7.2	85	0
15	109	7.2	79	16
10	96	6.0	48	67
20	93	5.7	47	100
12	103	6.7	65	1
6	99	6.3	52	69
21	91	5.5	41	92
8	89	5.4	33	81
11	92	5.5	45	96
19	93	5.6	45	61
13	90	5.5	42	100
9	90	5.3	34	81
City wide	99	6.2	55	

[1] District contains University of Chicago, with many children going to the University School (private).

[2] District includes North Side "Gold Coast," with many children in private schools.

Source: Robert J. Havighurst, *The Public Schools of Chicago*, p. 39.

the various school districts, and then grouped the 243 schools by their income ranks. The schools in a given group tended to be located about the same distance from the central business district, with the highest income schools farthest out.

As can be seen in Tables 3.4 and 3.5, the schools in the lower income areas had poorer records of achievement, intelligence, behavior, and drop-outs; while the schools in the higher income areas had more pupils chosen in elementary and junior high school to participate in a program for "gifted" children, and more senior high school pupils going to college. Also, the schools closer to the center of the city had higher proportions of families with mothers working, and with mothers

Table 3.4   *Income Levels and Characteristics of Pupils in "Big City" Elementary Schools*

AVERAGE INCOME, 1957	COMPOSITE SCORE, IOWA ACHIEVEMENT TEST, 6TH GRADE	IQ RATING	PUPILS SENT TO DETENTION SCHOOL (PER 10,000)	CONDITION OF SCHOOL BUILDING (PERFECT—1,000)
$3,000–$4,999	5.23	2.79	31.3	574
$5,000–$6,999	5.61	3.31	21.7	578
$7,000–$8,999	6.47	4.55	6.9	688
$9,000–	7.05	5.09	2.7	779

Source: Sexton, 1961.

Table 3.5   *Income Levels and Characteristics of Pupils in "Big City" High Schools*

AVERAGE INCOME, 1957	NUMBER CHOSEN AS "GIFTED" (PER 10,000)	PERCENT OF H.S. STUDENTS WITH FAILURE IN ENGLISH	PERCENT OF DROP-OUTS, 1957–58	PERCENT OF GRADUATING CLASS REQUESTING TRANSCRIPTS FOR COLLEGE
Below $6,000	1	16.8	19.2	23
$6,000–$6,999	6	10.9	15.8	34
$7,000–$7,999	20	9.3	7.9	46
$8,000–$8,999	36	8.5	7.2	61
$9,000–	79	6.6	3.6	81

Source: Sexton, 1961.

receiving Aid for Dependent Children, indicating that a father was not present in the home.

Effects on an Elementary School.

We have already seen (in Chapter 2) how the Leibnitz Elementary School changed during a five-year period from a school serving a stable working-class and lower-middle-class community into a slum school with an extremely high transiency rate. In 1955 this school had an SER of about 1. Then the process of subdividing apartments and renting them to working-class families with large numbers of children caused the socio-economic ratio to drop. In this case the crowding of the school, the introduction of a double-shift program, and the appearance of Negro children all combined to cause some people to move away. This resulted in a rapid lowering of the SER and by 1960 this was .06.

Such a school has the following characteristics: First, there is a wide spread of intellectual ability and achievement within a single grade. There are a few children of relatively high IQ, there are some average, and many below average. Their achievement, as measured by standard tests, shows a range of six or seven years in the intermediate grades. Some seventh-grade children will be reading at a tenth-grade level while others will be at the third-grade level. Second, there is a wide spread of educational motivation. A few children are extremely eager to achieve academically. They will work hard for the teacher, and their parents encourage them to work hard. Many other children are indifferent about school, or actively hostile to it.

Usually in such a school there is a system of ability grouping of the children, which aims to make the school tolerable for the minority of children who have average or better ability and who show substantial academic motivation. As long as the school maintains special classes for the brighter children, a few lower-middle class families will stay in the area and the stable lower-class families will be satisfied.

Polarization Between Central City and Suburbs

The migration out from the central city to the suburbs has consisted largely of middle-income white-collar people. As was noted in Table

3.1, this migration produced a kind of polarization of the metropolitan area, with the lower status and low income people making up the majority of central city residents, while the higher status and higher income people placed their stamp on the suburbs.

By 1960 it was definitely established that the suburban areas had higher socio-economic status than the central cities, and the basic facts are shown in Table 3.6. This Table combines occupation, income and education into a single scale of economic status, and compares the residents of central cities with the residents of the urbanized portion of the suburban area. It omits the residents who lived on farms or in non-urbanized villages in metropolitan areas.

Table 3.6   *Proportion of Population, White and Nonwhite, by Economic Status Residing in Central Cities and in the Urban Fringe: 1960*

PLACE	SOCIO-ECONOMIC STATUS SCORE			
	80–99 (*highest status*)	50–79	20–49	0–19 (*lowest status*)
Total Population				
Central Cities	13.7%	42.4%	35.2%	8.6%
Urban Fringe	22.8	50.1	23.4	3.7
White Population				
Central Cities	16.0	46.8	31.1	6.1
Urban Fringe	23.7	51.3	22.0	3.0
Nonwhite Population				
Central Cities	3.0	21.9	54.5	20.6
Urban Fringe	3.6	25.2	52.7	18.4

Source: U.S. Bureau of the Census. Current Population Reports, *Technical Studies*, Series P. 23, No. 12, July 31, 1964.

The urban fringe exceeded the central cities in the proportions of residents in the highest fifth on a scale of economic status, while the central cities had more than twice as high a proportion of residents in the lowest fifth.

Nevertheless, Table 3.6 indicates that the economic distinction between suburbs and central city is only one of degree. There are many low income people in suburbs and many high income people in central cities. Further study of metropolitan areas shows that the general pattern is set by the large northeastern and middle western metropolitan areas, while the smaller SMSAs and those in the South and the West do not fit the pattern.

The variation in degree of polarization of the larger areas is seen in relation to regions of the country in Table 3.7. This Table presents data on the proportions of the adult population (over 25) who have graduated from high school, comparing the central cities with the area outside central cities for 23 of the larger SMSAs. Those with a high

Table 3.7 *Polarization in Metropolitan Areas in Terms of Education of Adults Within Central City and Outside Central City (Percent at ages 25 and over who are at least high school graduates)*

SMSA	1960 Outside CC	1960 Central City	1940 Outside CC	1940 Central City
High Polarization				
Cleveland	55	30	45	21
Chicago	52	35	31	25
New York	52	37	33	22
Washington	65	48	43	41
Philadelphia	46	31	27	19
St. Louis	41	26	23	18
Newark	50	27	33	17
Milwaukee	53	40	29	22
Buffalo	44	30	23	20
Baltimore	41	28	21	19
Medium Polarization				
Detroit	47	34	27	26
Boston	57	45	39	32
Minneapolis–St. Paul	60	47	27	34
San Francisco–Oakland	58	49	41	37
Cincinnati	41	34	21	25
Atlanta	48	41	26	31
Kansas City	52	47	27	40
Pittsburgh	43	35	22	24
Low Polarization				
Los Angeles	54	54	42	42
Houston	46	45	27	36
Seattle	56	56	31	43
Dallas	48	49	31	40
San Diego	54	55	38	41

Source: 1940 Census of Population, v.2; 1960 Census of Population, Tables 73, 74, 76 of State Reports in Series PC(1)C and PC(3)1D, Table 8.

polarization, or a relatively large excess of high school graduates outside of the central city, are all in the Northeast and Middle West. Those with little or no difference between central city and suburbs are on the West Coast or in Texas.

The same regional difference is seen in Table A–3, which reports that college graduates are more likely to live outside the central city than in the central city, unless they are in the western states.

Table 3.8 throws more light on the matter with its report on regional differences in population growth in central cities and outside central cities. In 1930 the central cities of the North and East had practically stopped growing, while the suburbs were growing rapidly. In the West and South, however, central cities were growing vigorously, though not as rapidly as suburban areas. This means that the central cities of the West and South have had room to grow, partly by annexation of suburban areas and partly by building on vacant property.

Table 3.8   *Population Growth in Central Cities and Outside Central Cities by Regions: 1900–1960*

	NORTH AND EAST	SOUTH	WEST
	%	%	%
1900–10			
Central Cities	32.4	41.2	89.0
Outside Central Cities	21.7	18.3	64.7
1910–20			
Central Cities	24.6	37.8	37.7
Outside Central Cities	20.8	10.3	39.2
1920–30			
Central Cities	18.8	38.3	45.1
Outside Central Cities	31.7	19.6	63.8
1930–40			
Central Cities	2.4	14.4	11.9
Outside Central Cities	9.7	23.7	29.3
1940–50			
Central Cities	7.4	29.9	33.0
Outside Central Cities	24.9	43.5	79.3
1950–60			
Central Cities	0.3	28.5	31.9
Outside Central Cities	43.7	47.7	65.9

Source: U.S. Census Bureau: *U.S. Census of Population: 1960 Selected Area Reports. Standard Metropolitan Statistical Areas.* Final Report PC(3)–1D.

Thus they have maintained attractiveness for the more affluent residents.

The factor of size of the SMSA is brought out in Table 3.9, which shows the ratio of the number of families with incomes over $10,000 (in 1959) to the number with incomes under $3,000, and gives these ratios for central city and outside central city in SMSAs of various sizes. This table shows that the smaller SMSAs are quite different from the larger ones in this respect. The smaller SMSAs have smaller ratios of affluent to poor families. The smaller SMSAs (those below 250,000 in population) have more of their high-income residents in the central city than outside.

Table 3.9 *Ratio of Number of Families with Incomes over $10,000 to Families under $3,000 by SMSA Size: 1959*

POPULATION OF SMSA	ENTIRE SMSA	CENTRAL CITY (CC)	OUTSIDE CENTRAL CITY (OCC)	DIFFERENCE IN RATIO: (OCC-CC)
United States	124.2	93.9	169.4	75.5
Over 3,000,000	183.0	126.7	311.5	184.8
1,000,000 to 3,000,000	160.5	97.3	238.9	141.6
500,000 to 1,000,000	95.6	73.8	129.3	55.5
250,000 to 500,000	82.8	78.6	87.4	8.8
100,000 to 250,000	70.3	73.1	66.6	− 6.5
Less than 100,000	67.0	76.3	44.0	−32.3

Source: U.S. Bureau of the Census. *U.S. Census of Population: 1960, Selected Area Reports, Standard Metropolitan Statistical Areas.* True ratio is multiplied by 100.

The polarization of central city and suburb was further accentuated by the migration of southern rural Negroes into the central cities after World War II. Table A–4 shows how the growing numbers of Negroes were distributed between central city and suburbs. After 1940 the proportion of nonwhites in central cities increased rapidly, while the proportion of nonwhites outside of central cities decreased slightly. Moreover, as seen in Table 3.6, the nonwhite population did not reflect the economic polarization within itself that was true of the white population. Middle and low income Negroes were distributed evenly between suburbs and central cities.

As we shall see in the next section, there are forces tending to bring about a new balance between suburbs and central cities, and to reduce the polarization which probably has reached a maximum during the 1960's. Leo Schnore (1963) studied central cities and their suburban fringes in 200 SMSAs, and he noted that in the newer metropolitan areas, central cities generally outrank the suburbs in occupation, education, and income. Table A–5 shows how the age of the SMSA is related to polarization. He sees no basis for a prediction that the higher status groups in the new metropolitan areas will repeat the process of shifting to the suburbs.

Stratification of Suburbs

While the process of socio-economic stratification has gone on in the central city, the suburban area has not been an unmixed upper and upper-middle-class preserve, as might be supposed from the over-simple generalizations that sometimes are stated about polarization of suburb and central city. The area around the central city has independent villages and smaller cities which retain some of their character while the metropolitan area surrounds them and takes them over. There are favored directions of growth for high-status residential areas. The high-status suburbs may develop along a lake shore, or along the high banks of a river, or on the side of the city that itself has been a high-status section, or around a country club.

For example, the following account of the development of upper-class suburbs of Milwaukee shows the influence of a lake shore and a favored section of the central city. Richard Dewey (1948) described the experience of Milwaukee before 1950 as follows: "The clear-cut directional movement of the upper-class migration started with the move to the upper east side of Milwaukee proper, thence to Shorewood, Whitefish Bay, Fox Point, and River Hills. One climbs the social ladder by following this route, as is evidenced by the fact that the persons whose names are listed in the *Social Register* live almost exclusively in the areas named. Fox Point and River Hills have the greatest proportions of population listed in the *Social Register*."

In other directions from the central city there may be heavy industry, or a swampy region, or city dumps, which make these directions unsatisfactory for middle-class suburbs. Thus the suburban area takes on a social structure, and the suburbs become differentiated into communities which are predominantly upper-middle, or lower-middle, or upper-working class. The city dweller who aspires to a house in the suburbs will find that the amount of money he can pay for a house determines the type of suburb he will live in. If he is employed as a manual worker in an auto assembly plant or an electronics factory located 15 miles out of the city, he is likely to make a payment on a two-bedroom bungalow in a real estate development in which there are hundreds of similar houses, all variants of one basic design, all on small lots with a plot of grass in front, a garage and clothes-line in the rear. He will live in a working-class suburb. If he is a lawyer with an office in the city he will buy a ranch-type house on a large lot in an area where all other houses are of similar size and cost, in a new section of a well-established upper-middle-class suburb that has a reputation for good schools and a good country club.

The New York metropolitan complex shows this decentralized stratification more clearly than other centers, partly because of its size, and partly because it contains several large and mature industrial cities, such as Jersey City, Bayonne, Newark, Paterson, Passaic, and Elizabeth, none of which is part of the central city of New York. Members of the lower-working class live in Manhattan, Brooklyn, the Bronx, and in the Jersey industrial cities. Craftsmen and foremen live out beyond the lower-working class and also in some of the residential suburbs such as Mineola on Long Island, Tuckahoe in Westchester County, and Roselle Park in Union County. The upper-middle and upper classes live in Manhattan (on the upper East Side), in Westchester County to the north, Nassau County on Long Island, and Essex and Bergen counties in New Jersey.

The suburban stratification is partly due to decentralization of industry after World War II. After the war, there were various economic factors, as described in Chapter 2 that led to further decentralization of industry. In the 48 largest metropolitan areas, the proportion of manufacturing production workers living in the central cities declined from 67 percent in 1929 to 58 percent in 1954.

The older, larger, and closer-in suburbs by the 1960's were developing their own structure, like that of the central city. An example of this kind of situation and its influence on the high school is seen in the Madison Township High School.

Madison is a small, semi-industrial city which has been surrounded by residential suburbs since World War II. Several of these small suburbs have elementary schools of their own, but send their teen-agers to Madison High School. Until recently the high school had a SER of approximately 1, with a cross-sectional student body including about ten percent Negroes.

About five years ago a middle-class suburb five miles from Madison which had been sending its pupils to Madison High joined with a new suburb farther out to set up its own high school. This was somewhat disturbing to people in Madison, but just then a new middle-class residential area on the outskirts of Madison was being built, and it supplied a number of middle-class students who replaced the earlier group. This new suburb, Elmwood, continued to grow, and just last year established its own high school, which took away about one-fourth of the students of Madison High, and reduced the SER of Madison to .40. There is a Negro working-class suburb which sends its students to Madison, and appears to be content with this arrangement. But the faculty and the dwindling group of middle-class parents in Madison High are now fearful that their school will become a slum-type school, and they argue that the behavior of the Elmwood group in forming its own high school was undemocratic.

Types of Suburbs

In a contemporary complex metropolitan area there are suburbs of three major types. They are distinguished principally by differences in the ratio of the numbers of people who live in them to the numbers who work in them. More technically, this ratio consists of the number of members of the labor force who *live* in the suburb divided by the number of members of the labor force who *work* in the suburb. This ratio varies from 0.1, for a suburb in which nearly all the adult males commute to work in the central city, to 2.0, where most of the local adults plus a considerable number of people from outside the suburb come to work in the suburb.

A DORMITORY SUBURB is one in which at least half of the local residents work outside of the suburb, generally in the central city, though they may work in other parts of the metropolitan area. There is nothing but small local business in this suburb. There are middle-class and working-class dormitory suburbs. For instance, Glencoe and Park Forest of Chicago, Bronxville and Scarsdale of New York, Shaker Heights of

Cleveland, Clayton of St. Louis, the Shawnee Mission district of Kansas City, San Mateo of San Francisco, Pasadena of Los Angeles, are middle-class suburbs of the metropolitan areas named. Working-class dormitory suburbs are more difficult to find. They generally are quite young, having been formed since World War II. There are Negro working-class dormitory suburbs, as well as those occupied by whites. For example, the town of Robbins, southwest of Chicago, has 10,000 residents, all Negro and nearly all working-class. They work in the industries of the southern suburbs of Chicago. There are about a dozen dormitory suburbs populated largely by white working-class people in the Chicago area.

AN EMPLOYING SUBURB is one in which more than half of the local residents work in the suburb, while relatively few non-residents work there. It tends to be economically self-sufficient, and a kind of cross-section of the area in terms of socio-economic status. Those who work in this suburb are employed in local business, sometimes in a local college, in the area's airport, often in a light industry such as electronics or plastics, or in a business establishment such as the regional office of an insurance company. Examples in the Chicago area are Evanston, Blue Island, and Des Plaines. Owing to the post-war decentralization of industry, employing suburbs have grown rapidly since World War II.

A MANUFACTURING SUBURB imports workers for its industry. Most of the people living in this suburb work in local business and industry, which is likely to be one or more large manufacturing plants—steel products, electric products, airplanes, automobiles, chemicals, etc. Examples in the Chicago area are Chicago Heights, Cicero, and Melrose Park. In terms of socio-economic ranking, this type of suburb generally falls somewhat below average, having a higher proportion of manual workers than the average of the metropolitan area.

All three types of suburbs have grown rapidly since World War II. In the North and East the dormitory suburbs have grown more rapidly than the other types, in the large metropolitan areas. But this is probably not true of smaller SMSAs and of those in the West.

THE NEW BALANCE. It appears that a new balance between suburb and central city is becoming established. The economic and racial polarization between them has probably reached its maximum and is already receding. From now on it is likely that the suburbs and central cities will become more like one another, rather than more different from one another.

The forces which were to bring about the new balance were already dimly visible by 1960. For instance, one of the new post-war suburbs of New York City, Levittown on Long Island, became less middle class and more working class in composition between 1950 and 1960. Whereas 62 percent of the adult males were in white-collar occupations in 1950–51, the proportion dropped to 50 percent in 1961. (Dobriner, 1963, p. 98.)

The suburbs tend to decrease in average socio-economic status for two reasons. One is the decentralization of metropolitan industry and business, with light industry being located in suburban areas, big shopping centers being built there, and the central and regional offices of certain kinds of business, such as insurance companies, being located in suburbs. Many lower-middle- and working-class employees of these concerns seek to live nearby, and thus build up new "common man" residential areas. The other reason is that the older suburbs are becoming obsolescent, following the patterns of the central cities, and higher-status families move from there out to newer suburbs, or back into the central city.

There is also a "reverse migration" setting in from suburbs to central city. As urban renewal clears old buildings from attractive sites, new middle and high income homes and apartments are built, which offer space to people who prefer to live in the central city. There has been a good deal of such rebuilding since 1950, and probably more since 1960 than during the previous decade. However, the volume of reverse migration is low, according to the information now available. Karl M. Taeuber and Alma F. Taeuber (1964) studied migration between central city and suburban areas in the 12 largest metropolitan areas for the years 1955–1960. They found that migration from suburbs to central city within a given SMSA was one-sixth as great as migration from the central city to the suburban area. The in- and out-migrants were better educated than the non-migrants.

We may speculate that the volume of migration from suburbs to central city is increasing during the current decade. However, the people who migrate into the central city are probably largely older people without children of school age or young people who are just starting their families.

Another evidence of the growing similarity of suburbs and central city is the growth of Roman Catholic schools in the suburbs. Since

1950 the Catholic school enrollments in central cities have just about stayed constant, while their enrollments in suburban areas have increased sharply. This means that Roman Catholic city dwellers have been migrating to the suburbs, which earlier were largely Protestant.

Speaking of the *new balance* between suburbs and central city does not signify that the balance has arrived in 1965. The next ten years will see a substantial movement toward this balance, and it will be registered in the educational field as early as anywhere else.

The Pathology of Socio-economic and Racial Segregation

It may be argued that people are exercising a democratic freedom of choice when they form neighborhoods or residential areas of people like themselves. People tend to feel comfortable when their neighbors have the same style of life that they have. They like to have their children grow up with children from families like their own. Consequently, it may be argued, it is not only natural but also desirable that there should be homogeneous areas of the city, and that suburbs should be socially homogeneous communities.

On the other hand, one of the foundations of democracy is the cooperation of its members in government and other forms of social activity. Such cooperation is likely to be increased and improved if people of various social, economic, and racial backgrounds mingle freely and get to know and understand one another. This argues for heterogeneous residential communities, in which the children and the adults of various social groups associate freely in schools, churches, libraries, parks, and political and social activities.

Furthermore, a democratic society establishes and maintains as much opportunity as possible for social and economic betterment of the individual. This requires that the individual have opportunity to study with, work with, and grow up with people who have the characteristics he wants to acquire—the attitudes toward work, the language habits, the social manners—which he needs in order to achieve his socially valuable aims in life.

Arrangements for living and working in a metropolitan area are affected by these arguments. Since men can influence the social structure of the metropolitan area by adopting and applying social policies, they are continually working to direct and control the impersonal forces of society so as to improve the conditions under which they and their children live and work.

One aspect of society which everybody agrees is pathological is poverty and its correlates. Along with poverty go unemployment, crime, juvenile delinquency, bad housing, broken families, and residential segregation. The social measures so far adopted to combat poverty are not fully satisfactory. Public welfare payments to poor people, aid to mothers of dependent children who do not have husbands to support them, subsidized public housing in large segregated settlements, are well-intentioned, but they do not get at the causes of poverty.

Meanwhile, poverty tends to be segregated, and the segregation of the poor does not contribute to the cure of poverty.

One way by which poverty has been segregated in the United States is through subsidized public housing. The federal government has made grants to local government agencies for the clearing of slums and the building of housing projects which are then rented to low-income families at below-cost rents, depending on family income and size. The local housing authority, which receives the government funds, constructs the new houses and administers the project, generally locating the new project in an area that has been cleared of slum buildings. It generally builds high-rise apartment buildings, though sometimes it builds blocks of two- or three-story buildings spread over an area of one or two city blocks. The typical housing project contains two to three hundred apartments with a thousand or more residents. For example, Washington, D.C., in 1965 had 37 projects housing 8,400 families with 41,500 people. To qualify for public housing, a family's annual income in the Washington projects could not exceed $3,200 to $5,100, depending on the size of the family. Once a family was admitted, the income could rise to $4,000 to $6,400, again depending on size; and a family which succeeded in getting above these income levels was forced to leave the project.

After some initial attempts to maintain a policy of integrated residence in public housing projects, most housing authorities practiced segregation, operating some projects for whites and some for Negroes. In many cities, there was a predominance of Negro residents. For instance, the *Washington Post* of December 18, 1965, reported that 98 percent of Washington's public housing residents were Negroes. At the same time, 92 percent of Chicago's public housing citizens were Negroes.

Recently the public housing authorities have been trying to avoid segregation based on economic status and race through small four- or six-family houses which can be built on vacant lots in any part of the city. In spite of objections from some all-white and middle-class communities to having even small public housing units in their midst, other such communities have requested the local housing authority to build this type of project.

There is also some discussion of allowing residents of public housing projects to stay as long as they please, no matter what their income is, and using a sliding scale of rents which rises to a level which is the same as that for private housing when the family's income rises definitely above the poverty level. This would have the effect of building local leadership in housing projects based on the more successful families, which under current policies are expelled because they are economically successful. This would also result in making public housing projects more nearly self-supporting, and would bring public housing into competition with the real estate business, by giving people a choice between renting from a public housing project and renting from a private corporation or landlord at the same rates.

Is Segregation Always Bad?

Any form of segregation which is forced upon a person against his will is likely to be opposed and resisted by him. Therefore a democratic society tries to maintain as much freedom as possible for its members to go where they wish, to live where they wish, and to work where they wish. Segregation may be imposed as punishment, as in the case of prison for a person who has committed a crime or a child's being sent to his room for misbehaving.

If, under freedom of choice, people of a similar economic status, nationality background, or skin color get together in their own social organizations and residential communities, this is acceptable in a democratic society as long as they do not monopolize some scarce good, such as a lake shore, a park, choice schools, and the like. Thus a certain amount of freely-chosen segregation is to be expected in a democracy.

However, a democracy depends for its welfare on the welfare of all of its citizens, and therefore must provide opportunity for all of them to share in the things that are important to the good life for them —education, business activity, employment, use of public facilities such as hotels, restaurants, transit lines. A democracy cannot systematically deny full opportunity in these areas to any of its members and still be a democracy in fact as well as in name.

This is the reason that *de facto* segregation in school, whether along racial lines or along socio-economic lines, is bad for a democracy. Since it has been proven to the satisfaction of the United States Supreme Court that segregation by race in the public schools is a denial of opportunity to the minority racial group, racial segregation is now officially believed to be undesirable, whether it be expressed through law or through custom.

But socio-economic segregation is also undesirable, in the eyes of people who believe in democracy and who have studied the effects of such segregation or stratification in the schools. From social scientists who have studied the relation of schools to society, from judges who have studied the significance of the American constitution for the educational system, and from social philosophers and religious leaders, has come a common agreement on the importance of the school as a place where boys and girls from all social groups can learn together. It has been affirmed by the courts that schools which are limited by law or by residential segregation to Negroes are not good for Negro youth, and should be changed. It has been found by social scientists that schools attended predominantly by children of lower socio-economic status do not succeed in teaching these children as well as do schools of mixed socio-economic composition.

Effects of Socio-economic and Racial Stratification and Segregation in the Schools

Every school has its own special characteristics: special folkways, customs, and legends. Not only do schools have different insignia, songs, and symbols, but they differ in less tangible ways. In one school the relationships between teachers and pupils are unusually intimate and friendly; in another, unusually formal. One school has an atmosphere of regimentation; another emphasizes individual differences between pupils. In one school, competition is played up; in another, it is played down. There is often a special history and tradition that develops. In one case, students may feel fierce pride in their school and its accomplishments. In another, there may be a feeling of resignation among both children and adults, as if mediocrity is all that can be expected in any school endeavor.

The culture of the school has a profound effect upon what children and adolescents learn and the ways in which they learn. There is a saying that children learn not what is taught, but what is "caught." Much of what is caught (attitudes toward learning, toward authority, values of right and wrong, and so on) comes not from the formal curriculum but from the pervading culture of the school.

In a school there is usually a dominant group of students which defines and establishes the *ethos* of the school. When the dominant group of students is in accord with the values and expectations of the teachers and the parents, the resulting ethos or set of values has a strong effect upon nearly all students. When the parents and teachers expect a school to prepare most of its students for college, the school program reflects this expectation, and the students share the expectation. But when the parents have no educational goal for the children beyond high school, and if teachers get the notion that the students in this school cannot learn well, the ethos of the school reflects this set of expectations, and it affects the performance of most of the students.

In this same connection, a study (Wilson, 1959) of eight different high schools in the San Francisco–Oakland Bay area provided good evidence that the ethos of a given school affects the academic achievement and occupational aspirations of its students in measurable degree. The eight schools varied considerably with regard to the proportion of students who came from families of different occupational levels, and thus showed differences in regard to the climate of values that prevailed. It was found that in schools that were predominantly lower status (the majority of fathers were manual workers), the *proportion of middle-class boys* who planned to go to college was significantly lower than in schools of predominantly middle-class students. Congruently, a lower-status boy attending a school in which the majority of his classmates were middle class (their fathers were upper-level white-collar or professional workers) was more likely to plan to go to college than if he attended a school in which the majority of his classmates were working class. The investigator interpreted these findings as evidence that the school milieu and peer-group norms can significantly modify the effects of social class in influencing the adolescent's values.

Furthermore, Wilson found that the school environment affected the grades obtained by a boy. A working-class boy attending a school with a predominance of middle-class pupils was more likely to get good grades than a working-class boy *of the same IQ,* who attended a school with a predominance of working-class pupils.

Wilson (1963) also studied the elementary schools of Berkeley, California, and found that a child of a particular social class and ethnic group would achieve differently in a school of one socio-economic composition than he would in a school of another socio-economic composition.

A similar finding is reported by Havighurst and his associates in their study of school dropouts in River City. Boys and girls who dropped out without graduating from high school were paired with others of the same IQ and socio-economic status who did graduate from high school. The stay-ins lived in areas and went to elementary schools of higher socio-economic status than the dropouts, on the average. (Havighurst, Bowman et al, 1962, p. 184.)

The following two cases illustrate the influence of the ethos of a school upon the educational achievement. In both cases the boy was above average in learning ability, but not superior.

Case of Sidney, 17 years old.   Sidney started school in 1952, attending Kelly school, and transferred to Holmes, Roosevelt, and Douglas elementary schools in that order. As far as he remembers there was not much difference among them except for Roosevelt. The class at Roosevelt was behind the comparable class at Holmes, and Sidney just loafed through that year. Douglas was harder, and he worked harder.

Sidney started ninth grade at Washington High School in 1960. This school had an SER of .22 and had 35 percent of its ninth-grade class in Basic English, which meant that they were reading below the sixth-grade level. After four semesters, Sidney's family moved to the south side and he transferred to Jefferson High School, which had an SER of 2.50. He continued in the College Preparatory Course of Study. At Washington, Sidney had been an average student, with grades of C and B. His weakest subject was math. In his first semester at Jefferson school he almost failed, receiving grades of D and E. There were four courses he continued at Jefferson school which were started at Washington:

> *English:*   At Jefferson there was more required reading and thus a faster reading speed was important. They were more thorough in testing what was read. At Washington he could "bluff" his way through with little effort. He had developed bad study habits due to a lack of demand on the part of the teachers and his own "goofing off." His reading was slow although in grammar school he had had a high reading rate. The same series of books were used and others in addition were

of the same caliber in both high schools. However, at Jefferson they were further advanced.

French: At Washington, Sidney had six different teachers in his first semester. They started the first chapter six times. There was little work required. At Jefferson he found himself very far behind, and passed with a C after receiving a D at mid-term. At Jefferson the books were newer and much more was required.

History: He had taken a history course in his first semester at Washington and was considered an outstanding student, although he exerted little effort. His first semester at Jefferson, he took another history course and found it much more difficult.

Music: Both schools were just about equally good. Washington has an outstanding band and is noted for this. Sidney has a special interest in music and received top grades at both schools.

In Sidney's experience the teachers at Jefferson were older, better and more stable. Washington had many more subs, especially in history and language. Subs are very rarely used at Jefferson. Washington places a great deal more stress on sports, especially basketball, than Jefferson. In fact it stresses sports more than scholastic standing. Jefferson has more of a variety of sports and they are not stressed above scholastic standing.

Sidney has buckled down to work and is now making above average grades at Jefferson High. This will get him into a selective college. More important, since he is up against stiff competition at Jefferson, he will not find college work much more demanding than his high school work now is.

Case of Donald, 21 years old.   Donald graduated 10th in a class of 110 in an all-Negro high school with an SER of .28. With an IQ of 112, and scoring at the 83rd percentile of the college aptitude test, he had done constantly superior work in science and mathematics. It seemed a good choice when he entered the school of engineering at the state university. His father and mother were both high school graduates, and his father had a stable job as maintenance man.

Donald wrote, as a high school senior:

"For as long as I can remember, I have always wanted to go to college and become a mechanical engineer.

"I attend the AME Church where I help teach a young boys' class in Sunday School. The children are very nice and usually want to learn, so I get a joy from being able to share my knowledge with them. I enjoy reading and working difficult mathematical problems. My hobby is tinkering with motors of all kinds.

"My family is behind me one hundred percent."

His teachers recommended him highly, though one of them commented, "With a little more aggressiveness, Donald could develop into an outstanding college prospect."

Donald got all C's and D's in his first year and was placed on scholastic probation. The next year he repeated a mathematics course but did not get a good start and withdrew from school until the second semester, when he started again. This time he withdrew after six weeks, and gave up on his college career. He took a civil service examination and got a job in an office in the city government.

Donald had the misfortune to go through a high school with relatively low standards, and he never learned what was expected of a student who could do acceptable work in a good engineering school. It seems probable that if he had attended Jefferson school, the one Sidney is now attending, he would have learned the study habits and skills that he so badly needed when he entered college.

Both of these boys were affected by the school environment, which in turn was affected by the stratification of the metropolitan area.

Response of the School System

There are two alternative approaches to the solution of the problems of socio-economic and racial stratification in the metropolitan area. One is a process of adaptation to the trends of metropolitan evolution; the other is a bold and fundamental effort at reversing some of these trends, and at designing and building the metropolitan area of the future with appropriate physical and institutional features. Both approaches require cooperation by the schools, and both approaches involve considerable changes in school programs and school organization.

Adapting to Existing Trends

The policy of adaptation to existing metropolitan trends assumes that the future structure of metropolitan areas will follow present trends. The belt of lower-class residential area around the center of of the city will expand and grow wider. The flight of middle-class families to the suburbs will continue. Suburbs will increase in number and size and variety. Low cost public housing will gradually make a physical improvement in the "grey areas" and will result in physical renewal of slums. Expressways will give automobile owners quicker and more comfortable access to all parts of the area. The present trend toward residential segregation by socio-economic status will continue, together with at least as much racial segregation as now exists. Only a few small counter-trends will be seen, such as the construction of expensive apartment houses near the center of the city for well-to-do people who have few school-age children, and the growth of working-class suburbs.

Educational Adaptations

The major educational adaptations will consist of attempts to provide educational stimulation and opportunity to the children of the slum areas, combined with identifying the abler children and separating them in special classes in the school. This approach will involve:

1. A MULTI-TRACK SYSTEM which separates children into several different groups according to learning ability and social status. This has the effect of maintaining at least one sub-group with fairly strong academic motivation in a school that is located in a slum area or is threatened by encroaching slums. The children of higher social status tend to be placed in the superior group, which makes the school more tolerable for their parents. Whatever may be the value of homogeneous grouping in helping children to achieve according to the level of their intelligence (and this is repeatedly questioned by research studies), there is no doubt that teachers and parents alike favor a multi-track system in a school where the SER has fallen below the critical point. This is because the multi-track organization gives some assurance to middle-class parents and to working-class parents who seriously want their children to get the most out of education that their particular children will be given special help and special consideration.

2. ENRICHMENT PROGRAMS for working-class children who achieve fairly well. This is a supplement to the multi-track program, and involves placing the more promising children in smaller classes, giving them special counseling and guidance, encouraging their parents to take more interest in their education, and giving them access to museums, libraries, theaters, and concerts. A widely-known example is the Higher Horizons program of Junior High School No. 43, Manhattan, and the George Washington High School of New York City (Hillson, 1963). This program has stimulated a considerable group of boys and girls to graduate from high school and to enter college who would not have

done so if they had not received special attention. Financial assistance for college attendance is a necessary part of such a program.

Since the New York City project, scores of similar projects have been developed for high school youth who are doing fairly well in school but give evidence of being able to do really superior work if they are stimulated and given higher standards to work for. A number of private schools and colleges offer special summer schools for such youth, with frequently a preference for Negro youth, on the ground that there is more unrealized potential in this group than in white working-class youth, who have not suffered so much from discrimination. Also, several public school systems have experimental scholarship-fund programs which recruit potentially able youth in the early high school years and guide them toward college, with a promise of a college scholarship if they do well in high school.

3. ENRICHMENT PROGRAMS for culturally disadvantaged children at the pre-school and kindergarten-primary level. A number of large cities are trying out a type of program that gives special assistance to the primary grades in the slum schools, on the theory that many of these children lack parental examples and stimulation from parents to read and to achieve well in school. They fail to master the task of reading, and stumble along for the first few years in school, after which they become confirmed non-learners, and tend to be social misfits in the school during their adolescence. By putting specially-trained teachers into relatively small classes, by using a social worker or visiting teacher to bring the home and school into contact, and by giving the children a variety of enriching experiences which middle-class children are more likely to get in their homes, these children will get a better start in school and thus a better start in life.

Assisted with funds under the Economic Opportunity Act of 1964, and the Elementary and Secondary Education Act of 1965, a vast program of "compensatory education" is now under way at the pre-school and kindergarten-primary levels.

4. WORK-STUDY PROGRAMS FOR ALIENATED YOUTH. Under present conditions some 15 percent of boys and girls fail to grow up successfully through the avenue provided by the schools. They become non-learners, and react to the school either with hostility and aggression or with apathy after about the sixth grade. In slum areas this proportion is likely to reach 25 or 30 percent. These children are alienated from the values and ways of behaving of the school and other middle-class institutions.

It is these boys and girls who make teaching so difficult at the seventh, eighth, and ninth grades, and who make the junior high school and the early years of senior high school so difficult for academically-motivated youth in schools where the SER is low. For alienated youth, especially for the boys, there is a good deal of experimentation with work-study programs which aim to give these youth a chance to grow up satisfactorily through the avenue of work.

5. SUBURBAN DEVELOPMENTS.   If present trends continue, it appears that educational programs in the central city will be increasingly aimed at providing opportunities for working-class youth in relation to their abilities and needs, while the suburbs are likely to be the scene of ex-perimentation with ideas and materials aimed at higher standards of educational performance for middle-class youth. The suburbs will have more money to work with than will the central city, and their pre-dominantly middle-class character will make them responsive to pro-posals for the use of new methods, new kinds of school buildings, and new types of school programs.

Fundamental Urban Renewal

Many individuals, including some educators, are not satisfied with ac-cepting the present trends of metropolitan development and with adapting school programs to meet them. They believe that the civic problems of metropolitan growth call for fundamental urban renewal. These people—the prophets of urban renewal—are proposing new enterprises that will require substantial educational changes.

Urban renewal has the goal of restoring physical areas of comfort-able middle-class living in the central city and also of establishing areas of comfortable, slum-free lower-class living. Beyond this, urban renewal has a social goal of making the whole of the metropolitan area a good place for all kinds of people to live. The leaders of urban renewal often speak of their goal as that of increasing the range and amount of choice people have among good ways to live.

Educational Programs for a Transition Period

It now appears that a number of metropolitan areas are ready for a fundamental program of urban renewal that will have the cooperation of suburbs with central city. The evidence for this proposition will be developed in the next two chapters. Such a program would need to provide for a transitional period of perhaps twenty years, during which time the planned-for metropolitan organism would emerge from the present metropolitan chaos.

Certain educational policies would need to be adopted for the transitional period, aimed at: (1) stopping the flight of middle-class people from the central city, and (2) building self-contained communities of 50,000 to 200,000 people, which are cross-sections of the social composition of the entire area. Some policies would be temporary, while others would become permanent parts of educational policy for the metropolitan area of the future.

The call is for the *mixed school*—the school with a mixture of socioeconomic groups and a mixture of racial groups where there are such groups in the community. The mixture need not necessarily reflect the exact composition of the city, but it should not be more than perhaps 50 percent Negro, or 70 percent working-class, according to the judgment of practical people who have been working with the problem of social integration.

The mixed secondary school is practically a necessity for the success of what is being called *social urban renewal*. In distinction to *physical urban renewal*, social urban renewal consists of the redevelopment of the central city so that all kinds of people—rich and poor, colored and white—will want to live there and raise their children there. This means that there will be large areas of the central city in which middle-class and working-class people will live, and Negroes and white will live, within a few blocks of each other if not in the same block. But those who can afford to move to another area or to a suburb will not stay in a local community if they do not like the schools, and middle-class people will not live in an area where they must send their children to a school that is dominated by working-class children. White people will not live in an area where they must send their children to a school which is dominated by Negro children. On the other hand, working-class parents and Negro parents will send their children to schools dominated by middle class or by white children, because they think the standards of such schools are better.

Therefore, to serve the process of social urban renewal, the schools must be organized *as far as possible* as mixed schools. The phrase *as far as possible* is important here, because it may be impossible to organize all elementary schools as mixed schools, since they serve such small geographic areas and are likely to continue to serve a neighborhood. It may be impossible, also, to organize all secondary schools as mixed schools, in an area which is predominantly working class or Negro. In such a case, the concept of the regional high school district is useful. This is a district containing several high schools, where students have considerable degree of choice among the schools. There may have to be one school that is predominantly Negro in such a district, or one school that is predominantly working-class through its location; but there should be at least one and preferably more mixed schools in a high school regional district, thus making that region acceptable to all families in the region who insist on their children's attending a school with a substantial white middle-class college preparatory group.

This chapter can be summarized by saying that metropolitan development as it has taken place in America during the present century has made it more difficult for boys and girls to get a good education, both in and out of school. The schools have been handicapped by the growing economic and racial stratification of the metropolitan area. Urban renewal of a fundamental kind will restore and create educational values in the city. But urban renewal cannot take place without substantial changes in educational organization and policy.

Exercises

1. Study the suburbs of your metropolitan area. What was the pattern of growth? Where did the high-status suburbs develop, and why? Are there any working-class suburbs? How did they develop? Are there any Negro suburbs or suburban neighborhoods? How did they develop?

2. Select a particular suburb and study its development. How did it get started? Was it an independent community before it became a suburb? What was its social structure in earlier periods and what is it now?

3. Make a socio-economic classification of the suburbs or suburban districts in your metropolitan area, using the typology suggested in this chapter.

4. If you are acquainted with a school in an area that has changed its character rapidly, describe these changes and how the school was related to them.

5. Write a report on public housing in your area and discuss its contribution to making the area a better place to live.

Suggestions for Further Reading

1. An interesting set of readings about suburban life will be found in *The Suburban Community* edited by William Dobriner. Compare this book with *The Exurbanites* by Auguste C. Spectorsky.

2. Several of the large metropolitan areas have been subjects for extensive research and writing about their past, present, and future. A general discussion can be found in *The Exploding Metropolis* by the editors of *Fortune*, published as a paperback. Of special interest is the New York Metropolitan Region Study, made under the auspices of the Graduate School of Public Administration of Harvard University. The Harvard University Press is publishing a series of books on this research; the last volume to appear is entitled *Metropolis, 1985,* by Raymond Vernon. Jean Gottmann's *Megalopolis* gives a striking account of metropolitan development in the chain of urban areas stretching from Boston to Washington, D.C.

3. A provocative book by Jane Jacobs is *The Death and Life of Great American Cities.* Mrs. Jacobs believes that much of modern physical city planning is destructive of the values of neighborhood life. She argues for more attention to *social* rather than *physical* factors in urban renewal.

4 ⅋ Schools in the

Metropolitan Area

Among the 29,391 public school districts that existed in 1964, 1,231 of them accounted for 22 million pupils, or 56 percent of the total number. These districts all had more than 6,000 pupils, and nearly all were in metropolitan areas. In addition, there were another four thousand smaller districts located in metropolitan areas. Table 4.1 shows how school districts are distributed according to enrollment size in metropolitan areas. In 1960, 95 percent of public school enrollment in metropolitan areas was in school systems with more than 1,200 pupils.

Types of Schools in the Metropolitan Area

With such a large number of schools, and with such diversity as exists in a complex metropolitan area, it is useful to think about these schools in terms of types or categories. For the purposes of this book, a set of four categories will be used, which depend on the characteristics of the parents, the characteristics of the pupils, and the atmosphere and internal working of the school itself.

SERs in Various Schools.

In Figure 4.1 the social class compositions of three typical high schools are shown, together with their respective SERs. School B is a typical comprehensive high school in an employing suburb, or in a town or small city which has only one high school that serves all the students of a cross-section of the population. The total high-school population will not be distributed in the same way as the elementary-school population, or the ninth grade alone, because some of the high-school students drop out of school without graduating. Hence the actual SER is not .6, as it would be in a cross-sectional elementary school, but instead is approximately 1.0.

School B shows the SER of a high school in an upper-middle-class suburb, where there are very few working-class people.

School C shows the SER of a high school which serves a working-class area where there are no upper- or upper-middle-, and only a few lower-middle-class families. In such an area there may be an actual majority of lower-working-class residents, but since their children tend to drop out of school early, the actual composition of the high school shows a preponderance of pupils from upper-working-class homes.

Table 4.1   *Public School Systems Inside and Outside of SMSAs; 1961*

A. Enrollment Size of School Systems

NO. OF PUPILS PER SYSTEM	TOTAL NO. OF PUPILS IN SMSAs	NUMBER OF SCHOOL SYSTEMS	
		In SMSAs	*Outside of SMSAs*
1200 or more	21,296,000	2,556	3,282
300–1,199	968,000	1,410	5,233
150–299	105,000	481	2,600
50–149	54,000	585	3,629
15–49	15,000	540	6,041
1–14	1,246	120	4,511
Non-operating		912	5,119
	22,439,246	6,604	30,415

B. Number of Public Schools

IN SYSTEMS WITH:

	In SMSAs	*Outside of SMSAs*
20 or more schools	18,599	10,810
10–19	6,036	9,413
3–9	9,784	18,923
2	1,352	5,596
1	2,326	17,500
TOTAL	38,097	62,242

Source: U.S. Bureau of the Census, *Census of Governments: 1962, Vol. V, Local Government in Metropolitan Areas.* Tables 1, 2, pp. 22, 24.

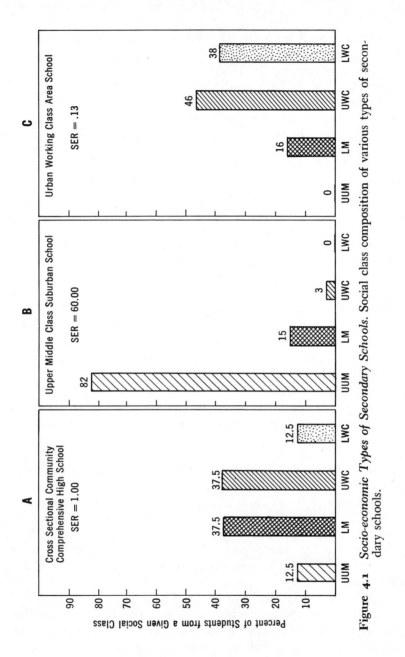

Figure 4.1 *Socio-economic Types of Secondary Schools.* Social class composition of various types of secondary schools.

There is probably a critical point in the SER of most schools, a point at which middle-class parents are likely to become anxious and will consider removing their children from the school. This is not to imply that parents tend to think in terms of the SER itself; but rather that middle-class parents, as they become aware of increasing proportions of lower-class students in a school, begin to fear the effects upon their own children. They may fear a drop in the academic standards of the school, or changes in curricular offerings, or unwelcome influences upon their own children's motivations for school achievement.

Parenthetically, it might be noted, with regard to the latter point, that such attitudes on the part of parents are not altogether unfounded. We have already referred to the study by Wilson (1959) that supports the generalization that when student bodies vary in their proportions of middle- and working-class, students develop different educational and vocational aspirations. Wilson says, "The *de facto* segregation brought about by concentrations of social classes in cities results in schools with unequal moral climates which likewise affect the motivation of the child . . . by providing a different ethos in which to perceive values." (Wilson, 1959, p. 845.)

The point at which a school becomes undesirable in the eyes of middle-class parents (the critical point in the SER) is subjective, depending upon the attitudes and experience of a particular parent, and depending also upon such factors as the tradition of the school, the racial composition of the school, the type of curriculum, and the quality of the teachers. However, there is enough consensus among middle-class parents about such matters so that they tend to agree on the question of when a school has become a "poor" school and when they begin to move out of the school district.

Secondary schools, more than primary schools, are vulnerable to desertion by middle-class parents when the socio-economic ratio reaches the critical point. As already indicated, in a community with a cross-section of the American population in terms of socio-economic status, the high school tends to have a SER of about 1.0. Thus, the SER is higher than that of an elementary school in the same community, because a number of lower-class boys and girls drop out of high school, leaving a disproportionate number of middle class. In an upper-middle-class suburb the SER is very high. In the central city, the slums continually encroach upon high schools in formerly middle-class areas, and reduce the SER in such schools toward the critical point. At that point there tends to be a rapid flight to the suburbs by middle-class families who have children of high-school age.

A High School in a Rapidly Changing Area

An example of what happens when the SER reaches the critical point is seen in the case of Benjamin Franklin High School, located in a large city which is now in stage IV of metropolitan development. Franklin High School is situated in what was a middle- and upper-class area about 1910, some six miles from the center of the city. In 1910 this was the school with the best academic record in the city, sending a high proportion of its graduates to college, and winning most of the prizes for academic excellence on the part of its students. The school's SER in 1910 was probably about 1.5.

Between the two world wars many of the upper-class people moved out to suburbs, and some of the upper-middle-class residents took over the old upper-class mansions, while other upper-middles moved out to a high school district farther out from the center of the city. Several areas of middle-class houses deteriorated, and some of the old, large apartment buildings were "converted" into small, low-rent apartments. A considerable number of working-class people moved in. On one edge of the high school district an area of old apartment buildings was turned over to Negro occupancy after the apartments had been "converted." By the beginning of World War II the SER of Franklin High was about .80.

Immediately after World War II, there was a further influx of working-class Negroes into a formerly middle-class area. However, there was also some new building of apartments, and some well-to-do Negroes began to buy the old upper-class mansions. The SER of Franklin High gradually dropped to .60 by 1955. With a large rate of dropouts of working-class pupils in the ninth and tenth grades, this meant that the SER of the ninth grade was .35, while that of the twelfth grade was 1.5. The SER for the ninth grade was well below the critical point for middle-class parents, and they began to move away from the area when their children were ready to enter high school.

At about this time the community sensed that a crisis had occurred. An organization was formed by the middle-class people in the district whose goals were "community conservation" and urban renewal. With the aid of government funds, deteriorated houses were torn down and replaced by middle-class houses. The high school was reorganized on the basis of a multi-track program, with the upper track consisting of college-going (and largely middle-class) pupils, thus achieving a high SER for this sub-group. These measures partially stemmed the outflow of middle-class families, and brought some new middle-class families with small children into the area.

However, in the same high-school district another area where there was no community conservation movement (the area served by the Leibnitz elementary school, already described) also "changed" sharply after 1955. Its graduates tended to force down the SER at Franklin High. At this writing there seems to be a close balance between the forces that tend to make Franklin High into a slum school, and those forces that will preserve it as a school with an academic ethos serving a community with a substantial proportion of middle-class families.

Socio-educational Motivation

What parents desire in the education of their children is a kind of school which stimulates children to do well academically; encourages them to finish high school and go to college; and offers something useful and interesting for children from all kinds of families. Looking for these things, they try to sense the spirit or *ethos* of the school. The SER can be improved upon as a measure of school ethos by replacing the percentages of children from various social classes with the percentages of children with certain kinds of socio-educational motivation.

If the latter data are available, the substitution would allow for the fact that children of any one social class have a range of educational motivations.

It is possible to describe four levels of educational motivation, each level indicating the kind of occupational aspiration held by the individual as well as the probable educational level he will attain.

Table 4.2 gives data of this kind for the ninth grade of a high school which represents a cross-section of the American society. In this school the SER is $50 \div 80$ or .6. The SER can be replaced by a *motivation ratio* which is computed as follows: $2A + B \div C + 2D$, where the letters refer to the motivational levels shown in Table 4.2. In this case the motivation ratio is $90 \div 60$ or 1.5. While this ratio is a better measure of the academic ethos of a high school than is the SER, it requires so much more knowledge about the students that it is likely to be used less frequently than the SER.

Table 4.2   *Socio-educational Motivation of Male Students in a Cross-Sectional High School (Percentages of Male High-School Students at 9th Grade Level)*

PROBABLE EDUCATIONAL LEVEL	CHARACTERISTIC MOTIVATION	SOCIAL CLASS				TOTAL PERCENT
		U + UM	LM	UWC	LWC	
College	A. Academically motivated— major white-collar job	10	16	8	1	35
High School Grad	B. Minor white-collar career	—	9	7	4	20
H.S. Grad & Dropout	C. Skilled blue-collar career	—	5	20	5	30
Dropout	D. Alienated	—	—	5	10	15
Total		10	30	40	20	100

$$\text{Motivation Ratio} \quad \frac{2A + B}{C + 2D}$$

Atmosphere and Internal Working of the School

The nature of a school depends on the teachers and on the educational program in the school as well as on the characteristics of the parents and of the pupils in the school. While these are all interrelated, they are not so tightly bound that one can predict accurately the school atmosphere on the basis of knowledge of the socio-economic status of parents.

To a considerable extent the atmosphere and the internal working of a school depends on the principal, the teachers, the supervisors and specialists, the parent-teacher organization, the librarian, the supply of books and teaching materials, and the curriculum. Therefore an attempt has been made to discover types or categories of schools by looking into the school itself rather than by looking at the socio-economic situation of the school.

This attempt has been carried out successfully by Russell Doll (1965) in his study of elementary schools in Chicago, and his study serves as the basis for the categories to be presented here. Doll studied intensively 40 elementary schools. He interviewed 185 teachers of grades four to eight, and made systematic observations of each school.

The visit to a school consumed a full day and often an extra day was added. In general, the research worker conducted the following: (1) interviews averaging 45 minutes with each teacher; (2) interviews and discussions throughout the day with the principal; (3) short observations of the children in the classroom; (4) observations of the children at recess, moving in and out of the building at lunch time and after school; (5) observations of teachers at their lunch time, at sign-out time, and at their break times; (6) observations of principals handling cases sent to the office or of parents coming to the school; (7) observation of the inside and the outside of the school building.

The interview with teachers was treated as confidential, and in almost every instance the interviewer and the respondent were placed in private quarters. Questions were asked concerning: (1) the ability of the teacher to use the curriculum guides and supplements, given the social composition of the school (the interviewer had already gained some idea of what the respondent thought the social composition of the school was); (2) the ability of the teacher to function as a teacher, again, given the social situation; (3) what the biggest problems were in the classroom; (4) what assistance was given, by whom, and how worthwhile was this assistance; (5) what were factors which assist the teacher in the classroom; (6) what type of cooperation from the community did the teacher receive; (7) what was the background of the pupils. (Havighurst, 1964, Ch. 8.)

Four types or categories of schools were identified, and given names as follows:

A. *High-status* schools—generally found toward the edges of the city, in high income areas, and in upper-middle-class dormitory suburbs.

B. *Conventional* schools—generally found in areas of lower-middle class dominance and in cross-sectional employing or industrial suburbs. May be found in upper-middle and upper-working-class areas.

C. *Common-man* schools—generally found in areas of stable working-class residence, in the central city and in working-class residential suburbs.

D. *Inner-city* schools—generally found in slum areas of low income, high transiency, high delinquency, both Negro and white.

Although these names come from geographical and social characteristics, the categories are really based on internal characteristics of the schools, as is seen in Table 4.3. Doll found that teachers can identify the category of school in which they work by using the chart of Table 4.3 as a check list. They agree fairly well among themselves and with a skilled observer in classifying their schools.

Although the chart of Table 4.3 deals with elementary schools primarily, the same kinds of distinctions can be made among high schools, especially at the ninth and tenth grades. The higher grades of the high school may be put into categories A, B, and C, with D missing because students drop out of a D-type school before getting to the 11th grade.

Table 4.3   *Check List for School Type*

A	B	C	D
1. CURRICULUM AND TEACHING MATERIAL			
Curriculum is enriched with extra work. Texts one year or more above grade level can be used.	Curriculum is used as planned. Texts at grade level can be used.	Curriculum is altered downward. Difficulty in the use of grade level texts.	Curriculum does not fit students' needs. Texts one to two years below grade level must be used in many cases.
2. TEACHING EMPHASIS			
Almost all of teacher's emphasis on academics. Students willing and able to cooperate in this regard.	Most of teacher's emphasis on academics. Some students unwilling or unable to cooperate in this regard.	Teacher's time divided between teaching academics and controlling student behavior. Some disorder in hall and around building but can be controlled.	Majority of teacher's time devoted to controlling student behavior. Much disorder in class and around building which is difficult to control.

A	B	C	D

3. "CULTURAL EXPERIENCE"

A	B	C	D
Wide and meaningful "cultural" experiences part of student's every-day life. School can enrich and support these cultural experiences.	Some exposure to "cultural" experiences. Student accepts and enjoys these "cultural" experiences when such experiences are encouraged by school.	Little exposure to "cultural" experiences and reluctance on the part of many students to accept these experiences when they are encouraged by school.	Almost no exposure to "cultural" experiences. Often a struggle for school to prepare students for these experiences. Resistance on the part of students toward these experiences.

4. RESPECT FOR TEACHER

A	B	C	D
Little or no disrespect from students and parents. Strong positive attitudes by almost all students and parents toward teacher.	A few instances of disrespect from students and parents. Positive attitudes by majority of students and parents toward teacher.	Wide range in attitudes of respect from students and parents. Some ambiguity in students' and parents' attitudes toward teacher.	Flippant attitudes and some disrespect toward teacher from many students and parents. Apathy on part of many students. Some damage to teacher's personal belongings.

5. ATTITUDES OF PARENTS

A	B	C	D
Majority of parents most helpful and even initiate helpful programs and carry them out. Teachers may even feel some parents are too "pushy" with children and that some parents "look down on teachers."	Parents accept what the school feels is best for the children and are willing and able to follow teacher's suggestion.	Many parents want children to do well but equate being good in school with doing well in academics. Teacher accepted as authority by majority of parents.	Many parents apathetic and many unable to offer any help to students even if they want to. Some hostility toward teacher on the part of some parents.

A	B	C	D

6. STUDENT HOSTILITY

A	B	C	D
Few or no fights among students. Hostility is verbal. Some teasing among students.	Hostility sometimes expressed in "shoving matches." Hostility is still mostly verbal.	Hostility expressed in some rough fights of "wrestling-punching" type. Verbal hostility may contain some profanity.	Hostility expressed in many rough fights, started easily with some being hard to stop. Verbal hostility contains some profanity.

7. CLIMATE OF SCHOOL

A	B	C	D
Climate of school set by academically oriented pupils. Children with discipline problems can be easily handled within framework of the school. Discipline problems are mild.	Children with discipline problems are seldom leaders of student behavior but can exert influence in some cases. Discipline problems can be handled within the framework of the school.	Children with discipline problems may be leaders for some students and sometimes upset academic classroom situations. Majority of discipline problems can be handled within framework of the school; a few cannot.	Children with discipline problems are influential in setting climate of the school. Many children with discipline problems require the help of outside agencies such as police or Family Service.

8. SOURCES OF STUDENT VALUES

A	B	C	D
Students receive their values through contact with stable and respected adults. Students will identify with peer group but also identify with future adult role.	Students influenced by a well-behaved peer group. Behavior somewhat patterned after models offered by movies or TV. Students still identify with future adult role.	Students strongly influenced by peer group. Behavior and dress patterned almost entirely on models offered by movies or TV. Many have no identification with future adult role.	Students heavily influenced by an alienated peer group. Many students influenced by delinquent adolescent and adult models. Many have hostility toward wider society and little identification with future adult role.

Table 4.4 shows data concerning two central city high schools. School C is on the border-line between an inner-city and a common-man type of school, and School B is a conventional type. They have SERs of .22 and 2.50 respectively.

Table 4.4   *Comparison of Two Contrasting High Schools (Schools C and B)*

	Grade 9		Grade 10		Grade 11		Grade 12	
	C	B	C	B	C	B	C	B
AGE	PERCENTAGE DISTRIBUTION OF AGES							
11-9 to 12-8	2	0						
12-9 to 13-8	6	16	0	0				
13-9 to 14-8	<u>31</u>	<u>53</u>	2	10	0	0		
14-9 to 15-8	39	23	<u>25</u>	<u>58</u>	4	14	0	0
15-9 to 16-8	18	7	43	23	<u>35</u>	<u>56</u>	10	14
16-9 to 17-8	3	1	24	7	38	28	<u>35</u>	<u>69</u>
17-9 to 18-8	1	0	5	2	18	2	38	<u>16</u>
18-9 to 19-8			1	0	4	0	15	1
19-9 & over								
Number	2,039	668	1,246	549	676	524	503	443
	PERCENTAGE ENROLLMENTS IN BASIC, ESSENTIAL, AND HONORS COURSES							
Basic course								
English	35	0	23	0	—	—	—	—
Mathematics	19	0	0	0	—	—	—	—
Essential course								
English	30	12	36	0	42	0	31	0
Mathematics	56	14	44	0	—	—	—	—
Honors course								
English	1	12	2	5	4	5	7	6
Mathematics	2	12	0	23	0	10	0	18

School B is in a section of the city with the highest socio-economic ratings on occupation, income, and education of adults. School C is in the lowest section of the city. Table 4.4 shows the ages of the students in each of the four high-school grades. The underlined figures indicate the age groups which are normal. For instance, a child who entered school at the age of six would be between 13 years, 9 months and 14 years, 8 months at the beginning of the ninth grade if he had made average progress, never failing a grade and never "skipping" a grade. School B has more than half of its students just at the "normal" age, and about 25 percent over-age. But School C has 61 percent of its ninth graders over-age, and 55 percent of its twelfth graders. School C has only a fourth as many twelfth graders as it has ninth graders. At least half of its entering ninth graders drop out of school within the first two years. School B has very few drop-outs. (The ninth grade is larger than it was two or three years earlier, and thus the apparent drop-out figures are exaggerated.)

The two schools show a great contrast in the proportion of pupils in the various "tracks" of the program. School C has four tracks or ability groupings, called Basic, Essential, Regular, and Honors. School B does not have the lowest, or Basic, track.

The two schools contrast sharply in their offerings of Basic, Essential, and Honors courses. Students with reading or arithmetic scores below a grade level of 5.9 are placed in "basic" courses. These pupils are three years retarded or more, since they are in the ninth grade or above. Furthermore, many of them are over-age, and therefore even further retarded. Those with a reading or arithmetic score between grade level 5.9 and 7.9 are placed in "essential" courses. They are from one to two years retarded if they are in the ninth grade.

School C has 65 percent of its ninth graders in Basic or Essential English, and 75 percent in Basic or Essential Mathematics. By the sophomore year there have been many drop-outs, but Basic and Essential English still enroll 59 percent of the students. An Essential Mathematics course continues with 44 percent of second year students. Essential English is continued throughout the four years, with 31 percent of the seniors in it.

In contrast, School B has nobody in Basic English or Mathematics, but has 12 and 14 percent of ninth graders in Essential English and Mathematics, respectively. After the ninth grade there are no Essential or Basic courses.

Honors courses enroll 12 percent of ninth graders in School B, in English and in mathematics, and they continue through all four years. But School C has only 1 percent of ninth graders in English Honors, and 2 percent in Mathematics Honors. Mathematics Honors does not continue, but English Honors continues, getting up to seven percent of the senior class.

School C has 15 classes in foreign language, while School B (with a lower enrollment) has 41. School C has a one-semester course in trigonometry for 11th grade students, and nothing beyond that, while School B has honors courses in advanced mathematics, analytical geometry, and calculus for 11th and 12th graders.

There are, in School C, about four percent of eleventh and twelfth graders who are in the top quarter of all students in the city in ability and achievement test scores. In School B, 63 percent are in the top quarter. Such a vast difference in the abilities and achievement of pupils means that the program of School B is probably better and richer for bright students. One might argue that the program of School C can be expected to be better for slow students. At least, it offers that possibility.

Both of these schools have unusually good faculties in terms of experience and interest in their work. The principal of School C has energy and insight and determination. Though this is his first year at this school, he has developed a plan for intensified teaching of Basic English which appears to be working well. He has also established bi-weekly meetings with new teachers to help them learn to teach in this kind of school.

School C may become a common-man type of school through the efforts of the principal and his staff. It is not likely that it can be transformed into a conventional type school as long as it serves its present clientele. School B could become a high-status school if it had a better principal and if he had the support of the central administration over a period of several years in selecting and training teachers and improving the library and the curriculum.

Types of Elementary Schools

High-Status Schools

A teacher in a high-status school said "We're so conscious of the gifted here. We've based our whole course of study on the gifted. It is the same with the curriculum guides. As for discipline problems, well, they are practically non-existent."

These are schools with a high degree of most desirable characteristics. The children are extremely well prepared for what the school demands, and parents are willing and able to supply equipment needs over and above what is needed, and are taking an active part in school life. The children have high academic scores and provide only a small number of discipline problems and, in the majority of cases, no active discipline problems at all. The disturbed children are few and for the most part can be handled in the school setting.

One teacher's description of a high-status school area is as follows: "The school community is an old established residential area made up of middle-class families who are economically comfortable. They are proud of their community. The parents are well educated and interested in the educational opportunities provided for their children and often compare these to neighboring schools in suburban areas. The majority of students are academically motivated. The PTA is a cooperative active group. On the whole the parents are eager to work with the school to ensure the success of their children in the educational program."

Teaching is most rewarding in this type of setting and once a teacher enters such a situation, it is very seldom that he leaves. In one such school the length of total teaching experience was as follows: a range of from one year to 32 years with the teacher of one year's experience having had a total of ten years of teaching experience in other situations. The total faculty median was 15 years. As one principal stated, "My teachers only leave to retire, or if they are married, when they become pregnant." There are also few sick days used by the teachers. "It's always a pleasant place here. We really do not have many teachers who take too many days off. In fact, they only take a day off when they are very sick."

Because of the high ability level of the children, the curriculum guides and supplements not only may be used to their fullest, but must even be supplemented. One teacher said, "The guides and supplements suit our students well. I think they're constructed in an excellent fashion. They are realistically attuned to my class, but nevertheless, I have to provide some degree of variety, no matter how good the supplement and guide are. This is because the majority of my children do reference work in the library."

The backgrounds of the students aid the teacher in the presentation of the curriculum and undoubtedly offer the necessary information and skills for success in school—which success again provides the teachers with a rewarding experience. As one teacher stated, "Given a good curriculum, you can really teach in this type of situation. Culturally, these kids have an advantage. I would say about 99 percent of my kids have an encyclopaedia at home, 75 percent have traveled to interesting places, and at least 60 percent have been to the city and have visited all the museums—the Museum of Science and Industry, the Museum of Natural History—and these children take advantage of the school library and the public library. Culturally, they rate high."

Conventional Schools

A teacher in a conventional school said, "This is just a nice typical school situation with nice typical kids." Conventional schools are those which have a majority of academically oriented children, but they also have a greater number of discipline problems and parental problems than have the high-status schools. However, these are not enough to interfere with the academic program. This type of school has a majority of children with a strong background of family experience preparing them for school work. However, such a school will have a visible minority of children with poor reading and below-average school achievement. While there are discipline problems, the majority of them can be handled between the teacher, the parent, and the principal. This is a school which is psychologically *in the city*, whereas the high-status school is more suburban in nature. The children and parents of the conventional school exhibit behavior and achievement patterns associated with the mainstream of American culture and society.

The areas in which conventional schools are found show a great diversity in socio-economic status and social composition. Since conditions within the school are the ranking criteria rather than only socio-economic factors, one may find conventional schools in a cluster of common-man and inner-city schools. In general, though, clusters of conventional schools are found in stable areas geographically removed from the inner-city, in areas with young families, in areas of new housing developments, or in other areas in which parents are experiencing upward mobility.

In the newly settled areas, the parents are not quite sure what their role is in relation to the school, and some either withdraw or become somewhat critical, more so than in the stable conventional schools. One teacher said, in a newly settled Negro middle-class area, "Oh, I get some parents up here who don't understand what we are attempting to do. They want to know what the school is doing for their child, and they think the school can do a better job. I tell them that we have to concentrate on the academics, and if they want their children to be taken to museums, to be taken to these extra events, it is up to them to take them. Eventually, they see our point and realize that they cannot expect us to turn out a good academic product and yet spend all our time in these acculturating activities." And as one principal in a similar area stated, "We attempt to explain the program to the parents, and many become involved on their own; but as concerns community outreach, I think at some point we reach a point of diminishing returns because a lot of these parents just won't be drawn into the framework of the school, and consequently one expends one's energy in areas that are not fruitful."

In general, in this type of school, the majority of parents and the community support the schools and the teachers. In one newly settled area, the principal reported, "I gathered together many of the important people of the community and told them the importance of our preparing the children to go to college. I outlined for them what the school was attempting to do and I told them what they could do to help the school. They loved it. I realize that this can't be done in all places and communities, but here, the parents respect the principal's word."

A teacher contrasted this attitude with a high-status school in which she once taught: "My children's attitude in this school, I think, is a little better than the _____ area. The attitude there on the part of the students and their parents was a superior one. It was one which considered the teacher *only* a teacher and one which said, 'My mother knows more than you do.' "

With respect to curriculum guides, a teacher in a stable area said, "I think they fit our children well, at least those with good backgrounds; but I wouldn't try to exceed the guides as they do in the schools north of us. We're just right now because our children are very eager to learn and we don't have to pull it out of them."

Conventional schools' discipline problems are not very severe. Those problems which they have may be handled in the school situation. As in the high-status schools, there is seldom if ever any overt hostility on the part of the student and very little verbal hostility directed towards the teacher. In very rare instances is there any physical hostility. The discipline problems consist of cases of the classroom being upset by behavioral antics or inattentiveness on the part of the children. A stable conventional principal says, "The crisis in this school is: 'Johnny pushed me going home' or else, 'Mary stuck her tongue out at me.' Our discipline problems are not really discipline problems,

but they are more or less just little misunderstandings among children.
I am usually able to handle them if the teachers send them down to
me. But in most cases, the teachers are able to handle them themselves.
We've got the kind of a kid where if a note is sent home, that's the
end of it for a while. Except for the emotionally disturbed children,
we have no problems; and with these children, you sometimes have
to have the parent in."

Teachers in conventional schools feel the pressure of lack of time,
as preventing *them* from teaching effectively. A teacher with eight years
of experience, who had a relatively slow group in a new area, said, "Most
of the children in my slow group have trouble using the text. This
means I have to do most of my presentation orally or with worksheets,
and these I have to mimeograph myself. I simply do not have enough
time for this preparation. There are always forms and reports to be
made out for the district office or for downtown. This takes up the time
for grading papers and other time I could be using in preparation. Since
my children can't use the text so much, I have to find time somewhere
for this mimeographing. As well as the fact that I have a husband to
look after. If I could only have some time each week, or a free period,
to get this stuff in order! My biggest problem is time."

Common-Man Schools

A teacher in a common-man school said, "They sure play rough, and
they get rough in fights, but they're not bad kids when you really get
to know them." As in conventional schools, common-man schools show
a great diversity in student body, parental cooperation, home background, and ability to use the curriculum. The student population
tends to be less academically oriented, more independent when dealing
with the school and the teachers, and less inclined to identify with the
school and its personnel than in the conventional schools. The mass
media set the behavioral patterns for many of the students. Parents, for
the most part, desire an education for their children and push verbally
in this direction, but are not quite certain what educational goals should
be achieved, nor how one goes about achieving them. Being good in
school behaviorally is equated with doing "good" in school academically.

The schools may or may not be close to the center of the city
geographically but they are definitely city oriented. They are attended

by a large percentage of second generation foreign-born and/or Spanish-speaking and Negro children.

A school with a long history as a common-man type is the John Paul Jones, which has always been in a working-class area. This school now has an SER of .26, which has probably been the same for 50 years. Originally settled by Irish, Germans, and Swedes who built their frame houses near a foundry and steel fabricating plant where they worked, the community was gradually populated by Poles, Lithuanians, and Czechs, who worked in the foundries and the car barns, and some of whom have recently become truck drivers and factory operatives.

A teacher who has taught at John Paul Jones for a long time describes the neighborhood as follows:

The neighborhood is an old one, but the buildings are kept in excellent repair. The great majority of the people are laborers, many truck drivers and factory workers. Many are third generation in the neighborhood. Lately there are a few transient families. Most of the families had little education and because of fairly comfortable living, they desire little education for their children. The only drawback to teaching in this school is the parents' lack of interest in education. They want their children to be clean, well-behaved, and healthy; but they really (for the most part) don't care if they're educated.

An observer of this community reports:

During the past 20 years there has been a good deal of moving out toward the suburbs by young adults, and there is some defensiveness in the attitudes of those who have stayed. Although there is a tendency to apologize for their having lived in the neighborhood so long when they feel they have "bettered themselves" economically, they are quick to point out that those who have moved "might be sorry." Although they will claim that someone who moves out is not really missed, one finds that they do keep in touch with one another and visit occasionally. Actually, the people are missed, but for a much deeper reason. Egress is a threat to their personal security, to the group as a whole, and to the stability of the neighborhood. Consequently, it is with great reluctance that they admit to each other that someone is "really going to move."

One man said, "It disturbed me to see many of my friends move out to the suburbs. I don't think I really miss them, though. But it was like breaking up the old gang. You knew they were there like you knew the support under the house was there."

There is no formal group, such as a Community Council, to maintain morale. Rather, there are a number of informal cliques which grew up for purposes of mutual support during the depression of the 'thirties; when young men went off to World War I; and when there was almost a mass migration after the war to what was locally known as the "Polish Gold Coast."

When a move seemed imminent, there was an increase in phoning and visiting. Although the conversation centered around the move, it followed a general pattern. First it was wondered whether or not the person did right, if he would be happy where he was going; and almost in despair, talk of who would move into the vacant house which was soon to stand as a threatening symbol of disintegration. These talks usually ended with an agreement that *they* would not move, that *they* were happy where they were, and, almost with a ceremonial incantation, "I'm sure we'll get good people in there." In this way they closed ranks, reverting back to the interpersonal relations which saw them through periods of stress in the "old days."

The people who stayed spoke of the advantages of low taxes and the comparatively cheap living in the area as compared to other parts of the city and the suburbs; the convenience of the schools, churches, and parks for the children; the proximity to transportation lines, shopping districts, and places of employment. Yet the transportation lines and factories were felt to be outside of the area; and in listening to people talking one got the idea that they felt the area to be a small village, total unto itself. "This area is nice and secluded. There's no main street or highway. And when you get off the bus and walk back into the neighborhood, it's nice to come back to. I can have leisure time and still be close to my employment. I save train fare and still the work place is far enough from my house." This factor of being near work and yet not having it within the area proper was mentioned by all the groups and serves further to give the illusion of "a small town."

Strangely enough, the idea of moving in the event that the school may not be providing the education which they desired for their children never entered into any remark by the residents. It was assumed that the school was performing a job which was totally unrelated to their everyday lives. And yet they regarded the schools, both grammar and high, as an important part of their children's lives in a functional sense. To them the school's main task was to prepare the child for a job. The school was important in that it served as a means of economic success, not so much in terms of preparing for college as in preparing for a life devoted to working in a blue-collar job or else, the pinnacle of success, "a good job in an office," or a "job as a secretary."

The John Paul Jones school and its community may go on as a kind of working-class backwater where non-mobile people can live and raise their children, but its residents are apprehensive of the threat of the expanding Negro working-class group who live only a quarter-mile away. These people have strong prejudices against living in the same neighborhood as Negroes, and will probably move farther out from the city center rather than stay in an integrated community. Industrial and employing suburbs are likely to have some common-man elementary schools.

One principal, with many years of experience in a stable common-man school, remarked, "The parents could keep closer watch on their children and on their activities. They shouldn't let them roam the streets as they do. There's also too much TV. Some parents seem rather messy, and surprisingly enough, come up to the school in slacks and the like. Many do not wear the proper street attire."

Parental interest does not extend to active participation in school affairs or school organization, although there is a core of parents who attempt to awaken interest. In rough common-man schools, this parental cooperation is even less, and the core smaller. This is not necessarily because the parents are at odds with the school, but they either are ill at ease or are busy with other, more pressing matters.

One stable common-man school teacher notices differences between his own students and the nearby conventional students. He commented, "Those from the conventional school are better academically and better in behavior. The kids in our school, although they're not problems, nevertheless are slower and don't reach as high a level of achievement, but they're good kids. We are very heavy with foreign-born and foreign-speaking homes, and this may be one reason for the low achievement."

In common-man schools receiving newcomers, discipline problems vary. They may begin to resemble rough common-man situations or, they may resemble inner-city schools. If the influx is gradual, if there is not too great a difference in culture and outlook between receiving and entering groups, the problems are reduced. In one stable common-man school receiving an influx of Puerto Rican and Mexican children, the principal stated, "Our area is experiencing some influx of new students, but they seem to be fitting in all right. This has raised some behavior problems, but we're able to cope with them. And since they're not coming in very fast, we have a stable student body as well as a stable faculty. If we didn't have this stability, I don't think we'd be able to do as good a job of easing the new students in."

However, in the common-man area experiencing quick transition, the situation becomes more serious. In a once heavily Russian and Italian immigrant area which is now receiving a Puerto Rican and working-class Negro influx, one assistant principal with many years of experience remarked, "The job is getting harder, because of the constant conflict in the school between the Puerto Rican and the Negro students. They carry their problems into the school and it has adverse effects. Thank goodness none of the teachers is leaving yet because of it. We have a tradition of keeping teachers for a long time at this school, even if this is what can be called a poor area. But if the situation ever gets to the point where the discipline problems mount, and impertinence to the teachers increases, they will leave."

But despite the problems, the teacher in the rough, common-man schools see themselves in a better situation than in an inner-city school, and seem to be, in the main, as positively oriented to the majority of these schools as those in the main-line schools. A teacher who had been in an inner-city school stated:

I feel like a different person here. I really do. I'm enjoying my teaching now and I feel like I'm getting some kind of a reward. A problem that is considered a great problem here just didn't count at the _____. Oh, we have problems at recess. We do have some pretty bad problem kids, but at the _____ we really had our problems. When I was going to transfer, the principal of this school visited me and told me that this school wouldn't be any different than the _____. But it is as different as night and day. And the strange thing is, these kids don't come from any worse backgrounds than the kids at the _____ do. At the _____, discipline was terrible. In the morning there would be kids left over from the previous day, lined up outside the office. One day I just went down and put my name on the transfer list and I came to this school. And it is different.

Probably the greatest difference felt by teachers who have taught at inner-city schools between the problems of the inner-city schools and these schools is in the degree, consistency, and direction of hostility which the teacher experiences. This hostility seems to be more direct, more frequent, and more overt in the inner-city schools.

The ability to handle the curriculum varies drastically from one type of common-man school to the other. In the main, the curriculum must be altered downward in all schools of this type, but more so in the rough common-man schools. Again, this adds more to the teacher's burden, for the teacher does not only have to teach, but also must construct a curriculum. One principal said, "When you have reading problems, you have problems in curriculum, I don't care how good the curriculum is. We can't find things to use in the eighth grade. What are you going to do with a kid that is reading at the fifth-grade level and is in eighth grade? To a great extent, it is vocabulary that is a problem. But the difficulty, and I say it again, is mainly in reading. The teachers have to prepare most of the work outside of the textbook, and this is killing."

For teachers in common-man schools the problem of time is a problem of getting enough of the child's time to accomplish something with and within him. The school time is especially valuable for learning because neither the child nor his family can be counted on to see that he studies at home or uses his out-of-school time in ways that improve his school work. The teacher must adapt curriculum material and prepare work sheets in any time she can find, outside of class. She must do an active job of teaching, in class. One teacher said, "There is one consolation. We know that the school does all. Anything positive that happens to these kids, we know we did it."

Inner-City Schools

A teacher in an inner-city school said, "Each day I'd enter the school, each day the problems would begin, and each day I'd say, 'Dear God, what can I do?'"

Inner-city schools face the gravest problems of any schools in the system. They also face the greatest challenge in any attempt to remedy the problems. For these schools, the problems are rooted mainly in the subculture and subsociety beyond easy reach of the schools and, indeed, beyond the effective reach of many agencies designed especially to deal with these subsocieties.

What we are calling the *inner-city school* is not necessarily a school located in the inner-city in a physical sense. There are actually a number of common-man schools and even some conventional schools located in areas where inner-city schools predominate. The inner-city school is a psychological as well as a sociological phenomenon. Whether a given school will have inner-city or common-man characteristics depends partly on the principal and his faculty and their relations with the parents and children.

For example, a teacher in an inner-city school in New York's Harlem says,

A few blocks from here there is a good school. It's eighty years old, with multiple wings and stairs like ours; there are hundreds of places for children to hide—and they never do. Every child in the school is in his room all day. Low truancy, zero lateness. Notes go home with aides at nine-thirty if a child isn't there. The school reads on grade level. The principal is a Negro woman, but that's not the point. She has the same cross section of teachers as anywhere else. They come from the same school board, same distribution of assignments. But this level is what she demands. Her being a Negro may play a part, though, because she *intends* her school to produce children who can read. From nine to ten o'clock the whole school is reading; ten to ten-thirty, phonics and nothing else.

So it runs that way because she runs it. A school can't be left to what emanates from the Board—which isn't putting real thought into teaching these children. . . .

The inner-city school suffers from a syndrome of problems. Covert and overt hostility to the teacher; lack of self control on the part of pupils; lack of experience and background needed for success in school; an outer society which hardens, alienates, and produces a negative type of maturation; and intellectual apathy in the student all combine to produce in many instances an unrewarding and impossible teaching climate. It is a situation in which the teacher's hardiness and physical stamina count as much as teaching ability. It is a situation in which the young experienced teacher survives better than the young inexperienced or older experienced teacher. It is a difficult situation.

The inner-city respondents felt to an overwhelming degree that they were cut off and abandoned. In most cases, the curriculum guides cannot be used, and it was felt that the curriculum planners were drifting even further away from an understanding of what is needed. With a feeling that their problems are not understood by the downtown office; that those who are to offer assistance, such as psychologists and consultants, are either too few in number or out of contact with their problems; that these problems are covered up by those in authority or that no one in authority or in the public really cares—buffeted by all those forces they feel are out of their control, the inner-city school teachers often give up in frustration after entering with dedication. As one assistant principal contemplating transferring said, "If I was a teacher instead of the assistant principal, I would have been out of here long ago. In fact, I never would have come if I had known what the school situation was. There are dangers that I face all the time that I shouldn't have to. Why do I have to pin boys to the floor? This has happened. Why do I have to take away knives? Why do I have to break up fights? I always thought that I was a teacher, but I'm no teacher. I'm a bouncer and a policeman with the assignment of dangerous duty."

A sixth-grade teacher with four years' experience in an inner-city school remarked, "My biggest problem is not teaching. My biggest problem is keeping some semblance of an academic environment in my room. Some of these children are so nervous that they just can't handle the school materials. I have five or six in my group that just cannot be reached. These poor kids are just starving for individual attention. But what can I do? These are the same ones that go through school with their problems; these are the same ones that will end up with problems when they reach the upper grades."

A newly assigned teacher who is having some degree of success in an inner-city school commented, "My class is not too bad. In fact, without bragging, I would say it's one of the better ones in the school. I'm very authoritarian and I have a booming voice, and this may be why I've got my class under control. But I don't see why this should be necessary in a school system. I don't know why I should be a warden. I don't know why I should have to spend most of my time just keeping the kids under control. Why, oh why can't I be a teacher?"

A mature woman had this to say:

Academics take second place. I wasn't aware of this, I just was not aware. I heard stories from other teachers, but you just never know. You never realize until you're exposed to it. I've worked since I was thirteen years old and I've never worked so hard in my life as I have in teaching. I never heard worse cuss words come from people than I have from these children. I don't know, I simply don't know how the others stand it. I try to use the theories that I was taught in school; I try to use the methods, but I just can't. And I have an advantage on a lot of these young teachers because I entered teaching late. I see a lot of those young teachers just out of college. Many of them are genteel and soft spoken. My heart just bleeds for them because I know what's going to happen. And again I ask, why does it have to be like this?

In most instances, the teachers are at a loss to explain the motivation behind the hostility. Even teachers with many years' experience in these situations feel at a loss at times. One teacher with 12 years' experience, and described by her principal as a superior teacher, stated,

They are hard to handle. They think little of talking back, even to me. They
know me. To some extent, this hurts. They can be extremely rude without
any type of provocation whatsoever. I realize what causes this. They bring
a lot of problems to the school. You know, I'm no stranger here. They know
me and I know them. But I had to fill in with a fifth-grade class and because
of the fact that I wasn't their regular teacher, I had a hard time. Now, this
is hard to take, this is hard to understand. You know, I come to the school
lots of times prepared for a good day. I have things planned. I know I'm
going to teach and I can get slapped down in just five minutes, and I wonder
why, why this happened. All you have to do is just make such a simple
statement as "Please hang up your coat." Then you get snapped back to
you, "I won't," or "I don't have to," or "Nobody's going to make me hang
up my coat and *you* can't make me hang up my coat." Then, with this greet-
ing you in the morning, how *can* you really teach? It just seems to be that
the whole class picks it up, like some type of a signal. Then *you* try to
control it.

Tardiness and a slow start in September also hinder the teaching
situation. Out of 2,000 enrollment in a particular school, there may be
as many as 200 children tardy in a single day, some arriving as late as
15 to 20 minutes after the bell. In the fall, children are still entering
the school at the end of September and as late as October. The principal said, "When they come in in September, they trickle in. We
really don't start school until October. The truant officer this year had
300 names he had to round up to get to school."

A man who had taught for four years at a large inner-city school
commented:

I'm not saying that the case is hopeless. I am saying that something is going
to have to be done on the home level before you can do anything in the
school. Look, you get kids coming in with no paper. They can't even get
up a dime to buy a pad of paper. So, what do you do? You make it up to
them, you supply the paper. What do you do in the situation in which
there's five, six, or seven kids sleeping in one room, and even more than
one kid in one bed? Many of these people don't have any medical aid, as
well as the fact that there's no challenge in their society for school. I had
a kid in my room who was walking around with an excruciating toothache
for three days. The parents had to wait a long time to get him into the
County Hospital to the dentist. So what do you do? It's not that I'm making a fortune. I hate to see the kid in pain, so I took him to the dentist.
The tooth had to be pulled. Here's a poor kid walking around suffering.
Can you study with a toothache?

As the sixth-grade teacher said, the major problem in the inner-city
school is to keep order, so that the children can study and the teacher

can teach. This is never a problem in the high-status school, and seldom in the conventional school.

Suburban School Systems

The most effective and most innovative school systems during the past 30 years are generally thought to be suburban systems. Every large metropolitan area has from one to four or five upper-middle-class residential suburbs which have a reputation for a first-class, high-status type of school system.

The high visibility of these few school systems tends to obscure the fact that there are 2,500 school systems in suburbs with 1,200 or more pupils, the great majority of which are conventional systems. Although they are generally housed in new buildings and they present a good physical appearance, these average suburban schools are no better than conventional schools in the central city.

Also, with the growth of working-class residential suburbs, there is a growing number of common-man schools in suburban areas.

There are also a number of small and relatively weak school systems in the lesser-developed suburban areas. Many of them are in the process of consolidation into larger systems.

Table 4.1 indicates that in 1962 there were in the SMSAs about 4,000 school districts with less than 1,200 pupils enrolled. Almost one thousand of them were "non-operating" districts, which means that they did not have schools of their own but paid the cost of sending their pupils to schools in adjacent districts. Of the remaining 3,000 small districts in 1962, a large number have been consolidated into larger districts since that date. Still, there remain several hundred school systems with less than 300 pupils, and over a thousand with enrollments between 300 and 1,200.

Private School Systems

Approximately 14 percent of elementary and secondary school pupils attend private schools, and the great majority of these are in metropolitan areas. For example, in the state of Illinois in 1960, 89 percent of the private elementary-school enrollment was concentrated in the state's six SMSAs, and 79 percent were in the Chicago SMSA; this compares with 71 percent of public elementary school enrollment in SMSAs and 55 percent in the Chicago SMSA.

The concentration of private school pupils in metropolitan areas is due to the fact that Roman Catholics tend to live in metropolitan areas, and 90 percent of private school enrollment is in Catholic schools. The remainder is about equally divided between other church-related schools and independent private schools.

As would be expected from the facts of out-migration of residents of the central city to the suburbs, the Catholic school enrollment has increased sharply in the suburbs in recent years, while barely holding its own or even diminishing in the central city. This is due to the increase of Negro population in the central city, which is largely non-Catholic.

Most parochial schools are of the conventional or the common-man types. A parochial school located in a slum area is likely to be a common-man type of school. This is due to the fact that the parochial schools draw children from the more stable working-class families in this kind of area, that the parents support the teachers in establishing an ethos for the school, and that the Catholic parochial schools tend to maintain a very orderly routine.

In the suburbs and also in many areas of the central city the Catholic schools are likely to be of a conventional type. There are a few high-status· type Catholic schools, generally associated with a Catholic college which is interested in the training of teachers.

Since about 1960 there has been a growing pressure on the private non-church schools in the central cities. These schools have traditionally served upper-class families and a few upper-middles. Now the upper-middle-class pressure is increasing in the central cities where the public schools are believed to be less satisfactory than they once were. For example, in 1964 the *New York Times* made a survey of 50 private non-church affiliated schools in New York City with a tuition range of $400 to $3,000. The *Times* writer found a large increase of applications with little or no desire on the part of private school directors to enlarge their schools.

Functional Types of Schools

Another way of categorizing metropolitan area schools is by their functions—the particular educational purposes they serve. The comprehensive elementary or secondary school, serving all kinds of pupils, is still the most common type, but there are others which have grown in number in recent years.

Schools for Maladjusted Children

Many of the large cities have one or more schools for socially maladjusted children. In New York City the so-called "600 schools" have this function. In Chicago there are two schools for boys and one for girls. Most cities have a residential school for children who are sent there by the courts because they have no families or their families have been judged unfit to look after them.

Although these schools are crowded, they have not been enlarged, as a rule. They are not adequately staffed for treatment purposes, and therefore they serve primarily as custodial institutions. Consequently the principals and counsellors and psychologists try to send pupils there only as a last resort, feeling that the best thing for the pupil is to be kept in a regular classroom as long as he shows any ability to adjust himself and as long as the teacher will tolerate him. These special schools are also limited to children of 12 or 13 years or older. Younger children who appear to be disturbed or disturbing are kept as long as possible in a regular classroom. There is now a tendency to set up special classes for maladjusted children in elementary schools, classes with small enrollment and specially-selected teachers to work with them.

Effective Schools

This is a name used by New York City for a group of inner-city schools that have been given special services not available to the other schools. New York City had 20 elementary schools in this category in 1965–66. They have an average class size of about 20 pupils, and they cost about $200 per pupil above the average per-pupil cost. This money is used for smaller classes, special teachers and counsellors, social workers, teacher-aides, and after-school classes.

The name may become applicable to the thousands of inner-city schools which now receive special services under Title I of the Elementary and Secondary Education Act of 1965. The federal government provides about $200 to $250 per pupil for pupils from poverty-stricken families, with the provision that this must be spent to supplement the basic school program. The great bulk of Title I money goes to central cities of metropolitan areas, and is spent on inner-city schools.

Middle Schools

The "middle school" is a school serving grades five through eight or six through eight. It is taking the place of junior high schools in some communities, and being introduced in other communities that have had a K–8 elementary school. The middle school is most popular in the larger cities, where it serves two purposes. First, it permits the use of a departmentalized faculty of teachers specially trained in the modern mathematics, or science, or the new methods in English, or the new materials in social studies. The school building may be specially equipped for team teaching with groups of various sizes. Second, the middle school offers a chance to get greater social or racial integration in areas where there is residential segregation in small areas, but Negro and white and other families live in an area that can be served by a middle school, an area perhaps of a one-mile radius.

Educational Parks or Plazas

A few cities in metropolitan areas are now experimenting with the concept of an "educational park." This is a relatively large area that contains a variety of educational institutions. It may contain schools ranging from kindergarten to junior college, in appropriate buildings. It draws from a relatively large area, several square miles at least, and thus provides for greater social integration along socio-economic and racial lines than can be achieved in local neighborhood schools.

The educational park may have a theater and auditorium, a swimming pool, gymnasium and playing field, a library, and other physical facilities that a neighborhood school might not afford. The educational park concept is promoted by the provision of federal funds for Supplementary Educational Centers under the Elementary and Secondary Education Act. Such a Center, built with federal funds, might be a nucleus for the development of an educational park.

The Comprehensive High School

The typical American high school has educational programs or curricula aimed to meet the needs of all the youth of the community. It is the "natural" type of school for a community up to 50 or 100 thousand, which needs only one high school. Beyond this size, the community's socio-economic structure affects the SER of the high schools. It is unlikely that a high school can be truly comprehensive if its SER is below .50 or above 2.0. A school drawing largely middle-class students will stress college preparatory work and may neglect the students who want to go to work immediately on leaving high school. On the other hand, a school drawing on a working-class area may stress vocational-type courses, and fail to provide the quality and variety of courses that are needed for college preparatory work in foreign languages, mathematics, and science.

Mr. James B. Conant (1959, p. 17) formerly President of Harvard University, and Ambassador to West Germany, in his study of the American high school, defined the objectives of the comprehensive high school as:

. . . *first*, to provide a general education for all the future citizens; *second*, to provide good elective programs for those who wish to use their acquired skills immediately on graduation; *third*, to provide satisfactory programs for those whose vocations will depend on their subsequent education in a college or university. If one could find a single comprehensive high school in the United States in which all three objectives were reached in a highly satisfactory manner, such a school might be taken as a model or pattern. Furthermore, unless there were some especially favorable local features which enabled such a school to attain these three objectives, the characteristics found might be developed in all the other schools of sufficient size in the United States.

Since state and regional differences do play some role in this vast country, I decided that I should attempt to locate satisfactory comprehensive high schools in different sections of the nation. To this end, I inquired through various sources as to the comprehensive high schools outside the metropolitan areas which had the reputation of doing a good job in providing education for students with a wide range of vocational interests and abilities. I specified that these schools should be of such a nature that less than half the boys and girls were going on to college and the distribution of academic ability roughly corresponded to the national norm (median I.Q. 100–105).

Upon examining 22 high schools that were nominated, Mr. Conant found eight which met his criteria for effective comprehensive high schools. These were all outside of SMSAs.

The high-status suburban high school may not be a very good school for the minority of its students who do not have college-going abilities or interests. Still, the high school of an employing suburb and the high schools of certain sections of the central city which have a mixed population in terms of socio-economic status are comprehensive in their student composition. Such schools could become highly effective in terms of criteria set forth by Mr. Conant for a good comprehensive school.

The Specialized High School

In the central cities, now, there is open question whether it would be better to develop more specialized high schools, or whether it would be better to work toward making most high schools comprehensive as far as the characteristics of the student body permit the maintenance of a balanced comprehensive program.

Large cities, especially in the northeast, tend to set up selective college preparatory high schools which draw from the entire city or from a sector of the city those students who have superior scholastic aptitude and who want to take the trouble to attend a specialized school. Along with this policy may go one of developing a number of specialized high schools for pupils with artistic and other talents. New York City's High School of the Performing Arts is an example. Many large cities have one or more vocational high schools which train students specifically for skilled trades. Still, the common practice is to include courses leading to vocational skills in trades, industry and business in the general high school.

In the decade of the 1960s, there is some experimentation with a kind of *pre-vocational high school*, for pupils who have not done well in academic work and are likely to quit school before high school graduation. This school, operating at grade levels eight to ten, attempts to teach simple vocational skills such as those involved in restaurant work, janitorial service, automobile service station work, and other simple service jobs. With the present high proportion of pupils of inner-city and common-man schools who are two or more years retarded in reading and arithmetic level when they reach age 13 or 14, it seems likely that such schools will multiply, either as separate schools or as separate divisions of comprehensive schools.

Diverse Functions of a Metropolitan School System

From the foregoing overview of types of schools in a metropolitan area it can be seen that the school system as a whole has a wide diversity of functions. These functions tend to be assigned to schools depending on their location in the metropolitan area, though some functions are more widely distributed than others.

High Status of General Education in American Society

The prevailing function of the schools in America is that of providing as much general education as possible for as many students as possible. The American one-track school system holds out the opportunity (unrealistically, for many pupils) of graduating from high school and going to college for all boys and girls. Hence any school program that implies a termination of formal education without a high-school diploma which can lead to college entrance is open to a kind of ideological objection on the part of many parents and some educators. However, it appears likely that some high-school programs are now developing which will not lead to a regular high-school diploma but which are aimed instead at getting a boy or girl into a stable job.

The Function of Social Integration

A major function of American public school education is to promote social integration—that is, to give young people of all socio-economic levels and all racial and ethnic groups a common school experience in which they learn to work and to live together, and to accept one another as equal members of a democratic society. This function argues for the mixed school, and will be discussed at length in Chapter 6.

Compensatory Education

As far as possible, the public school system is committed to helping children compensate for handicaps of various kinds—crippling conditions, deafness, blindness, innate mental retardation, and intellectual retardation due to inadequate family experience. This is the most striking function of the inner-city school, at all age levels from pre-school years to the late teens. Programs range from Operation Head Start to the Job Corps and the Neighborhood Youth Corps which are operated under the Economic Opportunity Act generally with the cooperation of school systems.

Adult Education

The most rapidly growing part of education in metropolitan areas is adult education. A program of adult education influences positively and immediately the economic and the cultural life of the area. The illiterate adult who learns to read and to calculate increases his own capacity to earn, and his city's economic capital. The adult who learns more about drama, literature, music, or painting becomes one of the participating audience needed to create a great cultural center. The adult who studies the social and civic affairs of a metropolitan area becomes one of a body of citizens capable of guiding the process of metropolitan development.

The American mass culture has the highest financial base in the world, and probably the lowest cultural level of the modern urban countries. This has been said in a variety of disturbing and stimulating ways by critics of culture in America and outside of it. They point out the great and growing amount of leisure "enjoyed" by American adults, and they find that wonderful opportunities for fuller living are missed through the indifference and insensitivity of many people.

In 1965 the Congress created the National Arts and Humanities Foundation with the objective of building up the cultural agencies of the country with federal government support. The Foundation is working through the larger metropolitan areas as regional centers for the development of theaters, symphony orchestras, ballet and opera companies. Schools and colleges are being encouraged to develop courses in the performing arts, to start the process of recruiting and training young people before they reach the more advanced stages of training to begin in the regional centers.

Adult education stands a good chance of being planned and supported on a metropolitan area basis, partly because it does not have a long history of small-district and neighborhood organization to shackle it to the past.

The Urban-Community School

The quality of the public schools is the greatest single factor in the decision of middle-income people to live in the central city or to live in the suburbs, and to live in one section or another of the central city or the suburbs. Knowing this as a fact, educators tend to divide into two groups with respect to their views on the proper ways to operate a school system in the contemporary metropolitan area.

One school of thought may be called the "four-walls" school. The basic principle is to do the best possible job of educating every boy or girl who comes into the school, whoever he is, whatever his color, nationality, IQ or handicap. This means building good school buildings, equipping them well, and staffing them with well-trained teachers. At its best, it means being courteous and friendly to parents and to citizens who are interested in the schools, but making it quite clear to them that the schools are run by professionals who know their business and do not need advice from other people. It means making use of the cultural resources of the city—museums, theaters, orchestras, TV programs— under a system which guarantees the safety of the children and meets the convenience of the teachers.

It means keeping the schools "out of local politics." Staff appointments are to be made on the basis of merit alone, and promotion of staff on the basis of performance. It means a limited cooperation with other social institutions, public and private. The welfare and public aid and public health agencies are asked for help when the schools need it, but they cannot initiate school programs. Youth welfare and delinquency control agencies have their jobs to do, which meet and overlap the work of the schools. On this common ground the schools' administration must have full control of the use of school personnel and school facilities. In the area of training youth for employment, the school system will use the facilities of local business and industry for on-the-job training according to agreements worked out. Over-all policy for vocational education is the responsibility of the school administration under the Board of Education, and local business and industry are not closely related to policy determination in this area.

The four-walls type of school system works for efficiency and economy, and attempts to free the creative teacher to do the best possible job of teaching under good conditions. The community outside of the school is regarded as a source of complexity and of tension-arousal if the boundary between community and school is not clearly defined and respected.

The other school of thought may be called the "urban-community" school. The educators who advocate this believe that the big city is in a crisis which has been in force for some years and will last for at least 10 years and requires the active participation of schools in the making and practicing of policy for social urban renewal. This big-city crisis is reflected in feelings of uncertainty and anxiety on the part of parents and citizens. There is danger of a collective failure of nerve which saps the vitality and flexibility of the city's efforts at urban renewal. Parents and citizens of middle income are tempted in this situation to escape to the suburbs, where life seems simpler and safer, especially for children.

The urban-community school attempts to act constructively in this crisis by involving the parents and citizens in the decisions about school policy and practice. The educator accepts the frustration of working with people who themselves are confused and uncertain about the schools, believing that the only way to solve the problems of the city is to work on a give-and-take basis with citizens and community organizations.

The urban-community school includes the intraschool program of the four-walls school, but differs at important points on the relation of the school to the community.

Those who take the urban-community-school point of view believe there is no viable alternative. They believe that the four-walls school actually causes some of the problems of the community through its rigid rules about attendance districts and about keeping the public away from the classroom. They believe that the schools by their policies and practices either attract or repel people in the local community. Under present conditions, the typical school system repels people whom the central city cannot afford to lose as citizens. Proponents of the urban-community school believe that the present trend toward economic and racial segregation in the metropolitan area will continue, and the central city will lose quality, unless the schools take a more active part in social urban renewal.

The Urban-Community School Program in Flint

The community school is made to serve the needs of its particular local community, and to serve people of all ages. For example, the Flint, Michigan, public schools have developed a program that might serve any medium-sized central city. Although the community school program in Flint, an automobile manufacturing city, began during the Depression of the 1930's, it has gained momentum since then and is now a regular part of the program of the Flint Public Schools. The program started as one of using the schools in the evenings and on weekends for recreation and diversion to men out of work and to their families. When full employment returned, the program became even more popular. Most of the elementary schools are open evenings and Saturdays. All of the 20 or more new elementary schools built since 1950 have a "community wing" consisting of a community room, a kitchen, a gymnasium, and an auditorium.

A visitor may observe the following:

Neighborhood elementary schools that are busier on almost any evening than during the day; 500 youngsters attending junior high school on Saturday mornings of their own accord to acquire skills they haven't found time for during the regular school week; an elderly woman going back to high school (one of 3000 persons enrolled each year in adult high-school education); a family reupholstering dad's easy chair in the school's arts and crafts room (part of 35,000 enrolled annually in 776 adult education courses); community players rehearsing their next production in the auditorium of an elementary school; a school person making neighborhood calls.

The Flint community school also provides the facilities for regular sessions of the neighborhood Teen Club (one of 43 such groups with a card carrying membership of 13,000); for 7000 children on tot lots during the summer; for meetings in the community room of men's clubs, P.T.A.'s and various other organizations; for square dances for parents, teen-agers and the younger ones, and other recreational activities held in the large gymnasium; for a Christmas party attended by 700 adults in a school with an enrollment of only 500. (Buehring, 1958.)

The Urban-Community School and Social Urban Renewal

A more controversial quality of the urban-community school than the one just illustrated applies to the school system rather than to one or another particular neighborhood school. The urban-community school in this sense takes active part in the reshaping and renewing of the urban community. It adopts attendance or districting policies which are aimed at serving the purposes of urban renewal. If one of these purposes is racial balance in the schools, the urban-community school system adopts practices that work for racial balance. If another of the purposes is to reduce dropouts from high school and to reduce youth unemployment, the urban-community school develops a program of work experience, or remedial teaching or other devices to reduce dropouts and to prepare marginal youth better for employment. The urban-community school cooperates with non-school agencies of urban renewal.

If it appears that parents and citizens of middle income are becoming concerned about standards in the city schools and are thinking of moving to the suburbs, the urban-community school attempts to act constructively by involving those parents and citizens in discussions and decisions about school policy and practice.

If the education of handicapped children is of low quality in the smaller suburbs, the urban-community school system gets together with other systems to form a cooperative program of special education for the handicapped. The urban-community school system in a metropolitan area also cooperates with other systems to maintain an area-wide program of educational television.

Metropolitan Area Cooperation of School Systems

The first steps toward true metropolitan area cooperation are likely to be taken by volunteer and non-official groups which meet to study the problems of a metropolitan area and to plan for possible cooperation. A School Superintendents' Study Group or a Metropolitan School Board Association are examples.

An example is the PACE Association which was established under the auspices of the Greater Cleveland Association Foundation. A committee of citizens made a five-month study of the Greater Cleveland (Cuyahoga County) school needs, and then published a Plan for Action by Citizens in Education (PACE, 1963). The report points out, among other things, that: *Inequalities among Cuyahoga County's school districts are so vast that they cannot possibly be justified by a community which believes in equal opportunity.* In one favored district, 60 professionals serve a thousand children; libraries, laboratories, and swimming pools abound and excel; more than $800 is spent annually to educate each child. But in less fortunate districts, only about 40 professionals serve the same number of children; the elementary schools have no libraries; and $400 is available each year for each child. Similar disparities occur in all aspects of education: housing, facilities, personnel, programs, services.

The major recommendation was that the Cuyahoga County Superintendents' Association, parochial school leadership, and the present informal group of Cuyahoga County school board presidents should launch a thorough county-wide study of cooperative programs and services. The concluding recommendation in the Report was that "A continuing tax-exempt Greater Cleveland Citizens Committee should be formed which, over the next seven years will (1) work with existing organizations to review this Plan for Action and help to carry out its recommendations; (2) foster a climate of opinion which demands quality elementary and secondary education for all Cuyahoga County children; and (3) provide a badly needed and long awaited county-wide mechanism for the many citizens who want to work in the best interests of all the schools."

Reviewing this chapter's discussion of schools in the metropolitan area, it appears that the diversity of schools and the diverse functions of the schools may best be organized and operated as a part of a broadly planned and executed program of social urban renewal that is as wide as the metropolitan area. This requires the school systems to cooperate with one another and also with other social systems of government, culture, business and social welfare in a program that is based on metropolitan planning, the subject of the next chapter.

Exercises

1. In the inner city of your metropolitan area, how would you change and develop the school program so as to promote urban renewal in one or

more specific neighborhoods? What cooperative relationships between school system and other agencies would be required?

2. Looking at the high schools that you know in your metropolitan area, which ones can be called truly "comprehensive"? What criteria do you use to define a comprehensive high school?

3. Study the activities of the War on Poverty in your metropolitan area. To what extent are these activities planned and administered through the schools? Is there any evidence that these activities will have a continuing influence on school programs if federal support for them is ended?

4. Analyze the opportunities in your area for a person to participate actively as an amateur and passively as a spectator of the spectrum of arts. To what extent is the school system acting to extend the quality and scope of such participation? How is your metropolitan area related to a State Council on the Arts, and to the National Arts and Humanities Foundation?

Suggestions for Further Reading

1. A variety of publications has recently become available describing practicable programs for socially disadvantaged children and youth. Some of these are: *Programs for the Educationally Disadvantaged*, U.S. Office of Education; *Promising Practices for the Culturally Deprived*, Great Cities Program for School Improvement; *Educating the Culturally Deprived in the Great Cities*, The Phi Delta Kappan; *Education in Depressed Areas*, edited by Harry Passow.

2. To see how an intelligent and able "outsider" examines the school system and what conclusions he arrives at, read the following three books by James B. Conant: *The American High School Today; Slums and Suburbs; Shaping Educational Policy*.

3. For an advance view of the development of American culture that may grow out of the work of the National Arts and Humanities Foundation, read the congressional act (copy from your Congressman) and also the report of the panel called together by the Rockefeller Brothers Fund, entitled *The Performing Arts: Problems and Prospects*.

5 ❧ School Systems, Urban Renewal
and Metropolitan Planning

The Development of Urban Renewal

There has been renewal of cities over a long period of time. Jerusalem was rebuilt by Nehemiah, Athens by Pericles, Rome by Augustus, Paris by Napoleon III, and Chicago by Mayor Daley. Sometimes a destructive catastrophe, such as an earthquake, a fire, or a bombing raid, sets the stage for creative renewal of a city. Thus sections of Rotterdam, Milan, and London have been imaginatively rebuilt after bomb damage in World War II.

More generally, in the twentieth century, urban renewal is a planned replacement of old and wornout parts of the city. The need for urban renewal made itself felt in the 1930's, just at the time that a number of Eastern and North Central cities had reached a stage of growth where large tracts of houses became obsolescent and substandard. This was also a time when the federal government was being called upon to provide jobs and materials for public works in order to rescue the country from the Great Depression. To stimulate the home building industry and at the same time clear out the worst slums, the Federal Housing Act of 1937 offered subsidies and loans to local agencies for the construction of subsidized public housing.

After the war, in 1949 Congress passed the Housing Act of 1949 which provided grants to local governments to acquire and clear the land in blighted areas, and then to sell the cleared land to private developers or to local housing authorities for public housing. By this time the goal was slum clearance and urban redevelopment rather than housing of slum-dwellers. In other words, the goal was *urban renewal*, a term which came into popular usage in the 1950's.

By 1965 the worst slums had been cut out of the major American cities. A slum section of over 400 acres in St. Louis was cleared. Much of Boston's oldest but least picturesque housing was torn out to make room for expressways. Hundreds of acres of tenement houses were torn down on Chicago's South Side. New York's Lower East Side, and the area in Washington southeast of the Capitol felt the iron ball of the building wrecker. Los Angeles cleared the area on which the new Civic Center is being built. The Golden Triangle of Pittsburgh was modernized with smoke abatement, new office buildings and hotels, and expressways.

Not only are slums cleared; a major aspect of urban renewal is the attempt to arrest and reverse the process of decay of the city center. This means the building of a second generation of new and ultramodern skyscrapers to take the place of the generation erected in the early 1900's. It also means the building of expressways to provide easy automobile transportation for commuters who do not use the old-fashioned rapid transit service. Furthermore, there must be new and attractive apartment housing within walking or taxi distance of the downtown offices and stores, for people who have the money and the inclination to live in upper- or upper-middle-class style without going out to the suburbs at the city fringes.

Meanwhile the federal government has continued to award large sums of money to what is now called "Housing and Urban Development." The Act of 1965 provided a variety of aids for housing, including substantial numbers of new low-rent public-housing units, subsidized low interest rates for housing for people of moderate income, and rent supplements to aid low-income families to secure better private housing. At the same time there is substantial money for the improvement of metropolitan areas through the purchase of land for recreational, conservation and other public uses, and for the construction of community centers, health stations, and water and sewer facilities.

The modern city must be an organ of the Great Society and also an organ of a democratic society. It must be a good place to conduct business—to interchange goods and services. It must be a good place to raise children. It must be a good place to enjoy at least a part of one's spare time.

Urban renewal has the goal of restoring physical areas of comfortable middle-class living in the central city and also of establishing comfortable slum-free housing for working-class people. Beyond this, urban renewal has a social goal of making the whole metropolitan area a good place for all kinds of people to live. The leaders of urban renewal often speak of their goal as that of increasing the range and amount of choice people have among good ways to live. This is more than physical urban renewal. It may be called *social urban renewal.*

By the middle 1960's it was becoming clear that physical urban renewal was not enough to accomplish the task of urban redevelopment. It was recognized that the cities were becoming better physically without improving socially or morally. In particular, housing was no longer the major problem. In 1940, the U.S. Census declared that about half of the housing in the country was substandard. This proportion decreased steadily until it was 19 percent in 1960. In the large cities, only 11 percent of housing was classified as substandard in 1960, and only three percent was labelled "dilapidated."

By this time there was wide and growing disillusionment with simple physical urban renewal. It appeared that many families who were dispossessed of their living quarters by demolition of slums were relocated in only slightly better homes at the cost of higher rents. The British sociologist Peter Marris (1962) after a study of American urban renewal in 1961, concluded that, "On the whole then, it seems fair to say that relocation has provided only marginally better housing, in very similar neighborhoods, at higher rents, and has done as much to worsen as to solve the social problems of the families displaced. The dispossessed enjoy as their reward a distant view of luxury apartments rising over their old homes."

He stated three conclusions about urban renewal:

1) That relocation has achieved little over-all improvement in the circumstances of the people displaced. They have tended to move into neighborhoods little different from those pulled down, which may rapidly degenerate.
2) Whether the interests of the people moved, or the revitalization of the city, are put first, urban renewal cannot achieve its ultimate purpose so long as slum communities are merely displaced or scattered. The renovation of one blighted area only accelerates the decay of others, and creates new slums.
3) Social welfare programs cannot succeed in integrating slum communities with the wider society. Faced with many handicaps, the slum dwellers retreat into a sub-culture which, though it increases these handicaps, protects them from humiliation. Hence they are not receptive to the values which welfare workers and social institutions represent as agents of society.

One of the first persuasive opponents of sheer physical urban renewal was Jane Jacobs (1961) whose *Death and Life of Great American*

Cities argued that the close-knit neighborhoods of the central city were being destroyed and replaced by impersonal and alienating housing projects, which lacked the human touch of the neighborhood delicatessen shop, drug store, and the sociability of the side walk and the front stoop of a tenement house. When a great public housing project was erected in East Harlem, with a wide rectangular lawn, the tenants said in no uncertain terms that they hated this lawn. When a social worker tried to find out why the tenants disliked the lawn, she concluded that it was for two reasons: the tenants had not been asked whether they wanted a lawn, and the bare lawn reminded them of things they no longer could have. One tenant said: "Nobody cared what we wanted when they built this place. They threw our houses down and pushed us here and pushed our friends somewhere else. We didn't have a place around here to get a cup of coffee or a newspaper even, or borrow fifty cents. Nobody cared what we need. But the big men come and look at the grass and say, 'Isn't it wonderful! Now the poor have everything.' " (Jacobs, 1961, p. 15.)

Mrs. Jacobs pointed to Greenwich Village in New York City and the Italian North End in Boston as examples of areas where old homes were renovated, the neighborhood was preserved, and people lived the good life, even though many of them were poor people.

Cities, for Mrs. Jacobs, are "problems in organized complexity." She believes that urban renewal experts have mistakenly seen cities as problems of simplicity and have tried to treat them with over-simple mechanical solutions.

Charles Abrams, writing in 1965, in *The City Is the Frontier*, calls the city a frontier not only because it is an asphalt jungle, a lawless place, but also because it is "our last unconquered environment." He believes that central cities can be made into areas where all kinds of people can work and live and enjoy life, but this will not be done by the real-estate business and the construction industry.

The Cultural Problem of Urban Renewal

The real problem is people, and not slums. Urban renewal has to influence people, and the physical improvement of their homes is not enough. A political scientist, Professor James Q. Wilson of Harvard University (1965), puts it this way:

We have three major problems in our cities: a poverty problem, a race problem, and a cultural problem. By culture, let me hasten to add, I do not mean the problem of maintaining the Metropolitan Opera, but culture in a broader sense: the cultural and educational prerequisites for a sound, stable family life which can prepare young people for taking advantage of the best opportunities that confront them. I mean culture, therefore, in an anthropological and not in a high-brow sense.

These are the real problems—poor people, disadvantaged minority groups, and people who come from families which have for generations provided no support for education, for intellectual attainment, for ambition, no reinforcement, indeed, for anything but for duplicating the tragic pattern of the past. For these three kinds of problems urban renewal, as it has been practiced in the United States until recently, is either irrelevant or disadvantageous. In the name of improving cities, or in the name of improving housing—in short, in the name of dealing with fictions—urban renewal has bypassed the real problems or, in some cases, made them worse. . . .

I think that we are at a point now at which we have to make some kind of fundamental reconciliation between what we are doing to the physical shells of our cities and what we hope to do with the people who live in those shells. It seems to me that if urban renewal is accelerated, as it may well be, before an institutional response has been devised to the problems of poverty, race, and culture, that these problems may be made worse or their solutions impeded. Urban renewal on a larger scale than is practiced today may continue to break up natural neighborhoods and the subcultures around which these neighborhoods are organized, weakening those institutions—schools, churches, and kinship ties—that are essential to dealing with fundamental human problems. A vast increase in the scale of urban renewal will further reduce the supply of low-cost housing faster than we increase the capacity of people to acquire higher-cost housing. And finally, an accelerated urban renewal program may very well increase the sense of family insecurity and decrease the attachment to neighborhood and to community which is already so weak that it constitutes one of the fundamental obstacles to the improvement of the people who are at the bottom of the social heap. . . .

Poverty in the United States, to a very real extent, is inherited—not genetically, of course, but culturally. Poverty is a vicious cycle of too-large families, too-weak families, families headed by mothers and deserted by fathers, families victimized by racial prejudice, by lack of education, and by the lack of a sense of opportunity and purpose. To eliminate this cycle, it seems to me, we must eliminate that whole pattern of joblessness which leads to the loss of self-respect, which leads to desertion, which leads to dependency, which breeds children who begin the cycle all over again.

I do not think that urban renewal, as it is presently constituted, can contribute significantly to the solution of these problems. And at the same time, I am convinced that these are the most important problems facing America domestically today. These people need a larger supply of low-cost housing, not a smaller supply. And it seems to me that, except in special cases where great national or community purposes are to be served, it is a mistake to continue a program, much less accelerate it, which has as its principal effect a reduction in the supply of low-cost housing. It seems to me that what we need today is to strengthen neighborhood ties and family ties and to encourage neighborhoods to become sufficiently stable so that a kind of neighborhood culture can develop, in which social controls are automatically exercised and do not have to be exercised by a police force which, in all too many of our large American cities, operates as a kind of army of occupation facing hostile natives.

Urban Renewal and the Schools

The inner-city schools are affected in several ways by urban renewal, some favorable and some unfavorable.

On the favorable side, urban renewal provides space in which to build schools, and space for playgrounds in areas where there were no parks or playgrounds before renewal. For example, in Chicago as of the close of 1964, urban renewal land had been sold or was in process of being sold to public and private schools for four new buildings as well as for the new site of the University of Illinois and an expansion of the Illinois Institute of Technology. At the same time, seven schools had secured land for playgrounds, and there were ten requests for playground space pending.

Also, a desirable element in urban renewal is the greater stability of families who secure apartments in public housing projects. School principals note that there is a great reduction of transiency in their schools when a large public housing project goes up nearby. Tenants do not move frequently. Many tenants are supported by public welfare funds, which give them a steady source of income and tend to keep them stationary.

On the undesirable side, urban renewal as it has been generally practiced has continued the pattern of economic and racial stratification which existed before. The subsidized public housing which took the place of slums has generally been concentrated into high-rise apartment buildings or two- or three-story row houses covering several city blocks. The average housing project has over a thousand residents, with three or four hundred school-age children. Some housing projects are so large that their children fill up an elementary school. One especially large public housing project in Chicago has a small high school and three elementary schools serving it, alone. In this project, in 1965, were 2070 children (not all of school age) who received Aid for Dependent Children; 661 families with annual income of less than $2,000; 612 school pupils severely retarded in reading, and 53 percent of the children in the first grade who tested on a test of reading readiness as not ready to learn to read.

Another subsidized housing project in Chicago, the Robert Taylor Homes, is a series of high-rise apartment buildings stretching for almost two miles along South State Street. Not only do the children living in these homes make up most of the enrollment of several elementary schools; at the close of 1964 there were 56 elementary school classes meeting in apartments in the Housing Project, due to lack of space in the neighborhood schools. The Robert Taylor Homes has practically all Negro occupancy. When it was proposed to build these high-rise homes, there was objection from some people on the ground that it would tend to segregate low-income Negroes, but the City Council voted to approve the project. Professor Roald Campbell (1965) later commented on this situation as follows:

> In many cases, housing patterns do more to determine the nature of the school than any action of the board of education. One might cite the decision to erect the Robert Taylor Homes, twenty-eight high-rise public housing apartments, down State Street in Chicago as one of the most dramatic examples. Apparently city council members were pleased not to have public housing dispersed over the entire city as had been advocated by Elizabeth Wood, then Director of the Chicago Housing Authority. In any case the two-mile strip of public housing on State Street did more to perpetuate *de facto* segregation in schools than any policy decision by the school board or any other body. But why was there not more collaboration between the board of education, the housing authority, and the city council? This lack of collaboration among agencies at both program and policy levels is a notable problem in our cities. . . .

What has happened in urban renewal in Chicago has happened in practically all of the big cities. The same mistakes have been made, from the point of view of those who are interested in social integration. Yet it was not necessary to make most mistakes. Subsidized housing in other countries is not generally built to entrench economic stratification. It is possible to build small public housing units spread widely over the city, so that families living in public housing have neighbors with average incomes and send their children to schools of mixed socio-economic status. In fact, the Chicago Committee on Urban Progress, reporting in 1965, went on record as opposed to the kind of public housing policy which had built these segregated projects. It said:

High density projects should be discontinued as a policy, but subsidized public housing, of appropriate scale and pleasing design, should be blended into normal residential neighborhoods in all parts of the city. . . . Experimentation should be initiated in designing public housing projects for resale to their occupants over a period of time, on a cooperative or condominium basis. (Chicago Committee on Urban Progress, 1965, p. 30–31.)

The Federal Department of Urban Affairs

Thus urban renewal as it was practiced from 1950 to 1965 was at best an uncertain force for the social health of the city. In this situation, knowing that the problem of the city was the major domestic problem of the time and that this problem was getting worse rather than better, the 89th Congress established a new cabinet post, and a new executive department—the Department of Housing and Urban Development. The first Secretary of the Department, Robert C. Weaver, had made it clear, as did President Johnson, that the entire metropolitan area was the province of the Department. He wrote in 1964, before his appointment to the President's Cabinet,

The city today is, or should be in my opinion, the heart, and in a sense the soul, of a metropolitan area. The suburbs around it, to a large degree, draw their life and their spirit from the city's economy and culture. The city should be revitalized as the anchor holding together our metropolitan areas. It does not perform this function effectively today.

I am not impressed by those who prophesy the demise of cities. I am convinced that the recent decline in the population of central cities has been due, in large part, to the concentration of new construction in the suburbs and the scarcity of competing living facilities in the central cities.

Affluent society should maximize consumer choices. As we are slowly providing attractive patterns of living in the central cities, largely through urban renewal, we are providing wider choices. In the decades ahead I hope the American people will respond to an increase in desirable housing both in the central city and in the suburbs, both rental and sales. In a word, a balanced supply of housing for a range of income groups in all parts of the metropolis should be sought.

For the ten or twenty years after 1965, the need is for social urban renewal to take the entire metropolitan area as the unit of planning and development. The following propositions outline the argument that will be followed in the remainder of this chapter.

1. A vast process of social urban renewal lies ahead, which will require not only money, but much clearer understanding of the problems of the city and the suburbs than underlay the early efforts at physical urban renewal.
2. Social urban renewal will take the metropolitan area rather than the central city as its field of attention.
3. Social urban renewal requires the cooperation of school systems with other social systems, especially local government, local business, and cultural agencies.
4. Successful renewal depends on planning on a metropolitan scale.

Metropolitan Areas as Units of Development

When one collects together the big department stores, the banks, schools, libraries, parks, factories, churches, play spaces, the mansions and the slums, the big and little homes, the highways and subways and railways, the suburban villages and the central city, the shopping centers and the still open fields, one has a metropolitan area. This is the area in which most of a man's material, cultural, and spiritual needs can be met. This is his ordinary living space.

The future of the suburbs depends on the central city, and the city depends on its suburbs. The suburbs are here to stay, and no amount of urban renewal in the central city can stop their growth. However, the isolation and autonomy of the independent suburban community has to be reduced. As the suburbs grow, they will get into trouble with each other if they do not learn to cooperate among themselves and with the central city.

Furthermore, the relatively privileged character of the suburbs in relation to the central city must be changed. No metropolitan area will survive as a middle-class suburban doughnut surrounding a central city slum ghetto.

There must be physical and political arrangements that tie the suburbs to the central cities, based on studies of the problems of the metropolitan area. There must also be bonds of conscience. The wealthy suburbs must show concern about the poor suburbs as well as about the central city. And the political power of the central city must be used on behalf of the entire metropolitan area.

The metropolitan area is a new kind of community, bounded and defined in different ways from the conventional civic units. The Committee for Economic Development (1960) states it as follows: "The metropolitan area is in effect a new community. Its boundaries often are hard to define. In some instances they change and expand frequently. The area ignores old geographic boundaries, jumping over and around rivers and land masses. It ignores the political lines of districts, villages, towns, cities, counties, and states." A new concept has arisen—the concept of metropolitanism, not urbanism or suburbanism.

Metropolitanism may be defined as a process of action and planning. It is the action of an increasing number of organizations that take the metropolitan area as their natural area of activity. There are many quasi-public and private organizations which operate within the entire area, regardless of local governmental boundaries. A chamber of commerce may cover the area, as well as labor unions, social clubs, and the telephone, power, and gas companies. School boards are often banded together into a metropolitan school board association. School superintendents often combine into a metropolitan area study group. A university is likely to serve the entire area. A symphony orchestra and a theatre group may be supported by the central city and suburbs alike.

Metropolitanism is also a process of planning for future development of the metropolitan area as a unit. The planning is done for such functions as transportation, recreation, teacher education, development of cultural agencies such as theatre, libraries, orchestras, and museums. By means of area-wide zoning, an orderly development may take place for industrial parks, regional shopping centers, residential areas, and recreational open spaces. Certain problems of urban-industrial development require solutions on an area-wide basis, such as: water supply; prevention of air, soil, and water pollution; sewage disposal; rapid transit; and preservation of scenic beauty.

Related to this process is a growing amount of *cooperation* among local units and organizations in the provision of services to the people. This is seen very clearly in the area of education, where school districts cooperate to provide educational television, vocational education for the entire area, special education for children with handicaps that are not widespread enough to allow a small district to provide its own program, and in-service teacher training.

Metropolitanism is a state of mind, as well as an action process. There is a growing consciousness of being a citizen of a metropolitan area, as well as of some smaller political unit. The metropolitan mind is not a characteristic of many people as yet. The metropolitan area tends to be an *unperceived community* for many people, quite different in their minds from their perceived communities of the church, the organization in which they work, and their local school district. It is interesting to speculate on the differences between metropolitan areas in the degree to which their residents perceive the area to be their community. Does San Francisco have a more highly developed sense of metropolitan community than Boston, for example? Differences in the extent of the sense of community may be due, in part, to the existence in some areas of certain problems, such as that of air pollution, which can only be solved by area-wide cooperation and action. Also, the increasing number of central city payroll or earnings taxes which bear upon suburban residents who work in the central city is making them concerned with the way the city government spends their tax money.

Goals of Metropolitanism

There are five main objectives of metropolitan development.

1. INCREASING FREEDOM OF CHOICE in living arrangements, work, and leisure activities. The goal is to give all kinds of people a free choice of where to live, where to work, and where and how to spend their leisure time.

2. EQUALIZATION OF OPPORTUNITY AND SERVICES among the parts of the area. This means financial equalization of tax support, as well as provision of good schools, police and fire protection, water supply and sewage disposal to all parts of the area.

3. EFFICIENT PROVISION OF SERVICES. Libraries, schools, health services, hospitals, and shopping centers must be provided efficiently,

which means that the smaller communities must cooperate to create a large enough population base for such services.

4. ADEQUATE PROGRAMS. The programs of libraries, schools, hospitals, and shopping centers should be maintained at a high level of quality.

5. SOCIAL INTEGRATION. The metropolitan area should be so structured as to bring diverse people together in schools, churches, and business and recreation centers. Although people should not be required to associate in non-public places with people of another color or economic level, this association should not be barred by residential and other forms of physical segregation.

The Facts of Fragmentation

Although the ideal of metropolitan development is one of cooperation, coherence and integration, the facts as of the 1960s are quite different. Metropolitan areas are highly fragmented, the suburbs most of all.

There are many government units in the average metropolitan area. According to the 1962 Census of Governments, there were 18,442 local governments in the. 212 SMSAs, on an average of 87 for each metropolis. These are all independent, with separate taxing powers, officials, and functions. They may be cities, villages, towns, boroughs, counties, and school districts.

Table 5.1 shows how the local governments are distributed among

Table 5.1   *Local Governments in Metropolitan Areas*

SMSA SIZE GROUP (1960 POPULATION)	NUMBER OF SMSAs	NUMBER OF LOCAL GOVERNMENTS (1962)	AVERAGE NUMBER OF LOCAL GOVERNMENTS
All SMSAs	212	18,442	87.0
1,000,000 or more	24	7,227	301.0
500,000–1,000,000	29	2,857	98.5
300,000–500,000	28	2,146	76.6
200,000–300,000	41	3,141	76.6
100,000–200,000	68	2,540	37.4
50,000–100,000	22	531	24.1

Source: U.S. Bureau of the Census, *Census of Governments: 1962*, Vol. 1, *Governmental Organization* (Washington: 1963), p. 11.

SMSAs by size. The Chicago SMSA had the most in 1962, with 1,060. Philadelphia had 963; Pittsburgh 806; New York, 555; and St. Louis, 439. But Baltimore had only 23 local governments while Madison, Wisconsin, with about 250,000 residents, had 178.

Table 5.2 shows the various types of local governments, and their numerical changes between 1957 and 1962. Local school districts dropped by 25 percent in these five years, while special districts increased substantially. The nonschool special districts have grown with the growth of metropolitan areas. These are agencies set up to perform one or two services for an area larger than a municipality. They provide such services as water supply, fire protection, sewage disposal, flood control, airports, and transportation.

Table 5.2   *Types of Local Governments in SMSAs, 1962 and 1957*

CLASS OF LOCAL GOVERNMENTS	NUMBER IN SMSAs, 1962	PERCENTAGE OF SMSA TOTAL	INCREASE OR DECREASE IN NUMBER, 1957–1962	PERCENTAGE CHANGE IN NUMBER, 1957–1962
All local governments	18,442	100.0	458	3
School districts	6,004	32.5	−1,482	−20
Special districts	5,411	29.3	1,675	45
Municipalities	4,142	22.5	298	8
Towns and townships	2,575	14.0	− 32	− 1
Counties	310	1.7	− 1	− 0.32

Source: U.S. Bureau of the Census, *Census of Governments: 1962*, Vol. 1, Governmental Organization (Washington: 1963), p. 11.

Although the number of local school districts has been reduced by consolidation of small districts, there still in 1961 was an average of 33 school districts per SMSA. As Table 4.1 shows, there were 1726 school districts operating in SMSAs with fewer than 300 pupils in 1961.

The fragmentation of a metropolitan area into many small school districts generally results in great discrepancies in the financial support of the schools between districts. For example, in the Chicago SMSA in 1961–63, there were two contiguous school districts which showed striking differences in school support. One district had within its boundaries a large industrial plant that paid a large tax bill. This district had a 64-cent school tax rate, one of the lowest in the state, and yet spent $1,030 per child in average daily attendance in elementary school. The neighboring district had no industry, though many of its residents worked in the plant in the adjacent district. The school tax rate was $1.85, one of the highest in the state, and yet provided only $348 per child in elementary school.

Movement Toward Metropolitan Cooperation

In order to overcome this fragmentation of local government, metropolitan areas have tried a number of forms of cooperation among their local units. These range from the governing of the area by a single metropolitan government to a combination of area-wide governments with local governments and on to a systematic cooperation among existing governments.

The one-government or metro-government approach has been adopted in only one large SMSA, Nashville. Nashville and Davidson County, Tennessee, combined the city and county governments into one government, and combined the school districts into a single county-wide district. This was done in 1962, after the voters defeated a similar proposal in 1958.

Dade County, Florida, saw the effort made in 1953 to abolish the city government of Miami and to make the county government the sole government of the area. When this was defeated by a close vote, a plan for a metropolitan charter was drawn up and approved by the voters in 1957. This was a "two-level" plan with a powerful county government combined with the limited action of local municipal governments, 19 out of 26 having less than 10,000 population.

A "federation" plan was adopted in Toronto, Canada, in 1954. This came about because the communities in the metropolitan area were suffering severely from lack of facilities, such as water supply, sewage disposal, good schools, arterial highways, rapid transit, and low-cost housing. There is an area-wide government which includes 13 municipalities. The metro government has much power, but the 13 municipal governments retain some powers. There is a metropolitan school board, which provides school sites and buildings and makes uniform per-pupil payments to the 11 locally elected school boards which operate the elementary and secondary schools.

Other plans and proposals for metropolitan cooperation have failed, such as the one proposed for St. Louis and defeated at the polls in 1959 and 1962. Cleveland voters failed to approve a county-wide charter plan in 1959.

One of the latest proposals for metropolitan government has come from Chicago, where the Committee on Urban Progress, a voluntary group of 47 citizens made a two-year study and concluded in 1965 with a set of recommendations for metropolitan development, the first step of which was a proposal that the Governor should appoint a Commission on Urban Area Government to develop a program of legislation and administration leading to the merging of the Chicago and Cook County governments and the creation of a number of special service districts for the Chicago SMSA in fields such as air pollution, transportation, public health, water supply, flood control, and sewage disposal. The Committee said:

The chief obstacle to rational and far-sighted control of urban expansion is political overlapping and fragmentation. For example, in the six-county area of northeastern Illinois 52 new villages and nine new cities were incorporated between 1950 and 1963. Two of the cities have populations below 1,500, and 23 villages have populations under 400.

The transportation network carries the lifeblood of the Chicago area, yet no single agency has the authority to coordinate these services or to plan the balanced development of a modern metropolitan transportation system. In Cook County alone 156 different governments can build highways—the county, the 30 townships, and the 125 municipalities.

Uncontrolled development in unincorporated areas may cause blight which threatens the standards of adjacent communities. Zoning regulations vary widely throughout the area as municipalities compete for industry and the tax revenue needed to support public services. Costs rise and efficiency suffers when problems common to an entire area are met in a piecemeal way dictated by political boundaries.

One particularly striking consequence of this diffusion of governmental authority is the difficulty of finding equitable ways to produce revenue for the financing of expanding needs. With the overlapping of administrative costs, all communities struggle with the job of supporting school systems tremendously enlarged by the flow of population to them.

In the central city, resources must be found to pay for what are really services occasioned by the needs of the suburban as well as the urban population. Consequently, the city taxes its property owners to provide expanded police protection, transportation facilities, parks, libraries, other recreational and cultural centers.

If the city declines in economic vigor, its capacity to support these necessary functions will be sapped. Without a vital urban nucleus the entire area loses focus and force. In short, the functional demands of our times have established the need for modernization of governmental structure. (Chicago Committee on Urban Progress, 1965, pp. 3–4.)

Thus the movement to create strong area or county governments is a live one, though it meets much opposition. Meanwhile, there has been a growth of voluntary cooperation among governmental units in the larger metropolitan areas.

Metropolitan Cooperation Among School Systems

School districts in a metropolitan area are moving toward closer cooperation in two ways—by consolidation and by voluntary cooperation.

The consolidation of small suburban districts has already been noted, and Table 5.2 shows that this has been going on rapidly. The small district with less than 300 pupils will soon disappear from metropolitan areas.

Voluntary cooperation among school districts has generally taken the form of a Study Council or Superintendents' Study Group, in which a local university works with the school superintendents of the area. This may lead to a more formal arrangement for voluntary cooperation, such as the Educational Research and Development Council of the Twin Cities Metropolitan Area, Inc. The superintendents of the Minneapolis-St. Paul area, together with members of the School of Education at the University of Minnesota, formed the Council in 1963. It consists of 35 public school districts in the seven-county metropolitan area, and these schools serve 44 percent of the pupils of the state of Minnesota.

During the first three years of the Council, a variety of research and demonstration projects were undertaken, including the following:

> Basic research studies: organizational climate and structure, school output measures, program evaluation, staffing of schools.
> Surveys: finance and taxation, expenditures, staffing.
> Developmental activities: workshops for teachers and administrators; programs for the mentally retarded; computer utilization project; production of a film to supplement the teaching of American poetry.

Metropolitan Planning for Development and Cooperation

The metropolitan area is a *product* of social changes. At the same time it is being recognized by more and more people and by more and more organizations as the best *agent* for directing and controlling social change in the interests of the people. Directing and controlling social change requires planning.

Planning by a government agency is now a respectable operation, though until World War II there were many people who thought that city planning and regional planning were un-American. They thought it was good for a business owner to plan ahead for the development of his business, but it was socialism for a city government to plan ahead for its development.

The physicial planning of a new city is an old practice, as old as the history of cities. The City of Washington was planned by Major L'Enfant. Salt Lake City was laid out by plan. But the nineteenth century saw relatively little city planning in the United States, less than in Europe, where Sweden adopted a city planning code in the 1870s. Probably the first conference on city planning in the USA was held in Washington in 1903. Most cities now have planning commissions, often only semi-official and composed of non-experts.

City planning now finds its strongest supporters among businessmen and newspapers. They have come to the conclusion that land use in urban communities cannot be left to the ingenuity and the capability of individuals without government control. The question today is not whether there should be government participation in community development, but rather what forms of comprehensive planning are best.

What Does Planning Mean?

Planning is a process by which responsible members of a community look ahead to future developments and prepare to guide them into desirable patterns of growth. The planning group may be official or unofficial, trained or untrained for the task. Sears, Roebuck and Company (1962) puts out a booklet on Community Planning and answers the question "Why do we plan?" as follows: (1) To meet events we expect to happen; (2) To accomplish things we want to happen; and (3) To avoid or prevent things we do not want to happen.

There are seven aspects of planning:

1. ARRANGEMENTS FOR CONVENIENT MOVEMENT OF PEOPLE AND MATERIALS. The increased use of automobiles and trucks has shifted the

load of transportation to streets and highways from electric trains, subways, street cars, and buses which used streets and highways less. Between 1950 and 1958 people decreased their use of public transit facilities from 17.2 billion to 9.7 billion rides per year. (Committee for Economic Development, 1960, p. 19.) To meet this problem new forms of rapid transit are being tried, and subways are being expanded. Also the cities have bought up expensive land and removed it from the tax rolls in order to build networks of automobile expressways.

2. RULES FOR ORDERLY AND ESTHETIC LAND USE. Zoning is the term applied to community control over the use of private and public land. Zoning is generally done by ordinance, and is enforced by law. Different districts are zoned for different functions, such as: retail or wholesale business, heavy manufacturing, light manufacturing, office buildings, single family residences, multiple family residences. If this is not done, people cannot plan to use property with confidence in the future. A man building a fine house may find himself next to a factory some years later.

The first comprehensive zoning law in the United States was put into effect in 1916. Most cities delayed, as did Detroit. The city charter of 1918 provided for a Planning Commission, but the Commission was not given enough money to accomplish much. The city enacted a zoning ordinance in 1940 and a master plan in 1948. But by this time there was little or no vacant land left, and the Commission had the problem of urban renewal on its hands.

3. LOCATION AND DESIGN OF PUBLIC BUILDINGS AND FACILITIES. A planning function is the designing and locating of public cultural, educational and recreational facilities. The quality of life in a city is enhanced by conveniently located and well-designed museums, convention halls, public libraries, art galleries and local community centers. In addition the location and development of parks, playgrounds, botanical gardens and zoos has a major influence on the satisfaction people get from living in a city. The park system established in Kansas City at the beginning of this century has kept that city attractive. The city of Dunedin, New Zealand, has now a belt of parks surrounding the central city, due to the wisdom of early planners in securing a "green belt" around the city's edges when it was smaller.

The location of school buildings is especially important in city planning, since the presence of a well-built school attracts and holds families with children. In planning for urban renewal it is desirable to locate school buildings in accordance with renewal policies, and consequently the city planning and school planning staffs are generally urged to confer and cooperate.

4. PROMOTION OF HEALTH AND PREVENTION OF HEALTH HAZARDS. City planning must anticipate needs for pure water and pure air. Hospital location is important. Measures for sewage disposal and smoke and fume abatement are parts of this function. This becomes crucial as a city gets to be very large.

5. PLANNING NEIGHBORHOOD SERVICES AND FACILITIES. The attempt to maintain and to encourage neighborhood life and neighborliness is a part of large scale planning of housing projects and new communities. These new and sanitary creations sometimes lack the homely touch of the old and deteriorating neighborhoods, where people knew their neighbors, had friendly relations with small tradesmen, and felt at home. The new planned communities in England have been organized around neighborhoods, each with an array of facilities including a health center, child care center, swimming pool, playground, social center and branch library. (Orland, 1952.)

6. URBAN RENEWAL. A program of urban renewal generally has behind it a master plan, drawn by a planning commission. The master plan does not have the status of a law. It is simply advisory, meant to guide public officials and private builders and investors. The planning commission generally publishes the master plan, with maps showing the areas of the city for which certain developments are suggested, and with a statement of the policies for transportation, land use and community facilities.

7. METROPOLITAN AREA PLANNING. With the population of metropolitan areas outside of the central city as large as the central city population, the need for area-wide planning has become clear. Transportation must be planned for the area as a whole. Sewage disposal, police protection, and industry decentralization present problems beyond the power of the many small suburban governments to cope with independently. Small separate school districts need to cooperate to provide educational services that they cannot give singly.

A regional plan for the 22 county New York area was drawn up about 1930 by the Regional Plan Association, a privately financed non-profit organization. Thirty years later a second regional plan was made, known as the New York Metropolitan Region Study, which dealt with the social and economic problems of the area, as well as its physical aspects. (Hoover and Vernon, 1959.)

There are metropolitan area plans for Greater London, extending about 30 miles out from the center of the city, and for the area comprised by the four Dutch cities of Amsterdam, Leiden, The Hague, and Rotterdam. Metropolitan Paris has had a master regional plan since 1935, which controls the planning of the smaller communities within the region.

The function of metropolitan planning is to coordinate the planning of the many local units, though it generally has no power to enforce its recommendations. It must persuade and advise. For example, the Northeastern Illinois Metropolitan Area Planning Commission works over an area of 3,700 square miles, containing 250 municipalities and 700 other government units. The Commission has 19 members, five named by the mayor of Chicago, one each by the six county Boards of Supervisors, and eight by the state governor.

In 1962 the National Municipal League identified 63 planning commissions operating in SMSAs and extending over several government units. Three fourths of them had come into existence since 1950. The federal government Housing and Home Finance Agency in 1963 listed 126 planning commissions operating over a metropolitan area or several areas in 142 SMSAs. This included county planning agencies, and used a more liberal definition than that of the National Municipal League. (Housing and Home Finance Agency, 1963.)

Thus metropolitan area planning is just finding itself. In some cases it is done by official government agencies, and in some cases by private organizations. In some cases its recommendations have the force of law, and in most cases they are advisory only. The American Institute of Planners in 1962 stated the following objectives of metropolitan planning.

Metropolitan planning is comprehensive planning applied to areas containing a large urban concentration where dominant economic, social and physical factors may over-arch local and even state boundaries. The function of metropolitan planning is to contribute to the formulation and implementation of optimal public policy for the metropolitan area.

Metropolitan planning functions at a new level in the governmental hierarchy, one which, however, includes fundamental roles for governments at all levels. On the one hand, metropolitan planning serves as a framework and a vehicle for the municipal, county and other local units of government and for relating these plans to the desirable development of the metropolitan area as a whole. On the other hand, planning at the metropolitan level seeks to integrate local and metropolitan plans with the plans of the state and of the nation.

The metropolitan planning agency should seek the development of a unified plan for land use, density and design, the provision and correlation of public facilities, services and utilities, and the preservation of open space and wise use of natural resources. It should strive to coordinate local planning, both public and private, with planning at the metropolitan level; similarly, the metropolitan plan should be coordinated with state and national plans—particularly those affecting transportation, public facilities and natural resource programs and functions that are metropolitan in scope. To this purpose, there should be a legal requirement that the agency review the content, conformity or compatibility of all proposals affecting the metropolitan area.

. . . The metropolitan planning agency should seek establishment and acceptance of goals, both long-range and immediate, for the metropolitan area's physical development (with due regard to economic and social factors). These goals should be the basis for the formulation of the comprehensive metropolitan area plan—and that plan, in turn, should serve as a framework within which may be coordinated the comprehensive plans of municipalities, counties and other units of government in the metropolitan area.

The metropolitan planning agency should seek to establish especially close relationships with other institutions concerned with metropolitan-wide development such as water supply and development authorities, mass transportation agencies, special districts, highway departments, park and recreation agencies and air pollution control bodies. Efforts should be made to participate in the decision-making processes of such agencies as a major means of accomplishing area-wide development goals.

The Metropolitan Area of the Future

New cities are being laid out all over the world. Some are capitals of developing countries, such as Chandigarh, the capital of the Indian part of the Punjab, on the plain of northwestern India. Another is Brasilia, the new capital of Brazil, located several hundred miles inland from Rio de Janeiro, the traditional capital city.

Many more cities are being planned without political significance in the industrial nations. Examples are seen in the "new towns" of Great Britain. After World War II the British government authorized the development of 15 new towns in the suburbs of the largest cities, eight near London and the others near Leicester, Newcastle, Glasgow, Edinburgh, and Cardiff. All were built around pre-existing small towns, and by 1963 their total population was about a half million, with none larger than 60,000. Though located near large cities, the new towns are intended to be partially autonomous through the development of local industry. The residential neighborhoods are each planned for a cross-section of people with various styles of life and incomes. All the dwellings are within walking or cycling distance of work, recreation, church, shopping centers, and schools. (Madge, 1962.)

Characteristic of the new cities and of the renewal of old metropolitan areas is the concept of a relatively self-sufficient sub-unit, varying in population from 50,000 to 400,000. This area should be small enough to be thought about and imagined by its citizens as a single unified community. For example, the reorganization of London creates 32 boroughs, varying in population from 146,000 to 341,000. Each borough council is responsible for health and sanitation, child services, welfare, libraries, and some public housing functions, while the Greater London Council has area-wide planning functions, traffic and transportation, ambulance and fire services. For education, the Greater London Council will be responsible in the 12 inner boroughs, and each of the 20 outlying boroughs will be responsible for its own school system.

In general, this concept calls for consolidation of suburban government and school districts into larger units, and for division of the large central cities into sub-units no larger than 400,000.

The specialists in city planning generally agree that in the big central cities there should be *decentralization* of residential areas, each area being self-contained with respect to the ordinary needs of social living—shopping facilities, schools, libraries, and churches. One type of arrangement is the *galaxy* in which the constituent cities are spaced more or less evenly over the territory, with a network of highways and transportation lines leading to the areas of specialized activity such as industrial sites, airports, freight docks, and financial centers. Another possible type is the many-pointed star or wagon wheel, with residential areas radiating out from a central business district, with industry located in certain sectors of the stars, and with transportation routes leading out from the center and crisscrossing with other transportation routes which form concentric circles around the area at various distances from the center.

In all cases there seems to be agreement on two matters: (1) that the SMSA should consist of residential areas which are relatively complete in themselves for the ordinary needs of family and cultural life; and (2) that many of these residential areas should contain cross-sections of the social structure, with people of the upper, middle, and working classes living in the same area. In particular, it is planned that many of the residential areas near the central business district should be populated by middle-class as well as working-class people.

Planning for Education in Metropolitan Areas

As soon as the citizens of a metropolitan area have become convinced that they need metropolitan planning and metropolitan action they are ready to create area-wide organizations with some definite responsibilities and functions in the metropolitan area. The first may well be a Metropolitan Area Planning Commission. This should be followed by a Metropolitan Education Authority and other organizations with governmental or quasi-governmental functions. The enabling legislation for such authorities is relatively easy to pass through a state legislature if the metropolitan area groups themselves want it, since it offers no problem or threat to the non-metropolitan areas. The federal government is likely to provide grants for metropolitan area agencies, and to make provision for metropolitan areas which cross state boundaries. The Department of Urban Development in Washington will promote such legislation.

Professor Norton Long of the Department of Political Science at Brandeis University believes that a metropolitan educational authority will be among the first area-wide agencies. He says (1962)

Despite the many advantages of autonomy, school systems in metropolitan areas will have to face the complications of a developing metropolitan community. As metropolitan areas become more than classifications in the census, they will produce common institutions and common loyalties. It is doubtful that the present gross inequities in educational opportunity will endure in the face of this trend. And, unless the federal government assumes a greater share of responsibility for the cost of education than it now does, it is likely that some form of metropolis-wide agency will be established to handle the problem of school finances.

Educators, whether they like it or not, are going to be involved in the politics of metropolitan change. Clarification of professional ideals as to what constitutes an adequate school system and the role of the schools in integration and assimilation will help the layman, politician, and civic leader alike to think constructively about how to guide the process of metropolitan change. We may hope that the professional commitment of educators will help them to find a more enlightened lead than that of the bureaucratic defender of the *status quo*. The challenge of metropolitan life is a challenge to embody the ideals of American education in significant practice. For every educator it means a chance to function on a plane of excellence at the top of his powers at a historic turning point in the culture.

The functions assumed by a Metropolitan Education Authority would probably be the following.

1. Planning of new suburban local school districts.
2. Administering a basic state aid fund so as to help equalize educational opportunity.
3. Maintaining a public university, with a teacher-training institution as part of it.
4. Administering a Metropolitan Area Educational Research and and Evaluation Council.
5. Administering a program of special education for the entire metropolitan area.
6. Administering an educational television station.
7. Recruiting and selecting and certifying teachers.
8. Administering a teachers' pension system.

The Functions of Local Education Authorities or School Boards

The creation and development of a metropolitan area authority would not weaken the initiative and responsibility of local school boards. On the contrary, it would aid them to work more effectively for the educational development of their own local schools. In the first place, there would gradually evolve a rational system of local school districts. This would involve the joining together of certain small suburban districts in units large enough to support a good elementary-secondary system. It would also involve the decentralization of administration in the central city. The central city might be divided into community areas of 50,000 to 400,000, each with its own local school board and district superintendent. These local school boards would have authority over the local schools, and might request the voters in their community areas to vote supplemental funds in addition to the support they receive from the state and metropolitan unit.

It would be the responsibility of the central city Board of Education to work with other branches of the city government to define the local communities in accordance with the goals of urban renewal and in cooperation with citizens' groups in the local communities. Some over-all strategy governing the socio-economic composition of the local school districts would have to be worked out, so that each local district had in it a variety of kinds of people.

A trend toward decentralization of school and other civic functions is manifest in a number of big cities. New York City is giving more responsibility to the local school boards which have had a nominal existence without much function for decades. Detroit is engaged in working out a district organization which facilitates a kind of "home rule" by communities of approximately 300,000 population. One advantage of such decentralization is manifest at this particular time— that is the possibility of encouraging community A within the big city to tackle its own problem in an intelligent and effective way, which might not be satisfactory to other communities (B and C) either because they have a different situation which gives them different problems, or because their local leadership is not yet ready for the actions that community A wishes to take. The stress and strains of the urban renewal programs of the coming two decades may be such that they are best met by decentralized action of smaller communities than by the big city itself. The big city may have to solve its problems part by part, section by section, with strategies adapted to the social goals and social attitudes of the various sections; but with financial support and a degree of coordination provided by the central city government and by the central city school board.

Results of a Survey of Metropolitan Cooperation

The writer made a modest survey of a sample of SMSAs in 1962, to find out how much cooperation there is among school districts within a metropolitan area and how much planning there is for such cooperation in the future. Omitted from the sample were the four largest cities —New York, Chicago, Philadelphia, and Los Angeles. Other large cities were included, ranging in size down to about 100,000. The procedure was to write identical letters to the superintendent of schools in the central city, the county, and one or more suburbs in each of 25 metropolitan areas. A total of 77 letters was sent out, and usable replies were received from 30 superintendents, representing 12 cities, 12 counties, and six suburbs. Eighteen states were represented in the replies, distributed over all sections of the country. It is probable that the people with the most interest in metropolitan cooperation or the most experience responded. Therefore the largely negative results of the survey may be taken to indicate that there is not much actual area-wide cooperation now going on.

In the great majority of situations there is no cooperation among school districts in a metropolitan area. However, a basis for such cooperation exists in several areas where there is a regional School Administrators' Association which meets monthly for exchange of information. "We have an association of superintendents that meets approximately six times each year. These meetings are informal with a rather loosely prepared agenda allowing individuals to introduce subjects which they feel might be of mutual concern. There is no real joint planning and no joint use of supervisory staff members."

One area goes further than this. "There is excellent cooperation between the larger city districts and the suburban school districts. Metropolitan area planning involves the cooperation of all the school districts. Such planning is the basis for future school site selection by individual districts."

There are two educational activities in which cooperation is prevalent. When educational television is available there is generally some cooperative direction. "A cooperative television board and planning council exists. School districts share in all aspects of educational television."

Another area of present cooperation is special education for handicapped pupils: "The Omaha metropolitan school district has special educational facilities for the physically handicapped and the emotionally disturbed, and other services for the handicapped child. The suburban schools use these facilities and pay tuition to the central city . . . and we do provide some service for handicapped children for the suburbs on a tuition basis."

COOPERATION AMONG SUBURBAN DISTRICTS. It is more common for several suburban school districts to join together for a specific service than for suburbs to secure this service from the central city.

. . . Being the larger of the suburban school systems we have, for example, provided area-wide service for mentally handicapped children to other suburban school systems. We have also provided several types of curriculum workshops for faculty members in which they and other suburban schools have been invited to participate.

A group of large elementary-school districts (5,000–15,000 average daily attendance) share the responsibility for operating special training classes; whereby one district operates the classes for the severely mentally retarded (trainable but not educable), another operates day classes for the hard of hearing, another for the blind, another for the orthopedically handicapped, etc. Interdistrict contracts have been worked out by which each of these classes serve the entire area. The effect of this is that the same service can be found in the suburban areas as is found in the cities.

COOPERATION INSTIGATED BY THE COUNTY SUPERINTENDENT. Frequently the county superintendent of schools takes the lead in organizing cooperation among suburban districts. ". . . Our County Superintendent of Schools Office serves as an intermediate unit and provides services which can be more economically provided on that level than on the local level such as processing warrants, furnishing legal services, TV, and audio-visual services and some supervisory and consultant help. A number of districts do join together on special projects and programs such as research and furnishing of special education; for example, we operate a program for partially-seeing students whereas an adjoining district is providing for cerebral palsied and still another for the mentally deficient."

However, this is by no means the rule. Another letter states, "Each school district is organized separately and financed separately. Except for I believe four of the smaller school districts, there is only casual relationship with the County School Superintendent's office. For the vast majority of our districts, our relationship is just as separate and independent as if we were in separate sections of the state."

ATTITUDES TOWARD COOPERATION. In some instances the central city is said to be in favor of area-wide cooperation, while the suburbs are opposed, and in other cases the reverse appears to be true.

There are no joint cooperative arrangements among the central city schools and the suburbs. There is no joint financing, no joint use of supervisory staff, no joint planning, nor is any effort made to secure a common collection of data. Approaches have been made to the suburbs to attempt joint planning, but to date the metropolitan area has been rebuffed in these efforts. As a result, the central school district has resorted to an extensive annexation program. (Superintendent of a central city.)

There is very little being done towards more area-wide planning, inasmuch as the city tends to ignore the surrounding areas, and seems to have an attitude that it is self-sufficient, and needs no assistance from the State Department of Public Instruction. We view this attitude as rather foolish, as many of our suburban schools are far more advanced in their thinking in curriculum planning than the central city. . . . (Superintendent of a suburban district.)

PROBLEMS SEEN BY SUPERINTENDENTS. Superintendents see the problem of unequal financial resources as a major one for metropolitan area schools. Some school districts are rich while others are poor. The rich districts do not wish to combine with the poor ones.

Another problem is that of communication between school districts, which have many needs to work together. "It seems to me that one of the biggest problems facing the school systems in our area is the necessity of frequent transfers because of the mobility of the population. This is true within the city itself and also between the city and the suburbs. We are all working to provide information to the receiving schools as rapidly as possible."

Related to this is the problem of communication between the school administration and the people of the area.

Our major problem as a suburban school district which faces rapid growth and expansion is that of communication. I have been superintendent of this district for approximately five years. During that time, 30,000 new individuals have moved into the community. Approximately 20,000 have left the community being replaced with another 20,000. In other words, of our 115,000 residents, nearly 50,000 were not here five years ago. It is difficult without a daily suburban paper, without a local television or radio station to bring pertinent information regarding the school district daily to the attention of our community. All major communication media represent the metropolitan area rather than any of its subdivisions.

The closest approach to a consensus among respondents is the suggestion that the county should serve as a coordinating unit.

. . . all suburban systems cooperate quite fully with each other inasmuch as they are all under the County Board of Education to a certain extent, and look to this office for leadership.

Some evidence of county-wide study of problems has become apparent in recent years. The Tulsa Metropolitan Area Planning Commission now has statutory planning responsibility for all the area within five miles of the city limits of Tulsa. In addition, this agency has planning contracts with most of the small county towns lying outside the five-mile limit. The effect of this arrangement is to provide metropolitan planning to a large portion of the county area and nearly all the population of the county. This is regarded as a very healthy development.

One of the features of our County Office of Education is that of data processing. At the present time one independent district is taking advantage of our data processing. Two or three additional independent districts are planning to buy this service next year. . . . Our office supplies supervisory service, coordination of curriculum, legal and technical advice, recommendation of teachers, recruitment of teachers, etc.

. . . Perhaps a county coordinating group which could be served by a full-time executive secretary would be useful. Through such an agency the common problems could be explored fully and highlighted with sufficient data so that constructive action could result.

I would like to see a federated system for the County that will bring the school more closely to the people and still finance the schools with a county-wide tax distributed through the County Auditor's office, and the amount of county tax money not be deducted from State distribution.

. . . the County School Office provides extensive arrangements for cooperation among the several local districts. For many years highly trained county office staff have served local districts in curriculum development areas, school management areas and in statistical operations. In the past five years, tri-county committees on school financing have arrived at consensus.

Conclusions

This analysis of metropolitan area development sees the next few years as crucial ones for the achievement of democratic social values. Essential for this achievement is the creation of effective cooperative machinery for central city and suburbs, and this requires a moral commitment by people living in suburbs and central city. This moral responsibility, if developed, will lead toward a civic and educational reorganization of the metropolitan area. There will be a transition period of perhaps two decades during which a rationally organized metropolitan community will emerge from the present chaos.

Exercises

1. On the basis of your knowledge of your own metropolitan area, how would you subdivide it into "core areas" of relatively self-sufficient

character? What would be the socio-economic and racial characteristics of these units?

2. If you know two metropolitan areas of approximately the same size, write a paper on their sense of community. Is one of the two much more conscious of itself as a metropolitan area than the other? What is the evidence?

3. Most metropolitan areas have a planning council or commission. Study the work of this council or commission in your area, and find out how the schools are related to their work.

Suggestions for Further Reading

1. For a substantial discussion of forms of metropolitan growth and co-operation see Chapters 13–16 of *The Metropolis* by Bollens and Schmandt.

2. State governments are moving to assist metropolitan areas to reorganize their local government systems. The principal agency promoting this activity is the Advisory Commission on Intergovernmental Relations, made up of state and city officials, with an office in Washington, D.C. The Commission has issued a *State Legislative Program* which contains suggested state legislation that would improve government in metro-politan areas.

3. For a critical study of the relations between local governments and suburban school systems, read *Government and the Suburban School* by Roscoe E. Martin.

4. A stimulating description of the spatial patterns of the future metro-politan areas is given by Kevin Lynch, city planner at the Massachusetts Institute of Technology.

6 ॐ Schools and the Negro Revolution

Introduction

The history of the United States is one of progress toward a democratic cultural pluralism. People from a variety of nations came to this country as poor people or as people who disagreed with the dominant political or religious power in their native countries. They were free in this country to practice their way of life. As a rule, they prospered. As a rule, they merged their way of life with the developing American way, contributing some of their own cultural traits and taking on others that were new to them. This was cultural pluralism.

One European immigrant group after another became assimilated in this way. Commencing before the middle of the nineteenth century, the Irish, the Germans, the Scandinavians, Italians, Poles, Hungarians, Czechs, Greeks, and Russians, came to this country, one group after another, and prospered. Generally they settled in communities or in sections of cities where they could maintain their own language and religions and family cultures for the first one or two generations. Eventually they moved out into the wider stream of American life, choosing freely their occupations and the places where they would live. With the passage of time these ethnic groups tended to lose many of their nationality traits.

The process of assimilation of European immigrant groups was at its height from about 1840 to 1930. After World War I, restrictive immigration policies cut down the flow of new immigrants from foreign lands, but the development of industry in the United States required an even greater supply of new and unskilled labor. The new supply came largely from the rural areas of the United States, where the farm population was excessive. Large farms were becoming mechanized, and the small subsistence farms of the southern hills were being abandoned or combined into large commercial farms which required less manpower.

After World War I, the need of American industry for unskilled and semi-skilled labor was met largely by rural Americans. They moved from their rural homes to nearby industrial centers and cities. From here they moved to the rapidly developing industrial centers in the Great Lakes area and the West Coast. They settled in the areas of the cities that had formerly been occupied by European immigrants who had moved up the social scale and out to more desirable residential areas. This great internal migration was interrupted by the Depression of 1930, and was stimulated again by the developing war industries of World War II, and by the economic boom of the post-war period.

The migration of southern rural whites and Negroes to the cities and industrial centers was accompanied by a migration of Puerto Rican workers to the cities of the eastern seaboard and of Mexican workers to the cities of the Southwest.

It was these groups that filled the places in the central cities left behind by middle-income people, old Americans and ethnic Americans, who moved out to the edges of the cities and to the suburbs, producing the socio-economic and racial stratification described in Chapter 3.

What is appropriately termed an "urban crisis" came upon the great cities shortly after World War II, as the central cities grew old and obsolete, physically, while the suburbs grew larger and more prosperous.

The new central city population appeared to be having trouble in taking full advantage of the economic and cultural opportunities of the United States. The educational level and the economic level of the central city resident did not rise as rapidly as did these indices for the country as a whole. And there was some evidence that the Negroes were having special difficulty, as a group.

For example, Table 6.1 shows how the Negroes and the Orientals (Chinese and Japanese) have fared in socio-economic status in recent decades. While the Orientals have gained greatly in these areas relative to the whites, the Negroes have not done so.

Urbanization of Negroes

During the past half-century the Negro has become urbanized. That is, while in 1910 73 percent of Negroes were living in rural or semi-rural conditions, 73 percent in 1960 were living in towns and cities of 2,500

Table 6.1   *Socio-economic Status of Nonwhite and White Male Population: 1940–1960*

	PERCENT OF EMPLOYED NON-FARM MALE POPULATION IN WHITE-COLLAR JOBS		
	1940	*1950*	*1960*
Japanese	45	36	56
White	39	39	42
Chinese	35	42	51
Negro	9	11	14
	PERCENT OF MALE POPULATION, AGED 25+, WITH FOUR YEARS OF HIGH SCHOOL AND OVER		
Japanese	34	57	69
White	24	34	42
Chinese	11	27	40
Negroes	7	12	18

Source: Calvin F. Schmid and Charles E. Noble (1965).

or more. Half of the Negroes in 1960 were living in cities of 50 thousand or more.

Urbanization of Negroes has taken place with about equal speed in all parts of the country except the South, where there is still a considerable number of rural Negroes. Table 6.2 shows that about 95 per-

Table 6.2   *Whites and Negroes in the Urban Population, 1960, by Region*

REGION	PERCENTAGE OF THE POPULATION LIVING IN URBAN PLACES	
	White	*Negro*
Northeast	79.1	95.7
North Central	66.8	95.7
West	77.6	92.6
South	58.6	58.4
United States	69.5	73.2

Source: *U.S. Census of Population*, 1960. *U.S. Summary*, Tables 155 and 233; PC(2)–1C, Nonwhite Population by Race, Table 1.

cent of Negroes outside of the South were living in urban places in 1960. Table 6.3 shows how the proportions of Negroes have changed in

Table 6.3 White and Nonwhite Population Trends in the Big Cities 1900–1960 (*Population in thousands*)

	1900		1920		1940		1950		1960	
	Pop.	Non-W. %	Pop.	Non-W. %	Pop.	Non-W. %	Pop.	Non-W. %	Pop.	Non-W. %
New York	3437	1.8	5620	2.7	7455	6.1	7892	9.5	7782	14.0
Chicago	1699	1.8	2702	4.1	3397	8.2	3621	13.6	3550	22.9
Philadelphia–Camden	1294	4.8	1824	7.4	1931	13.0	2072	18.2	2003	26.4
Los Angeles–Long Beach	105	2.1	632	2.5	1669	3.9	2221	7.9	2823	12.2
San Francisco–Oakland	410	0.7	723	1.1	937	1.4	1160	7.9	1107	14.3
Detroit	286	1.4	994	4.1	1623	9.2	1850	16.2	1670	28.9
Boston	561	2.1	748	2.2	771	3.1	801	5.0	697	9.1
Pittsburgh	452	3.8	588	6.4	672	9.3	677	12.2	604	16.7
Buffalo	352	0.5	507	0.9	576	3.1	580	6.3	533	13.3
Washington, D.C.	279	31.1	438	25.1	663	28.0	802	35.0	764	53.9
Baltimore	509	15.6	734	14.8	859	19.3	950	23.7	939	34.7
Kansas City, Mo.	164	10.7	324	9.5	399	10.4	457	12.2	476	17.5
Atlanta	90	39.8	201	31.3	302	34.6	331	36.6	487	38.3
Birmingham	38	43.1	179	39.3	268	40.7	326	39.9	341	39.6
Montgomery	30	56.8	43	45.6	78	44.2	107	39.9	134	35.1

Note: Nonwhite includes orientals, who are present in noticeable numbers in San Francisco and Los Angeles, but not elsewhere in this list.

populations of major cities. The northern cities had slow increases between 1900 and 1940, and very rapid increases between 1950 and 1960.
The southern cities generally saw some percentage decrease after 1900,
with fluctuation after 1940. The southern rural population lost both
Negroes and whites during this period.

The urbanization of Negroes and their migration to the industrial
centers of the country posed the problem of cultural pluralism in a
new and most difficult form. As long as most Negroes lived on a subsistence level in the rural South, they tended to be ignored by the rest
of the country. But as soon as they moved into the cities, they would
either become integrated socially into the cities or they would become a
highly visible social group, suffering from discrimination and lack of
cultural development and becoming a burden on the conscience of a
democratic society.

A minority of Negroes became integrated into the social and
economic life of the cities. They followed the familiar pattern of other
immigrant ethnic groups. They worked hard and saved their money.
They secured as good an education as possible for their children. These
children moved up the socio-economic ladder into professional and
business occupations. Thus a Negro middle class developed.

But the majority of newly-urbanized Negroes did not have this
experience. They and their children are still set aside from the mainstream of American life, even though they live in the midst of the great
cities. They are segregated residentially, with only a few exceptions.
They are in segregated schools, with relatively few exceptions. They are
marginal to the labor force, the last to be hired and first to be fired.

The working-class urban Negro presents a social problem. The
causes of this problem are certainly multiple. One cause is economic
discrimination, which prevents the Negro from getting into certain
skilled trades, and limits the number of places where he can find work.
Another cause is inferior education in the past and to some extent in
the present. Still another cause is weakness of the Negro working-class
family. The question of the Negro working-class family is a disputed
one, during the past decade, and deserves careful study.

The Negro Working-Class Family

The Negro in the United States has been studied by sociologists
throughout this century, and they have agreed that the Negro family

differs in general from the white American family as well as from the families of various European ethnic groups. To a considerable extent these differences are due to the fact that, under slavery, the Negro family barely existed. Negro slaves could not legally marry in the United States, Negro men and women who were living together and had children could be separated and sold separately, as could their children. Negro slaves had no legal protection. Other slave-holding societies recognized and protected the slave family, but not the American.

After the emancipation of the slaves, most of them continued to live in the rural South, where they developed a simple folk culture and a simple family structure to go with it. Women continued to have the dominant role in the Negro family, as they had before emancipation. The Negro male was greatly restricted in his access to jobs, to rights as a citizen, and to the initiatives which are expected of a man and the head of a family in American society.

After World War I there was a substantial migration of Negroes to the northern cities, which continued through the 1920's, and it soon became evident that the working-class Negro family would not stand up as a stable structure for child-rearing and marital relationships under these conditions. Professor Franklin Frazier, the Negro sociologist, wrote the following in his book, *The Negro Family*, published in 1939.

First, it appears that the family which evolved within the isolated world of the Negro folk will become increasingly disorganized. Modern means of communication will break down the isolation of the world of the black folk, and, as long as the bankrupt system of southern agriculture exists, Negro families will continue to seek a living in the towns and cities of the country. They will crowd the slum areas of southern cities or make their way to northern cities where their family life will become disrupted and their poverty will force them to depend upon charity.

The impact of hundreds of thousands of rural southern Negroes upon northern metropolitan communities presents a bewildering spectacle. Striking contrasts in levels among these newcomers to modern civilization seem to baffle any attempt to discover order and direction in their mode of life. (Frazier, 1939, p. 487, 298.)

Frazier's prophecy is supported by a mass of facts about Negroes in urban areas. Negroes live under great economic disadvantages, and the children of working-class Negroes grow up in families that are less stable and have less masculine influence than working-class white families.

For example, Negroes have consistently suffered more unemployment than whites, as can be seen in Table 6.4. The unemployment rate has been about twice as high for nonwhites as for whites. The Negro family is much more likely to be headed by a woman than is the white family, as is seen in Table A–6. Almost one-fourth of Negro families are headed by a woman. This condition is more pronounced in urban than in rural areas, as can be seen in Table A–7. Among other char-

Table 6.4   *Unemployment Rates, by Color, Excluding South, 1930–1960*

COLOR	PERCENT OF LABOR FORCE			
	1960	*1950*	*1940*	*1930**
White	4.8	4.9	14.8	7.4
Nonwhite	10.1	11.4	29.7	11.5

* Based on a different definition than the rates for the other years. Includes persons aged 10 years and over.
Source: Bureau of Labor Statistics.

acteristics, the working-class Negro male is less likely to be visible to the census-taker than the corresponding white male. This is seen in Table A–8, which reports the ratio of males to females, by color and age. In the 20 to 40 age group, the Negro males are undercounted by about 15 percent, according to census experts. In this age range a considerable number of Negro males are just "unattached" to any family or institution, and therefore are not reported to the census enumerator. This is an example of the fact that a substantial group of Negro men do not fill the usual male role in family life.

The facts which have been cited apply to the Negro working-class family and not to the Negro family in general. But the proportion of Negroes in the working class is so high that data for Negroes in general tend to reflect the Negro working class. There is evidence that the Negro population is becoming divided into a stable middle-class group of families that is growing stronger and more successful, a stable upper working-class group that is holding its own, and an increasingly unstable and disorganized lower working-class group. For example, middle-class Negroes have fewer children than middle-class whites. This is seen in Table A–9. Nonwhite women who married middle-class men at the age when middle-class women are most likely to marry (22 or over) had 20 percent *fewer* children than white women of similar social circumstances. On the other hand, nonwhite women who were married at ages 14 to 21 to men of the lower working class had 20 percent *more* children than white women of similar social class.

Negro School Children

It is not surprising that Negro children do less well in school than white children, on the average, when one considers the disadvantages under which the Negro working-class children live. In comparing Negro with white children on school performance, the groups differ in socioeconomic status as well as in race. Seldom has a comparison been made where the socio-economic status of the two racial groups was the same. In a few studies where the socio-economic status was the same for the two racial groups, the results tend to indicate that white children achieve slightly higher than Negro children, after they have been in segregated schools for a period of time. Most of the comparisons are similar to those in Tables A–10, A–11, and Table 3.3, where the socio-economic status is not kept constant. These tables, taken from recent surveys of the public schools of Philadelphia and Chicago, show clearly that Negro children are below white children in scholastic aptitude and school achievement.

Table 3.3 of Chapter 3 shows how the elementary-school children of Chicago ranked in IQ and school achievement at the 6th grade and in "readiness" for reading at the 1st grade. Chicago's 21 school districts are ranked by socio-economic status of the adults, and the average IQ, sixth grade school achievement and reading readiness is given for each district, as well as the percentage of Negro pupils. It will be seen that the lowest seven districts in socio-economic status all contain from 61 to 100 percent Negro school pupils, and tend to be the lowest in school aptitude and achievement. Less than half of the first graders scored average or above on the Metropolitan Reading Readiness test given at the beginning of the first grade. A score of "below average" on this test indicates that a child will have difficulty in first-grade work, and will not learn to read during the year unless he is given a good deal of individualized help. The Table also shows the test data for two districts which are in the top third in socio-economic status and have 37 and 77 percent Negro pupils. Although slightly below the other districts of high socio-economic status in school aptitude and achievement, those districts with a large proportion of middle-class Negro pupils are clearly superior to the districts which are populated mainly by working-class Negro families.

Table A–11 is taken from the Survey of Philadelphia Public Schools made in 1964–65, and shows how the white and Negro pupils who entered school in 1949 compared in IQ. The whites are obviously superior, and they are also superior in socio-economic status. Table A–10 shows what became of the first-grade class of 1949, as far as it was possible to keep track of them for the subsequent 12 years. The white children clearly performed better in school than the Negro children.

School Factor Versus Family Factor

It became quite clear during the 1960's that a massive effort must be mounted to assist Negro children to do better in school. The question was not *whether* to make such an effort, but *how* to do it. The answers to this question were being hammered out on the anvil of controversy through the 1960's, and they were by no means clearly stated by the middle of the decade, when President Johnson called for action in his Commencement Address at Howard University on June 4, 1965.

Our earth is the home of revolution. In every corner of every continent men charged with hope contend with ancient ways in the pursuit of justice. They reach for the newest of weapons to realize the oldest of dreams—that each may walk in freedom and pride, stretching his talents, enjoying the fruits of the earth. . . .

But nothing in any country touches us more profoundly, nothing is more freighted with meaning for our own destiny than the revolution of the Negro American.

In far too many ways American Negroes have been another nation, deprived of freedom, crippled by hatred, the doors of opportunity closed to hope.

In our time change has come to this nation too. The American Negro, acting with impressive restraint, has peacefully protested and marched, entered the courtroom and the seats of government, demanding a justice that has long been denied. . . .

We seek not just freedom but opportunity—not just legal equity but human ability—not just equality as a right and a theory but equality as a fact and as a result.

For the task is to give 20 million Negroes the same chance as every other American to learn and grow, to work and share in society, to develop their abilities—physical, mental and spiritual—and to pursue their individual happiness.

To this end equal opportunity is essential, but not enough. Men and women of all races are born with the same range of abilities. But ability is not just the product of birth. Ability is stretched or stunted by the family you live with, and the neighborhood you live in, by the school you go to, and the poverty or the richness of your surroundings.

The answer to the question centered around the relative importance of the family and the school in the mental development of the child.

There are four factors which determine the level of achievement of a child in school. One of them is the inborn ability or disability of the child. Another is the kind of family life or family training he experiences. A third is the quality of the schooling he gets. The fourth is his self-concept or aspiration level. He has it in his power, after several years of school experience, to determine how hard he shall work in school, and toward what goals.

There are inborn or biological differences of intelligence, but these are between individuals, not between large social or racial groups. No doubt there are inborn differences of potential intelligence among the children of a particular family; and every class of 30 children has 30 different levels of inborn intellectual potential.

The schools receive children with a wide variety of inborn intelligence and also with a variety of family experience which helps or hinders school learning. The schools provide a program of teaching and an environment in which pupils are learning. The pupil's self-concept grows out of his family and his school experience.

Thus the two factors about which society may be able to do something after a child is born are the school factor and the family factor. A very good family experience can make a child with only average inborn ability look good in school. A very good school can make a child with only average innate ability look good. A very good school may also compensate a child in whole or in part for a weak family factor, and a very strong family factor may compensate for a weak school factor.

Since about 1955, studies of the bearing of the family factor on mental development have led to a revision of earlier beliefs about the relative importance of the family and school factors, with greater emphasis being given to the family factor. Research on the cognitive development of children, summarized by Bloom (1964), points to the family as the major influence, and to the pre-school years as the crucial ones for mental development. The child's mind grows upon the language he hears, and the family provides his language environment. If the language is barren, the child's mind is stunted. If the language is rich, and if the family includes the child as an active person, his mind is stimulated to grow.

Every child's mind must feed on the language provided in the home. If families differ systematically in the nature of the language they use, their children's minds must differ systematically. There is now substantial evidence that families do differ in this respect, and that the better-educated parents, with higher socio-economic status, provide a more stimulating and more elaborate language environment. The sociologist Basil Bernstein (1960, 1964) has analyzed family language patterns in the several social classes, and has concluded that working class and rural families, as a general rule, but with exceptions, restrict the mental development of their children because they use a restricted language in the home. A child who has learned a *restricted* language at home is likely to have difficulty in school, where an *elaborate* language is used and taught by the teacher; and the difficulty of this child is likely to increase as he goes further in school, unless he learns the elaborate language that is expected in the school. On the other hand, the child who has had experience with an elaborate language in the home from his earliest years has a relatively easy time in school, because he must simply go on developing the kind of language and related thinking which he has already started.

These studies have led to a number of experiments with pre-school and kindergarten classes for children of lower-working-class families. Martin Deutsch in New York and Fred Strodtbeck and Robert Hess in Chicago have worked with socially disadvantaged children (mainly Negro children) at ages three to five, attempting to supplement the family factor. Deutsch (1965) summarized the situation with the following comments:

Strong evidence can be adduced to support the assumption that it is the active verbal engagement of people who surround him which is the operative influence in the child's language development. The structuring of these verbal engagements in terms of the family's conditions and style of life, and the further relationship between style of life and social class membership leads to the analysis of children's language skills and verbal behavior in terms of their families' socio-economic status. In the cognitive style of the lower-class family, Bernstein (1960) points out, language is used in a convergent or restrictive fashion rather than a divergent, elaborative fashion. An exclamation or an imperative or a partial sentence frequently replaces a complete sentence or an explanation: if a child asks for something, the response is too frequently "yes," "no," "go away," "later," or simply a nod. The feedback is not such that it gives the child the articulated verbal parameters that allow him to start and fully develop normative labeling and identification of the environment. Family interaction data which we have gathered in both lower-class socially deprived and middle-class groups indicate that, as compared with the middle-class homes, there is a paucity of organized family activities in a large number of lower-class homes. As a result, there is less conversation, for example, at meals, as meals are less likely to be regularly scheduled family affairs. In a recent paper we reported that children from fatherless homes have significantly lower IQ scores by the time they get to the fifth grade than do children who come from intact homes, and we hypothesized that this finding was a consequence not so much of the absence of the father, as it was of the diminution of organized family activity. . . .

In general, we have found that lower-class children, Negro and white, compared with middle-class children, are subject to what we've labeled a "cumulative deficit phenomenon," which takes place between the first and fifth grade years. Though there are significant socio-economic and race differences seen in measured variables at the first-grade level, it is important to note that they become more marked as the child progresses through school. While we can accept that some of this cumulative deficiency is associated with inadequate early preparation because of corresponding environmental deficiencies, the adequacy of the school environment also must be questioned: in a model system, one should expect linearity in cognitive growth.

Deutsch says that socially disadvantaged children need compensatory education at the pre-school level as well as a more effective school age education. He and others are proponents of *Operation Head Start*, which in 1965 commenced a massive pre-kindergarten program for disadvantaged children with financing under the Economic Opportunity Act. However, they feel that the schools must do a much better job than they now are doing with socially disadvantaged children.

The question is yet to be answered as to what balance of effort should be put on pre-school work and on work with school age children. If stress is laid on pre-school work, this emphasizes the family factor and seems to say that the lower-working-class family, and especially the Negro lower-working-class family is inadequate for rearing children in a complex urban society. If stress is laid on work with school age children, this emphasizes the school factor and seems to say that society has fallen down on the job of educating lower-working-class children and should improve its schools so as to do a better job.

When stress is laid upon the family factor, some people see an inference that Negroes are to blame for the shortcomings of the Negro working-class family, though they also recognize that society, through slavery and discrimination, is responsible for the Negro working-class family. Emotions are aroused. Some Negroes and some civil rights workers as well as some people who are emotionally identified with the working class tend to charge the schools with the responsibility for present defects in Negro children, while some educators and some social workers and some social scientists see the most of the difficulty in the Negro working-class family. The Negro Revolution of the 1960's is operating in this situation of emotional tension among people who want to improve the situation for the Negro working class but see the basic cause and therefore the basic solution differently. The Negro Revolution is working out its strategy in this situation.

The Negro Revolution

What has been called by many Negroes themselves the *Negro Revolution* is anything but a revolution as people have understood that term in the past, although it is something like the Industrial Revolution in the peaceable yet drastic quality of the social change it carries with it. The Negro Revolution was first taken seriously by many Americans on August 28, 1963, when two hundred thousand Negro and white Americans marched to the Lincoln Monument in Washington, to demonstrate the urgency of action for political and economic equality for the Negroes of North America.

Organizations to support the Negro Revolution have grown in strength and in number since World War II. Principal pre-war organizations were the National Association for the Advancement of Colored People (NAACP) and the Urban League. Later came CORE, the Congress of Racial Equality, and the Southern Christian Leadership Conference, organized by Martin Luther King. These are not aligned with any political party and do not have any political program beyond that of getting civic and economic and educational opportunity for Negroes.

It is characteristic of the leadership and the direction of the Negro Revolution that it seeks to make the fruits of democracy as available to Negroes as they are to other groups. The American Negro has no other culture than the American culture. The Negro Revolution seeks to join, not to destroy, the American way of life.

The Problem of the "Negro Role"

The basic obstacle to the Negro's full participation in the American way of life is his assignment to the Negro role. Just as other ethnic groups have had negative roles ascribed to them in the past, which they have learned to overcome, the role of the "lazy nigger" must be overcome. The Irish overcame the role of "shanty Irish"; the Swedish immigrants had to go through a period when they were called "dumb Swedes"; and the Poles more recently have overcome the connotations of the term "Polack."

While an ethnic group is in a subordinate position in a society, there generally exists a stereotyped role which members of the group are expected to fit. The role of a lazy, shiftless, and dull person has been assigned to the Negro and has turned into a reality for some Negroes by racial segregation and by economic and political and social discrimination.

The Negro Revolution is engaged in changing the Negro role to one which connotes success in urban industrial society. The new Negro role is one that encourages Negro children to work hard in school, to set high educational and vocational goals for themselves, and to become confident of their ability to do anything that those of another color can do.

There is one positive role for Negro boys and men, which attracts them—that of the athlete. Commencing with prize-fighting, and moving on to track athletics, baseball, basketball and football, Negro boys have embraced this role and worked hard and successfully to live up to it. Their latest conquest has come in the upper-middle-class sport of tennis, where Arthur Ashe, a Negro, made a place for himself on America's Davis Cup team.

The more widely universal role that is coming for Negro boys and girls requires integration in economic life, political life, and especially in the schools. Already large numbers of Negro children are successfully learning this role, as is proven by the growing numbers of Negro college graduates, of Negro businessmen and professional workers including school teachers.

The strategy of the Negro Revolution varies from one part of the country to another, and from one time to another, though it always emphasizes one or another of the following: better schooling, employment opportunity, better housing, better family life, access to community services.

Since the schools to which most Negro children go are public schools, and since better education is an obvious and basic need for Negroes, and since there has obviously been discrimination against Negro children in the matter of education in the past, the schools have been a continuing focus for the efforts of the Negro Revolution. Therefore the story of progress toward integration in the public schools and toward better education for Negro youth will be summarized.

Integration in City Schools: 1954–1966

The twelve years from 1954 to 1966 have seen the attention of educators forcibly focussed on the place of Negro pupils in the public schools. The problem has been concentrated generally in the cities. Only in the South have there been enough Negroes in rural communities and small cities to make segregation a problem in these schools. In 1960, 73 percent of all Negroes were living in places of 2,500 or more, and 50 percent were living in cities of 50 thousand or more.

The period since 1954 can be divided into three phases.

Phase 1. *Response to the Supreme Court Decision: 1954–1958*

When the United States Supreme Court declared the maintenance by law of a separate public school for Negroes to be illegal, there were at first only mild reactions. These reactions varied with the region of the United States.

A. THE DEEP SOUTH. In the Deep South there was at first very little response of any kind. This was followed by a period of several years spent in trying out various schemes to get around the Court's decision. Virginia, for example, made it legal for the state to pay tuition of pupils in private schools where public schools did not exist, and Prince Edward County proceeded to close its public schools. Negro children were left to fend for themselves, and had no public schooling for several years. Not much happened in the southern cities until the Little Rock incident exploded.

B. BORDER CITIES.   In the larger border cities—Baltimore, Washington, Cincinnati, Louisville, St. Louis and Kansas City—there was immediate compliance with the law in formally desegregating the schools. However, the residential distribution of Negroes was such that segregation continued, on a *de facto* basis, for the vast majority of Negro pupils. Since the 1954 decision coincided in time with the largest north and westward Negro migration that had ever happened, the incoming Negroes quickly filled up whatever vacant houses were available in areas partly but not entirely Negro, and thus made it economically easy for whites who were living in school districts inhabited largely by Negroes to sell or rent their homes and to move to suburbs or other sections of the city where there was no immediate prospect of integration.

However, there was a movement of small numbers of Negro pupils into previously all-white schools, partly in the suburbs where the number of Negro families was relatively small and they did not "threaten to overwhelm" the white families. Open attendance rules in a number of these cities facilitated the movement of small numbers of Negro pupils to previously all-white schools.

C. NORTHERN AND WESTERN CITIES.   The northern and western cities were experiencing a major in-migration of Negroes, without the decades of previous association between the races that had given people in the border cities a chance to work out forms of accommodation which allowed a certain amount of social integration without great tension. *De facto* school segregation grew up in these cities rapidly, supported by patterns of residential segregation that had been established earlier for the relatively small group of Negroes then living in these cities.

There was, however, the beginning of conscious attacks on the segregation problem in a few cities. New York City took the lead. The Board of Education on December 23, 1954, unanimously approved a statement which included the following paragraphs:

The Supreme Court of the United States reminds us that modern psychological knowledge indicates clearly that segregated, racially homogeneous schools damage the personality of minority group children. These schools decrease their motivation and thus impair their ability to learn. White children are also damaged. Public education in a racially homogeneous setting is socially unrealistic and blocks the attainment of the goals of democratic education, whether this segregation occurs by law or by fact.

In seeking to provide effective democratic education for all of the children of this city, the members of the Board of Education of the City of New York are faced with many real obstacles in the form of complex social and community problems. Among these problems is the existence of residential segregation which leads to schools predominantly of one race on the elementary and junior high school levels. In addition, prevailing racial attitudes and misinformation of some white and Negro parents reflect outworn patterns of segregation as well as limited educational and vocational horizons which make it difficult for them to accept school procedures contrary to their attitudes.

In spite of these and other difficulties, the Board of Education of the City of New York is determined to accept the challenge implicit in the language and spirit of the decision of the United States Supreme Court. We will seek a solution to these problems and take action with dispatch implementing the recommendations resulting from a systematic and objective study of the problem here presented.

We believe that an effective method of obtaining these ends is to set up a Commission of the Board of Education charged with the responsibility of determining the facts and recommending whatever further action is necessary to come closer to the ideal, viz., the racially integrated school. This Commission will obtain all the necessary facts from various community groups, parent and teacher organizations, the findings of systematic studies and other sources. It is imperative that members of this Commission approach their responsibility with the understanding that racially homogeneous public schools are educationally undesirable. It is now the clearly reiterated policy and program of the Board of Education of the City of New York to devise and put into operation a plan which will prevent the further development of such schools and would integrate the existing ones as quickly as practicable. The Commission must also address itself to the closely related and crucial problem of raising the educational and vocational aspirations of talented students from economically and socially deprived groups. (New York City Board of Education, 1954.)

The Commission on Integration appointed by the New York City Board of Education made an extensive report with recommendations that it expected would reduce segregation; and the Board of Education adopted many of these recommendations on June 28, 1956, and instructed the Superintendent of Schools to implement them.

In Detroit, the Board of Education in 1958 appointed a Citizens

Advisory Committee on School Needs, under the chairmanship of George Romney, who was later to become Governor of the State. This Committee made a variety of recommendations, including the suggestion that a new Committee on Equal Educational Opportunities be set up to study the problem of racial segregation and make recommendations. This was done.

In most northern and western cities, however, the official policy of the school administration was that the schools should be "color blind." This meant that the school system was to take no formal notice of the color of pupils or teachers, to keep no records of color, and under these conditions to strive to do the best job possible of educating all children in accordance with their needs and abilities.

In this situation the forces of economics and population produced more and more segregated Negro schools, due to prevailing attitudes of the white population, who abandoned most residential areas as soon as it became evident that a sizable fraction of the school children were Negro.

Thus the year 1958 saw a much larger Negro population living in segregated residential areas and attending *de facto* segregated schools than had been true in 1954 in the North and West.

Phase 2. Rise of Concern and Controversy: 1958–1963

When it became more and more evident to white and Negro people alike that residential and school segregation were increasing in the northern and western cities and were not decreasing in the South, there came about an increasing concern on the part of Negro groups as well as of white and mixed groups which were interested in the public schools and their relation to society's problems. This was accompanied and perhaps caused to some extent, by the worsening of the economic position of low-income Negroes, which followed the temporary economic depression of 1958. For instance, as President Johnson pointed out in his Commencement Address at Howard University on June 4, 1965, the unemployment rate of Negro teen-age boys in 1948 was actually less than that of white boys; but by 1964 the Negro male teen-aged unemployment rate was 23 percent against 13 percent for white males of the same age group. Between 1949 and 1959 the incomes of Negro men relative to white men declined in every section of the country. From 1952 to 1963 the median income of Negro families compared to whites dropped from 57 percent to 53 percent. In the years 1955 through 1957, 22 percent of experienced Negro workers were unemployed at some time during the year. In 1961 through 1963, this proportion was 29 percent. Thus the Negroes at the bottom of the social economic ladder were losing rather than gaining ground.

In both the South and the North, Negroes began to assert their impatience with the slowness and inadequacy of efforts at integration in the schools. At the same time the Negro protest against segregation in public facilities and in places of business began to make itself felt. Only a few years before, Mrs. Rosa Parks had quietly started a revolt in Montgomery, Alabama, against segregation on city buses. The rule in Montgomery had been that the first ten seats were always held for whites whether they were on the bus or not; the remainder of the seats could be occupied by Negroes, but if more white people got on the bus after the first ten seats were full, the Negroes must give up seat after seat, moving back toward the rear of the bus. Mrs. Parks was a middle-aged Negro woman. She describes what happened on that November day in 1955.

Well, in the first place, I had been working all day on the job. I was quite tired after spending a full day working. I handle and work on clothing that white people wear. The section of the bus where I was sitting was what we call the colored section, especially in this neighborhood because the bus was filled more than two-thirds with Negro passengers and a number of them were standing. And just as soon as enough white passengers got on the bus to take what we consider their seats and then a few over, that meant that we would have to move back for them even though there was no room to move back. It was an imposition as far as I was concerned. . . . Just having paid for a seat and riding for only a couple of blocks and then having to stand, was too much. These other persons had got on the bus after I did—it meant that I didn't have a right to do anything but get on the bus, give them my fare, and then be pushed wherever they wanted me. (Highlander Folk School, 1956.)

Mrs. Parks refused to leave her seat. The bus driver called a policeman who took Mrs. Parks to jail. This started the Montgomery Bus Protest, a movement on the part of Negroes to boycott the city bus line. The Protest won, and the buses of Montgomery were desegregated.

Martin Luther King rose to leadership during this period, and his methods of non-violent resistance to southern segregation practices spread throughout the South.

A. THE DEEP SOUTH.   Controversy flared in southern cities as the public schools slowly commenced to desegregate. In Little Rock, President Eisenhower called out the National Guard in 1957 to maintain order while a few Negro students enrolled and attended a white high school. In New Orleans, federal marshals walked with a handful of Negro children every day for months past a picket line of white adults who were keeping their own children out of the elementary school in protest against the introduction of these Negro pupils. In Atlanta, the process of token integration of high schools went more smoothly. By 1963 there was token integration in a few southern states.

B. BORDER CITIES.   In the border cities a number of school systems made ineffectual efforts to reduce the amount of *de facto* segregation. Washington saw the most determined action at this time, and some improvements were made in the public schools which probably produced better schooling, but did not stem the flight of white families to the suburbs. In St. Louis there was a good deal of unrest, which resulted in the appointment by the Board of Education of a Citizens Committee to look into problems of segregation and to propose remedies. The Baltimore Board of Education appointed a Citizens Committee with a similar mandate.

C. NORTHERN AND WESTERN CITIES.   The greatest concern over *de facto* segregation was expressed during this period in the northern and western industrial centers. In New York, Detroit, and Cleveland the school systems explicitly worked to reduce segregation by relatively mild measures. Open attendance rules were extended. A small amount of transportation was provided to encourage Negro pupils to attend integrated schools. New York City went farthest with free transportation.

Court cases were brought increasingly on behalf of Negro pupils, to force school boards to reduce segregation. In 1961, a federal judge held that the New Rochelle, N.Y., Board of Education was defining school attendance areas so as to promote segregated education. The New Rochelle Board was ordered to abandon this practice.

Several cases were brought by Negro plaintiffs to force school boards to take active steps to reduce segregation or "racial imbalance" as it was called.

The response of most school administrators and boards of education in northern cities was to defend the "neighborhood school" policy as the best form of school attendance rule, even if it brought about segregation. And during this period, several court cases were decided in favor of school boards which followed the neighborhood school policy—that is, which set up attendance districts for specific schools regardless of the race of the children, but only to direct children to schools as close to their homes as possible. The courts generally held that school segregation resulting from residential patterns was legal, as long as the board of education did not deliberately draw attendance lines so as to segregate pupils by race.

Phase 3. The Negro Revolution: 1963–1966

The controversy came to a head, both in the South and the North, during the period from 1963 to 1966. This was the time of the rise to major influence of Dr. Martin Luther King, and the time when he was awarded the Nobel Peace Prize. In August, 1963, came the March on Washington, in which many white churchmen joined with Negro and white leaders of organized labor and of civic oragnizations to give recognition to the Negro movement and to dignify it. During this period came two major laws to support the Negro Revolution. The Civil Rights Act of 1964, among other things, prohibited a number of types of discrimination that had been practiced against Negroes. Specifically, it required all state and local agencies as well as private persons or agencies who receive federal government funds to give written assurance that "no person shall be excluded from participation, denied any benefits, or subjected to discrimination on the basis of race, color, or national origin." The U.S. Commission on Civil Rights (1965) had found that in some circumstances,

Libraries receiving Federal aid either have not allowed Negroes to use the facilities or have subjected them to segregation or discrimination.

Elementary schools built and operated with Federal aid have discriminated in the admission and treatment of students.

Hospitals constructed with Federal funds either have refused to admit patients because of their race or have discriminated in their placement after admission; they also have refused to allow Negro physicians to practice there.

Vocational training programs established with Federal funds have not been available to all students.

Employment offices financed entirely by Federal funds have refused to refer all job applicants to available openings on a nondiscriminatory basis. Agricultural Extension Service offices operating with Federal funds have been established on a segregated basis and have provided unequal service to Negroes.

Dormitories have been built with Federal grants in colleges that have discriminatory admission policies.

Employers receiving business loans from the Federal Government, designed to increase employment opportunities, have discriminated in their hiring policies.

The requirement that school systems receiving any Federal payments must submit "assurances of compliance" with the law had the effect of stimulating desegregation in the schools.

The Voting Rights Act of 1965 further strengthened the movement for Negro civil rights in the southern states.

A. THE DEEP SOUTH. The conflict over Negro rights broke into violence in some areas of the South, especially Mississippi and Alabama. Negro civil rights groups were aided by student groups and others from the North who came to assist in the drive for registration of Negro voters, and to teach in the summer schools.

Still, the civil rights movement made substantial gains. Even in the embattled state of Alabama there was some resolution of the conflict. For instance, in the small city of Tuskegee, Negro voters found themselves in the majority. They proceeded to elect a bi-racial city council, and to get several Negroes appointed to the police force and to jobs in the City Hall. However, the majority of the council and of the city employees remained white. The formerly all-white high school was integrated, though the all-Negro high school was maintained, allowing for a viable racial balance in the integrated school.

During the summer of 1965 and the following school year a number of in-service teacher-training institutes were held in southern universities and southern counties, supported by the U.S. Office of Education under the Civil Rights Act. These were aimed at preparing teachers and school systems for the process of desegregation. The amount of explicit attention to desegregation varied, depending on the local sentiment, but there was always an emphasis on the ways of working with socially disadvantaged children, regardless of color, and there was always an unspoken assumption that desegregated schools were coming.

A number of county school systems maintained in-service training programs in 1965–66, in which for the first time, all the Negro and white teachers of the county took part in integrated study groups.

Most of the school systems of the South were started on the process of integration by 1966. The *New York Times* of September 4, 1965, reported, "Under the threat of a loss of Federal assistance, the South is admitting probably 7 per cent of its Negro children to classes with white children this fall—a percentage that compares reasonably well with the national average. And for the first time school desegregation has come to the Black Belt and to hundreds of rural southern towns, with virtually no violence or resistance."

Faculty desegregation also got under way in some southern cities. For example, Little Rock public schools in 1965 assigned four Negro teachers to teach in predominantly white schools, and four white teachers to teach in Negro schools. It was announced that there were 260 Negro pupils in schools which formerly were all white.

B. BORDER CITIES AND NORTHERN CITIES. The drive for integration in the border cities and northern and western industrial cities reached a peak in this period. Civil rights organizations joined together, and were aided by federated church groups acting through such agencies as a Council on Religion and Race. Civic organizations became involved, and the most prominent domestic issue during this period was the schools. The majority of big cities saw school boycotts aimed at inducing the Board of Education to take more active measures against segregation.

A number of state legislatures passed laws requiring the public schools to reduce segregation as much as possible. Several city school systems began to publish annual data on the numbers of Negro and white children in the various schools, and also the numbers of Negro and white teachers.

The pressures mounted that were pushing local school boards toward positive action on integration. Several state departments of education took action. The strongest of them was the action by the New York State Commissioner of Education, James E. Allen, who in June of 1963 requested all school districts in the state to report to him concerning racial imbalance, and if any school existed with 50 percent or more of Negro pupils to report on plans for eliminating racial imbalance. On the other side of the country, the California State Department of Education set up a Commission on Equal Opportunities in Education, which actively promoted integration of schools in that state.

A number of the major city school systems issued formal statements about integration. Those by the Superintendents of the New York City and Detroit Schools are reported here:

New York City

Responsibility of the Schools in Integration (A Reaffirmation of Policy Originally Adopted in 1954). Statement by Calvin E. Gross, Superintendent of Schools, October, 1963.

It has been said, correctly, that the schools alone cannot eliminate prejudice, discrimination and segregation. It is equally true that this task will not be accomplished with less than an all out effort of the schools.

Our schools must not be neutral in the struggle of society to better itself. We must not overlook the harmful effects of discriminaion on the education of all children. Moreover, within the limits of our control, we must not acquiesce in the undemocratic school patterns which are a concomitant of segregated housing. Furthermore, we must continue our policy of not tolerating racial or religious prejudice on the part of any member of our staffs. If education is to fulfill its responsibility, it must recognize that the school world has a significant influence on each child's attitudes and affects the future of democracy.

To further its integration policy, the school system has responsibilities to its pupils and personnel and to the communities.

1. For pupils—We must seek ways to give every child an optimum opportunity for fulfillment and success:

     a. Our school system must vigorously employ every means at its disposal to desegregate schools and classrooms and to bring about true integration as soon as possible.

     b. We must continue to develop educational programs which prepare all pupils to live constructively in a pluralistic society.

     c. We must provide whatever services and materials are essential to meet the special educational needs of those pupils whose progress has been impaired by an accumulation of the ills of discrimination. Simultaneously we must lift the goals of those whose environment has kept their aspirational levels at a low plane.

2. For school personnel—We must develop personnel practices which will maximize the success of the integration program:

     a. We must provide appropriate education and training for school personnel so that every staff member may gain an appreciation of the strengths inherent in the variety of backgrounds that compose our total population.

     b. In recognition of the value to the children of association with professionals of different backgrounds, our staffing procedures must provide for better ethnic heterogeneity in school faculties.

     c. It is essential that capable and experienced teachers and supervisors be distributed in accordance with educational needs.

3. With communities—We must work closely and cooperatively with communities:

a. We must support the efforts of those communities which are struggling to overcome past frustration and failure and to surmount present deprivation.
b. We consider it our obligation to help develop the kind of community attitudes which will help in the implementation of the integration policies of the City public schools.

Detroit

Special Report to the Board of Education by S. M. Brownell, Superintendent of Schools, May 5, 1964.

The Detroit Board of Education is on record with adopted policies and procedures intended to provide a racially integrated school system, to promote intergroup understanding, to eliminate racial discrimination from any school practices, and to attain equal educational opportunities for all children. These policies and procedures statements include, among others:

1. The Intercultural Policy of 1945.
2. Fair Employment Practices Acts in 1955 and 1956.
3. Endorsement of the goals of Equal Educational Opportunity in 1957.
4. Approval of recommendations made by the Citizens Advisory Committee in 1958.
5. Passage of the Non-discrimination By-laws in 1959.
6. A Policy on School Overcrowding and Relief Measures in 1961.
7. An Open Enrollment and Transfer Policy in 1961.
8. Approval of recommendations made by the Committee on Equal Educational Opportunities in 1962.
9. A "Statement Concerning Non-discrimination in Schools" in August 1962.
10. A statement on "The Treatment of Minorities" in Textbooks in December 1962.

Role of the Schools

These examples indicate the clear and consistent intent of the Board of Education that citizens and children will find Detroit schools free from racial bias and equal in the opportunities provided for each child, and that all school employes will conduct their activities so as to conform with and contribute to the attainment of these goals.

The opportunities to obtain public school education, employment, and public accommodations without discrimination because of race, religion, color, national origin or ancestry are civil rights in Michigan. Schools, as an arm of state government, have a responsibility to further the understanding and the fulfillment of these rights for all citizens. In these days there is fear and unrest in many parts of the United States as to whether these civil rights will be secured and maintained for all citizens. There is also recognition in Detroit that there is still much to accomplish to achieve fully the goal of the Board of Education for a school system with equal educational opportunity for all and with freedom from any racial bias.

Achieving and maintaining a school system which is racially integrated requires not only that there is no racial discrimination in the determination of the school which a child shall attend; it means also that the organization, administration, and operation of all facets of the school system are without discrimination as to race. The selection, promotion, and placement of personnel need to be without regard to race. Pupils, as they progress through school, should have opportunities to work together in bi-racial or multi-racial situations which contribute to improved understandings of the dignity and worth of persons who differ in race. Curriculum content has to be provided which adds interracial understanding and appreciation of the contributions of all racial and ethnic groups to the advance of local, national, and world culture. Curriculum activities have to be conducted in ways which motivate racial pride by all races and their inter-racial understanding, appreciation, and good will. Personal relationships of employes with pupils, parents, and with each other need at all times to be examples of freedom from bias or discrimination due to race, color, or creed.

Closely related to maintaining an integrated school system is the maintenance of equal educational opportunities for *all* children. The greatest number of pupils needing the greatest educational assistance at this time are those in the lower socio-economic levels.

The majority of school boards, while issuing statements saying that they favored integrated school experience for as many pupils as possible, added that there were limits beyond which the school system could not go in fostering integration, and that the major limiting factor was the "neighborhood school policy," which places a high priority upon the pupil's attending school near his home. Since the big cities have a great deal of residential segregation by race, the neighborhood school policy makes it very difficult to get integrated schools, especially at the elementary school level.

Thus the majority of school systems were adapting their school attendance patterns and policies to the residential patterns of the city, and the school boards and superintendents were arguing that the schools could not and should not attempt to alter the patterns of the city. They should educate the children who came to the schools in accordance with neighborhood school policy, and they should do as good a job as possible within this framework.

On the other hand, the civil rights organizations and a growing number of educators argued that the school system should take an active part in promoting the changes in the city known as "social urban renewal," which are aimed at creating or stabilizing areas of integrated residence in the city, attractive to middle income families. The school system would need to operate with flexible attendance rules and with a close relationship with local community organizations to accomplish this. Thus there was talk of an "urban-community school" philosophy, which was opposed to the conventional "four walls school" philosophy.

Two school procedures which came into use during this period to facilitate integrated school experience for children and to stabilize integrated residential areas were the Princeton Plan, and Transport Plans.

Princeton Plan

This is the pairing of schools so that they share the same attendance district. It takes its name from Princeton, New Jersey, where it has been operating successfully for some years. This plan has been adopted with success in a number of communities where the residential pattern is such that the districts served by two schools, one all or largely white and the other all or largely Negro, can be converted into a single larger district with all the children attending one school for the first three or four grades, and then attending the other school for the next three or four grades. When the socio-economic status of the Negro and white group is rather similar, the Princeton Plan seems to work fairly well.

Transporting children to relieve overcrowding was tried in a number of cities where there were overcrowded segregated Negro schools and underfilled schools in other parts of the city. Children were permitted in many cities to attend underfilled schools on an "open attendance" plan, but relatively few took advantage of this opportunity when they had to provide their own transportation. In a few cities the Board of Education provided buses to transport pupils in groups from overcrowded schools to underfilled schools. This might be done by transporting entire class groups, such as a sixth grade class, which then would simply occupy the classroom in the "receiving" school, but remain a part of the "sending" school for administrative purposes. Or, it might be done by transporting children from an entire block in an overcrowded area to a "receiving" school, where they would be distributed among the various grades a few in a room, and thus become a part of the receiving school.

Transporting children as a direct means of achieving integration was advocated by some civil rights groups. A drastic procedure would be to transport Negro and white pupils to schools according to a plan which would produce integrated schools throughout the city. This would involve transporting some white children to previously all-Negro schools and some Negro children to previously all-white schools. Such a plan has not been considered seriously by any Board of Education, but it has been held out as a possible danger by some groups who oppose integration and seek to influence the community against the milder forms of integration by claiming that the more drastic forms will follow.

Increasingly, during this period, the more positive forms of integrative procedure were being pushed forward and being tried out. This was partly due to pressure by groups working for integration, and partly due to a mounting series of court decisions that required active integrative practices.

The Legal Aspects of Integrated Schools

Since 1962 there have been a number of lawsuits in states outside of the South which raise the following questions:

Do school boards have an affirmative duty under the equal protection clause of the Fourteenth Amendment to eliminate or reduce racial imbalance not caused by deliberate action of local or state authorities?

Are the constitutional rights of Negro pupils infringed by *de facto* segregation which results from good faith adherence to a neighborhood school policy?

Are the constitutional rights of white pupils violated when school boards take racial factors into account in drawing or redrawing school boundary lines or in adopting other plans to reduce or eliminate racial imbalance in the schools? (National Education Association, 1965.)

As of 1966, the court decisions were balanced. In the Gary, Indiana, case, the federal district court held that there is nothing in the law requiring the school board to change a set of school attendance boundaries honestly and conscientiously constructed without a purpose to segregate the races, so as to balance the racial composition in the various school buildings. This decision has been followed by the federal courts in several cases, and the U.S. Supreme Court has refused to review these cases.

Another federal district court decided differently when Negro children claimed that the strict neighborhood school policy violated their constitutional rights. In the Manhasset, New York, case, all Negro elementary school children, together with a few white children, were enrolled in one of the district's three elementary schools. The court held that the maintenance of neighborhood school attendance lines by which all Negro elementary school children were separated from 99.2 percent of white children, coupled with an inflexible no-transfer policy, was equivalent to state-imposed segregation in violation of the Fourteenth Amendment. The school board was ordered to discontinue its no-transfer policy with respect to the children in this school.

The California Supreme Court made a similar ruling in the Pasadena case in 1963. It held that where there is racial imbalance in the school owing to residential segregation, the right of children to equal opportunity for education and the harmful consequences of segregation require school boards to take steps, in so far as is reasonably feasible, to alleviate the racial imbalance in the schools regardless of the cause.

In New York and New Jersey, the courts have upheld the actions of school boards in fixing boundary lines of schools so as to produce an ethnic balance among students. The New York Court of Appeals distinguished between an obligation on the part of the school board to reduce *de facto* segregation and the *right* (not the duty) of the school board to correct racial imbalance. The court held that an otherwise reasonable and lawful zoning plan does not become unlawful because racial factors were taken into consideration. The U.S. Supreme Court declined to review the case, and other New York and New Jersey courts have held that the school board is not prohibited from taking race into account in changing school boundary lines, school pairing plans and open enrollment plans designed to correct racial imbalance and to reduce or eliminate *de facto* segregation in the public schools.

In 1965 the State of Massachusetts went further than any other had gone up to that time by passing a law "providing for the elimination of racial imbalance in the public schools." The law states,

It is hereby declared to be the policy of the commonwealth to encourage all school committees to adopt as educational objectives the promotion of racial balance and the correction of existing racial imbalance in the public schools. The prevention or elimination of racial imbalance shall be an objective in all decisions involving the drawing or altering of school attendance lines and the selection of new school sites. . . .

Whenever the state board of education finds that racial imbalance exists in a public school it shall notify in writing the school committee or regional school district committee having jurisdicton over such school that such finding has been made. The school committee shall thereupon prepare a plan to eliminate such racial imbalance and file a copy of such plan with the board. The term "racial imbalance" refers to a ratio between non-white and other students in public schools which is sharply out of balance with the racial composition of the society in which non-white children study, serve, and work. For the purpose of this section, racial imbalance shall be deemed to exist when the per cent of non-white students in any public school is in excess of fifty per cent of the total number of students in such school.

Said plan shall detail the changes in existing school attendance districts, the location of proposed school sites, the proposed additions to existing school buildings, and other methods for the elimination of racial imbalance. Said plan shall also include projections of the expected racial composition of all public schools. Any plan to detail changes in existing school attendance districts, the locations of proposed new school sites and proposed additions to existing school sites and proposed additions to existing school buildings with the intention of reducing or eliminating racial imbalance, must take into consideration on an equal basis with the above-mentioned intention, the safety of the children involved in travelling from home to school and school to home. Said plan may provide for voluntary cooperation by other cities and towns in rendering assistance and in making available facilities to effectuate said plan.

No school committee or regional school district committee shall be required as part of its plan to transport any pupil to any school outside of its jurisdiction or to any school outside the school district established for his neighborhood, if the parent or guardian of such pupil files written objection thereto with such school committee. . . .

The school building assistance commission shall, notwithstanding any contrary provision of chapter six hundred and forty-five of the acts of nineteen hundred and forty-eight, as amended, increase the amount of grants for schoolhouse construction to sixty-five per cent of the approved cost, whenever the board of education is satisfied that the construction or enlargement of a schoolhouse is for the purpose of reducing or eliminating racial imbalance in the school system and so notifies the school building assistance commission. (Commonwealth of Massachusetts, 1965.)

Phase 4. Integration: 1966–1970

These paragraphs are being written early in 1966, and the reader may want to compare the author's prophecy with reality as it unfolds.

By 1966 there was substantial improvement in the situation of Negroes as compared with 1954. The Civil Rights Act and the Voting Rights Act had given Negroes much more political power in the southern states and more economic opportunity throughout the country. There was a general movement toward providing greater job opportunities for Negroes. Negro clerks could be seen in department stores, young Negro men and women worked at the counters of airlines, and Negro air stewardesses appeared on airplanes. Negroes were working as bank tellers. The proportion of Negro teachers had increased substantially in northern school systems. On television the scenes showing people in everyday groupings such as business and club meetings, school and college classes, and cocktail parties had unobtrusive Negro members. To the casual observer the American society showed a greater degree of racial integration than it had shown ten years earlier.

There was actually more economic opportunity available for Negroes in minor white-collar and technical jobs than there were Negroes with adequate training for those jobs.

Yet it was clearly evident that there was more unemployment among Negro working-class males than ever before, that there was a higher rate of illegitimate births to Negro women, that the working-class Negro family was not growing stronger. It was also evident that a higher rather than a lower proportion of Negro children were attending effectively segregated schools in the northern cities, and that the rates of educational retardation and of school dropouts among Negro youth were as great as they had been a decade earlier.

The public schools were more than ever seen as the crucial institutions for helping Negroes improve themselves, and critics continued to blame the schools for much of the difficulty experienced by Negroes. Two massive programs had been set up by the federal government aimed to assist Negro children and their families. The Elementary and Secondary Education Act promised to give school systems substantially more money to work with children of poor families, which meant Negro children predominantly in most big cities. The Economic Opportunity Act provided funds for pre-school classes, and for work-training and education of youth who were not doing well in school.

At this time the controversy over the Family versus the School factors gave rise to two opposed schools of thought among people who were working for the betterment of Negroes.

Those who emphasized the Family factor wished to expand pre-school classes for socially disadvantaged children, educational work with their mothers and fathers, spread of birth control knowledge and devices among working-class people, and a variety of forms of assistance and support through social workers to the working-class family. For them the school system could go on with its present program for school-age children, with whatever improvements might be made, including smaller classes and remedial instruction for disadvantaged children.

Those who emphasized the School factor were after new forms of education, not just more of the old forms. They recognized that the schools were not succeeding adequately with lower working-class children, and they called for new and radical changes in the schools. It was up to the schools to find ways of teaching these children successfully. For example, the *Washington Post* of December 19, 1965 carried an account of a statement written by Judge David L. Bazelon, Chairman of the Advisory Committee of the Model School Division, which had been proposed by Superintendent Carl F. Hansen in June, 1964, and had been adopted for the Cardozo High School and its 18 feeder junior high schools and elementary schools. Money had been provided to support this model program for, as Superintendent Hansen described it, "an across-the-board experiment—curriculum development, utilization of teachers, the management of the system itself—with provision for rapid feedback of results and rapid exploitation of new opportunities." After a year and three months of the experiment, Judge Bazelon charged that "Entering a school in the Model School District today, one finds few activities, atmosphere, teaching methods, or equipment different from what one found before the model school notion was expressed. . . . The concept of a sub-system advised by a citizens' advisory committee appears to have been abandoned before it began." The most that was accomplished, it was charged, was an extension of "more of the same." More after-school reading periods, more remedial teaching, and smaller classes. Instead of changing the school system so that the children would learn better, it was claimed that the schools were trying to change the children to make them fit the school program.

Judge Bazelon was advised by, among others, Dr. Kenneth Clark, the Negro psychologist who has been a leader in urging reform of the schools. Dr. Clark does not claim to know how to do the job, but he insists that it can and must be done.

Another proponent of school reform is Frank Riessman, a psychologist who is especially critical of what he terms the "middle-class emphasis" of the schools. He believes that children from working-class families have certain positive qualities and learning abilities which are overlooked by educators oriented to middle-class ways of living and learning.

He claims that these children, in contrast to middle-class children, have a mental style that is:

Physical and visual rather than aural.
Content-centered rather than form-centered.
Externally oriented rather than introspective.
Problem-centered rather than abstract-centered.
Inductive rather than deductive.
Spatial rather than temporal.
Slow, careful, patient, persevering (in areas of importance), rather than quick, clever, facile, flexible.

Their education should take account of and build upon these characteristics. He points out that the main problem of this type of child in school is his language difficulty. He says: "Thus, it would seem essential that the method of teaching formal language to deprived children take advantage of their communication style by employing teaching techniques that stress the visual, the physical, the active, as much as possible. We must be careful not to try to make these children over into replicas of middle-class children. The educational system should be pluralistic enough, broad enough, to find a place for a variety of mental styles." (Riessman, 1962, p. 73, 80.)

Riessman has not pointed to empirical evidence that working-class children are better than middle-class children in these respects. Probably most students of human development would agree that children of stable working-class families are slightly below children of middle-class families on a number of mental abilities, and have less disadvantage in these abilities than in certain other mental skills which require more vocabulary knowledge and more abstract reasoning ability. But the children of lower-working-class families may be far below the children of upper-working-class families in all of these positive traits.

The educators who use conventional methods and "more of the same" when working with disadvantaged children remain unconvinced that they should make radical changes, and ask just what changes are suggested and what evidence there is that these would work better than existing methods.

Equality of Opportunity or Equality of Achievement?

Those who insist that the schools can and must produce better achievement on the part of lower-working-class children, and who at the same time feel that the school factor is more important than the Family factor in the strategy for betterment have been aroused and angered over a comment that was made in the "Moynihan Report" of the U.S. Department of Labor. The report states that the fundamental problem posed by the Negro Revolution is that it is a movement for *equality* as well as for liberty.

The ideal of equality does not ordain that all persons end up, as well as start out equal. In traditional terms, as put by Faulkner, "there is no such thing as equality *per se*, but only equality *to*: equal right and opportunity to make the best one can of one's life within one's capability, without fear of injustice or oppression or threat of violence." But the evolution of American politics, with the distinct persistence of ethnic and religious groups, has added a profoundly significant new dimension to that egalitarian ideal. It is increasingly demanded that the distribution of success and failure within one group be roughly comparable to that within other groups. It is not enough that all individuals start out on even terms, if the members of one group almost invariably end up well to the fore, and those of another far to the rear. This is what ethnic politics are all about in America, and in the main the Negro American demands are being put forth in this now traditional and established framework.

Here a point of semantics must be grasped. The demand for Equality of Opportunity has been generally perceived by white Americans as a demand for liberty, a demand not to be excluded from the competitions of life—at the polling place, in the scholarship examinations, at the personnel office, on the housing market. Liberty does, of course, demand that everyone be free to try his luck, or test his skill in such matters. But these opportunities do not necessarily produce equality: on the contrary, to the extent that winners imply losers, equality of opportunity almost insures inequality of results.

The point of semantics is that equality of opportunity now has a different meaning for Negroes than it has for whites. It is not (or a least no longer) a demand for liberty alone, but also for equality—in terms of group results. In Bayard Rustin's terms, "It is now concerned not merely with removing the barriers to full *opportunity* but with achieving the fact of *equality*." By equality Rustin means a distribution of achievements among Negroes roughly comparable to that among whites.

As Nathan Glazer has put it, "The demand for economic equality is now not the demand for equal opportunities for the equally qualified: it is now the demand for equality of economic results. . . . The demand for equality in education . . . has also become a demand for equality of results, of outcomes."

The principal challenge of the next phase of the Negro revolution is to make certain that equality of results will now follow. If we do not, there will be no social peace in the United States for generations. (U.S. Department of Labor, 1965, p. 3.)

Some of the proponents of basic school reform have in effect argued that the schools must keep on experimenting with better methods for lower working-class youth until these youth are equal in educational achievement to the youth of other social groups. This can and must be done, they say.

The proponents of the Family factor approach argue that equality of educational results can only be achieved by improving the lower working-class family as an institution for rearing children. They argue that a child whose cognitive development has been neglected in a typical lower working-class family until he is of school age can never catch up. And that one who has been only partially handicapped by an inadequate family environment during pre-school years may be further handicapped by an inadequate family environment during his school and adolescent years.

The basic disagreement will be worked out and perhaps partially reduced during the next few years, as educators experiment with a variety of ways of helping the socially disadvantaged child, and as social scientists learn more through research about the mental development of children. There are ample funds for the experimentation and the research.

The Setting in 1966–1970

Although there is disturbing evidence about the Negro working-class family, and although the extent of segregation of Negro children in the public schools has increased in the northern cities and decreased only slightly in the southern states during the past ten years, the situation in the second decade of the nineteen-sixties is definitely more promising for urban schools than it has been during the preceding fifteen years. First of all, there is a much better understanding of the nature of the problem of educating socially disadvantaged children than there has been, and therefore society will do a better job with families and also with children in school. Beyond this, there are two trends among Negroes that are working to increase the status of Negroes and improve the educational situation for Negro children.

One trend is the movement of Negro middle-class families out of the inner city ghetto to the outer sections of the central city and to the suburbs. For example, the school-age population of Negro suburban residents is increasing more rapidly than the school-age population of Negro central city residents in most metropolitan areas. Thus, the non-white population for ages 5–19 in the Chicago suburban area increased between 1950 and 1960 from 9,700 to 22,600, or 133 percent, while that of the city of Chicago increased from 103,000 to 226,000, or 120 percent. This was a small difference, but according to estimates of the Population Research and Training Center of the University of Chicago, the increase between 1960 and 1965 was 55 percent in the suburbs and 34 percent in the central city. The suburbs are slowly but steadily opening up to Negro middle-class families, and the majority of Negro children in the suburbs are in integrated schools. Those Negro middle-class families who live in the central city are also tending to live on the outer edges of the segregated Negro areas and therefore likely to have their children in integrated schools.

The other trend is the decreasing rate of growth of the Negro school population in the northern cities. This is especially important in connection with plans for stabilizing integrated schools in the northern cities. Most such plans failed during the 1950's and the early 1960's due to the rapid increase of the Negro population in the northern industrial centers. Only in towns with a relatively small and stationary Negro population was it possible to create stable integrated schools. In the cities with rapidly growing Negro populations, such as those listed in Table 6.3, the Negro school population grew so rapidly that, when combined with the usual pattern of residential segregation, a school on the fringe of a Negro area one year would probably be surrounded by a Negro residential community two years later.

This rapid growth of the Negro school population was so striking and so widely publicized that it often gave rise to a kind of panic among white residents who thought they might be located in the path of Negro advance, and who moved farther out from the center of the city, or to a suburb, thus assisting the process of segregation and defeating efforts at stabilizing integrated communities within the city.

It now seems clear that the Negro school age population will stop its rapid growth in the northern centers by about 1970, for two reasons. One reason is that the migration of Negroes from the rural South to the urban industrial centers has slowed down since 1960 and probably will slow down even more. The migration of the immediate post-war years and of the early 1950's resulted primarily from recruiting efforts by employers who needed unskilled and semiskilled workers. These employers no longer need increasing numbers of such workers. Their factories and business establishments are becoming automated, and they are producing more goods and services with fewer employees. They can expand their business without expanding the number of their workers. The growth of the Negro population in northern and western cities will be mainly a natural increase due to excess of births over deaths rather than an increase due to in-migration.

The other reason for slowing down of the growth rate of Negro school children is that the birth rate of Negro children has decreased substantially in northern centers since 1960. This is partly due to the growing use of contraceptives by Negro women of the working class, but mainly due to the fact that the numbers of child-bearing Negro women have actually decreased during the 1960's. This can be seen by studying Table 6.5, which reports the age distribution of nonwhite females for 1950 and 1960 in two cities, Chicago and Kansas City, which probably are typical of cities of the North Central and of the western regions. Both cities show for 1950 a bulge in the numbers of females aged 20–44, compared with those who were older or younger. Chicago had 47.5 percent of nonwhite females in the 20–44 age range— the principal child-bearing age—and Kansas City had 44.2 percent. These high percentages reflect the fact that large numbers of young and vigorous Negro women (and men) had migrated to these cities in search of employment during the war years and immediately afterward, they had most of their children between 1950 and 1960, as is suggested

Table 6.5   *Age Characteristics of Nonwhite Females, Chicago and Kansas City: 1960 and 1950*

	CHICAGO		KANSAS CITY	
	Percent of Total		*Percent of Total*	
	1950	*1960*	*1950*	*1960*
0–4	10.3	15.0	8.5	14.7
5–9	7.4	11.8	6.6	11.0
10–14	6.4	8.4	6.0	8.0
15–19	6.2	6.2	6.0	6.1
20–24	9.7	7.6	8.6	6.5
25–29	11.3	8.0	9.7	6.8
30–34	9.7	8.4	9.0	7.7
35–39	9.2	7.6	9.1	7.3
40–44	7.6	6.2	7.8	6.2
45–49	6.6	5.2	7.5	5.4
50–54	5.0	4.3	6.2	4.7
55–59	3.5	3.8	4.6	4.4
60–64	2.5	2.7	3.5	3.5
65–69	2.2	2.1	3.5	3.2
70–74	1.2	1.4	1.8	2.2
75+	1.2	1.5	1.7	2.4
20–44	47.5	37.8	44.2	34.5
Median Age	29.4	25.6	32.0	27.7
Total No.	265,000	436,000	29,166	43,935

Source: U.S. Census Vol. 1, 1950 and 1960.

by the high percentages of children aged 0–9 in 1960, as compared with 1950. By 1960, the percentages of females aged 20–44 had dropped to 37.8 and 34.5 percent respectively. This means that the most rapid growth of school-age children took place between 1955 and 1965 and is continuing to 1970, when it will taper off.

As the numbers of school-age Negro children cease growing in the central cities, and as the Negro population gradually spreads into the suburbs, it will be much easier to maintain stable integrated schools than it was between 1955 and 1965.

What Lies Ahead for Integration?

When these considerations are combined with the expectations we may reasonably entertain concerning social urban renewal, it appears not unreasonable to be optimistic about the programs of school integration during the coming decade.

The Negro middle-class families will grow in number and will generally be able to place their children in integrated schools and to live in integrated residential areas, if they wish to do so.

The Negro working class, both in the North and the South, will gain integrated schools much more slowly. This is primarily due to the existence of large areas of segregated residential quarters, large enough to have a hundred thousand or more people in them. Integrated schools may be established and maintained around the edges of these segregated areas. High schools throughout the city may be opened to Negro students who wish to attend them. But these efforts amount to nibbling away at the problem. Such a nibbling process is desirable, if nothing more thorough can be accomplished. Possibly as many as fifteen to twenty percent of Negro working class pupils can be placed in integrated schools in this manner.

In cities of 100 thousand or less with a minority of Negro residents, integration will proceed fully in the North and West, and more slowly in the South.

Thus the principal obstacles to integrated schools will be located in segregated housing, as well as in the attitudes and entrenched practices in the southern states.

Exercises

1. What are the principal intergroup conflicts (economic, ethnic, religious, or racial) in your community? In your school or college? Interview a member of each of the groups in question and obtain their views regarding the ways in which conflict could be alleviated.

2. Work out a teaching unit for elementary or high school on *The Negro in American Life*. What books and pamphlets would you assign students? What topics would you suggest for individual projects? How would you treat contemporary Negro protest movements?

3. Investigate a school which has had a successful program of racial integration. Talk with some of the teachers and parents as well as the principal. Analyze the reasons for success.

4. Investigate a school in which efforts at racial integration have been unsuccessful. What are the reasons for failure?

Suggestions for Further Reading

1. For reports on recent studies and for various points of view on the problem of the disadvantaged Negro, read: Silberman, *Crisis in Black and White;* Clark, *Dark Ghetto;* Pettigrew, *Profile of the Negro-American.*

2. For general information and for various points of view on socially disadvantaged children and the causes of their disadvantage, read: Frank Riessman, *The Culturally Deprived Child;* Benjamin S. Bloom, *Stability and Change in Human Characteristics;* Bloom, Davis, and Hess, *Compensatory Education for Cultural Deprivation.*

3. For an analysis of the crisis in the public schools, as seen and analyzed by school survey teams working in two large cities, read William R. Odell, *Educational Survey Report on the Philadelphia Schools;* and Robert J. Havighurst, *The Public Schools of Chicago: A Survey Report.*

4. For more information on the social and economic conditions of working-class Negroes, read the famous "Moynihan Report" around which a major controversy developed in 1965 and 1966. See *The Negro Family: The Case for National Action,* published by the U.S. Department of Labor.

5. For a stimulating set of essays on the position of the Negro, read the two-volume report on *The Negro-American,* edited by Stephen R. Graubard. *Daedalus,* Fall, 1965 and Winter, 1966.

7 ❧ Teachers in Metropolitan Schools

Introduction

Although 65 percent of school teachers work in metropolitan areas, they do not distribute themselves randomly over the various types of schools in the area. Parallel with the great diversity of schools is a diversity of teachers in terms of experience, age, and other qualities.

For example, Table 7.1 shows the differences of experience among

Table 7.1   *Characteristics of Teachers in Various Types of City Schools: Chicago, 1964*

| | TYPE OF SCHOOL | | | | |
	High Status	Conven- tional	Common Man	Inner City	Total
Percent of total enrollment	8	18	21	53	100
Median years' experience of regularly assigned teachers	19	15	9	4	
Percent regularly assigned teachers	94	91	86	64	
Percent of full-time sub- stitute teachers*	6	9	14	36	
Percent distribution of regularly assigned teachers	11	23	22	44	100
Percent distribution of substitute teachers*	1	6	11	82	100

* Full-time substitute teachers are those who have a teacher's license, who are teaching full time and assigned to a particular school, but have not passed the examination for a certificate in Chicago schools.

Source: Robert J. Havighurst, *The Public Schools of Chicago*, p. 170.

teachers in the various types of elementary schools in Chicago. The types of school have been described in Chapter 4. The striking thing about this Table is the difference in experience between teachers of high-status schools and teachers of inner-city schools. Teachers of high-status schools have a median of 19 years experience, while those of inner-city schools have only four years of experience.

Similar information is given in Table 7.2 concerning high-school

Table 7.2   *Characteristics of High-School Teachers Related to Socio-economic Area of School: Chicago, 1964 (Percentage Distribution for Each Type of Area)*

	AREA SERVED BY HIGH SCHOOL				
	Upper- or middle class	*Mixed middle- and working-class*	*Stable working-class*	*Lower-class or slum*	*Total*
SEX					
Male	47	44	54	52	47
Female	53	56	46	48	53
AGE					
20–25	14	16	17	23	18
26–30	18	15	22	21	18
31–40	23	22	23	28	24
41–50	12	17	14	12	15
51–65	31	26	21	15	23
66+	2	3	3	2	3
EXPERIENCE					
1 year	5	7	11	11	9
2	5	8	11	14	10
3–5	19	20	23	29	22
6–15	35	31	28	31	31
16+	36	34	27	16	29
NUMBER	242	1,187	391	504	2,328
Percent of total	10	51	17	22	100

Note: The data are taken from a 60 percent sample of questionnaires returned by 65 percent of Chicago high school teachers.

Source: Robert J. Havighurst, *The Public Schools of Chicago*, p. 343.

teachers in Chicago. In this Table, teachers were asked to describe the socio-economic character of their school. Of those who said they taught in an "upper- or middle-class school," 36 percent had 16 years or more of experience, while 16 percent of those who said they taught in a "lower-class or slum school" had 16 or more years of experience. Age differences showed the same effect.

New York City shows a similar difference between the inner-city schools and other schools, as is indicated in Table 7.3. The New York City Board of Education gives examinations for permanent licenses, and those teachers who do not have such licenses are generally the younger ones with least experience. Table 7.3 compares "special service" schools

Table 7.3   *Teachers on Permanent Licenses in Various Types of Schools: New York City, 1963*

	PERCENT OF SCHOOLS WITH A GIVEN PERCENT OF TEACHERS ON PERMANENT LICENSES					
TYPE OF SCHOOL	65+	50–64	35–49	−35	TOTAL	NO. OF SCHOOLS
	Elementary Schools					
Special Service	22	34	29	15	100	206
Other	62	30	6	2	100	350
Total	47	31	15	7	100	556
	Junior High Schools					
Special Service	2	36	52	10	100	59
Other	34	41	24	1	100	71
Total	19	40	36	5	100	130

Note: A "special service school" is a school in a disadvantaged area, with low school achievement. It is similar to the "inner-city school" of Chicago.

Source: Sheldon and Glazier, *Pupils and Schools in New York City*, Tables 25 and 32.

with all others. The "special service" schools are like the inner-city schools that we have defined in Chapter 4. This Table shows, for instance, that only 22 percent of special service elementary schools have 65 percent or more of their teaching positions filled by teachers on permanent licenses, while 62 percent of other schools are in this condition. On the other hand, 15 percent of special service schools, compared with two percent of the others, have less than 35 percent of their teachers on permanent license.

It is well known that there is a shortage of elementary-school teachers, though not of secondary-school teachers. Most elementary-school teachers are women, and many of them teach for a few years and then raise a family, often returning to school work after their children are grown. But whether there is a shortage or not, the youngest and least experienced teachers tend to be assigned to the "difficult" schools.

Social Origins of Metropolitan Area Teachers

In the decades prior to 1920, teachers were recruited in large numbers from middle-class urban families, and from rural families of probably upper-middle and lower-middle class. Relative to the general population, persons who entered the teaching field had large amounts of formal schooling and probably were persons who regarded teaching as a calling. In those years, teaching was one of the few occupations available to respectable and educated women; as the schoolmaster made way for the schoolma'am, a sizable number of teachers were women from upper-middle-class and upper-class backgrounds. While teaching has always offered an avenue of opportunity for certain groups of young people, especially rural groups, the over-all proportion of teachers who came from lower-status levels was probably smaller some decades ago than at present.

As America became increasingly urban; as the educational system mushroomed, with greater need for teachers; with the growth of teacher-training institutions, with an increasing proportion of young people obtaining college education; and as more occupations became available to women; the social composition of the teaching profession changed.

There have been a number of studies of various groups of teachers and of various groups of students preparing to be teachers. While these studies show that there is considerable variability according to the region of the country and according to the size and the type of college attended, nevertheless they indicate that a large group of teachers is still drawn from business and professional families and that significant proportions come from farm families and from skilled laborers' families. The overall majority, however, is coming increasingly from lower-middle and upper-working classes.

In recent years there has been a further increase in the heterogeneity of social backgrounds, with the most pronounced changes being a drop in the number of teachers from farm families and an increase in the number from urban working-class homes.

Table 7.4 shows the distribution by age and family origin of a national sample of teachers drawn in 1960–61 (NEA, April, 1963). Of the total group, about 27 percent came from farm families and another 30 percent from blue-collar families (i.e., their fathers were unskilled, semi-skilled, or skilled workers). However, these proportions are quite different in different age groups. For example, of the oldest teachers, those aged 56 and over, almost 40 percent came from farm families; while of the youngest teachers, those under age 26, it was only 27 percent.

Table 7.4   *Age of Teacher in Relation to Father's Occupation: National Sample*

OCCUPATION OF TEACHER'S FATHER	PERCENTAGE IN EACH GROUP					
	56+	46–55	36–45	26–35	Under 26	Total
Unskilled worker	1.9	5.0	4.9	10.8	7.6	6.5
Semi-skilled or skilled worker	14.4	22.8	24.0	27.9	23.6	23.4
Farmer	39.2	34.5	28.7	13.9	20.3	26.5
Clerical or sales worker	9.0	5.2	6.0	9.2	6.3	7.1
Managerial or self-employed	23.6	18.7	21.7	24.6	21.9	22.0
Professional or Semi-professional	11.8	13.8	14.7	13.6	20.3	14.5
Number reporting	263	464	387	509	237	1,860

Source: National Educational Association, Research Division. *The American Public-School Teacher*. Research Monograph 1963–M2.

These figures are for the country at large. There are differences, however, when large school systems are compared with small. In the largest school systems, the proportion of teachers who come from farm families is much lower and the proportion from urban working-class families is much higher than the national averages. As can be seen from the detailed listing of fathers' occupations of teachers in the Chicago public schools in 1964, less than five percent came from farms, while almost half came from working-class homes (see Table 7.5).

SUBURBAN TEACHERS. The "typical" suburban or high-status school probably has a teaching staff which is rather similar to that of the high-status school in the central city. However, since there is a growing diversity of suburbs there is also a growing diversity of schools. The

Table 7.5   *Father's Occupation of Chicago Public School Teachers, 1964*

OCCUPATION OF TEACHER'S FATHER	PERCENTAGE OF TEACHERS					
	ELEMENTARY SCHOOL			SECONDARY SCHOOL		
	Male	*Female*	*Total*	*Male*	*Female*	*Total*
Semi-skilled and unskilled	26	15	17	20	9	14
Farm laborer or renter	1	1	1	1	1	1
Skilled worker, foreman or similar	33	31	31	30	24	27
Farm owner	3	3	3	4	4	4
Clerical and small business	17	23	22	20	26	23
Professional and Managerial	20	27	26	25	36	31
Number	720	4,430	5,150	1,123	1,250	2,373

Source: Adapted from Robert J. Havighurst, *The Public Schools of Chicago*, pp. 417–418.

distribution of teachers by age and experience among suburban schools and also among the schools of the smaller SMSAs almost certainly reflects the socio-economic characteristics of the schools.

Social Origin as a Factor in Educational Performance

It is important to know something of the social origin of any given teacher if we are to understand his performance in the teaching role. In this connection, however, we must look at social origin in relation to personality. It has been said, for instance, that social origin is the single most important fact in predicting a teacher's behavior. This is a gross oversimplification. Although a given teacher's social origin may have had an important influence upon his or her personality, it is virtually impossible to cite generalized effects that would be true for all teachers of any single origin. For example, a teacher who comes from a middle-class family is not necessarily ineffective in dealing with lower-class children. Some middle-class teachers, coming from fairly relaxed home environments, may emerge as adaptive personalities, who readily take on the color of their social surroundings. For them, it would be relatively easy to get along sympathetically with children and parents quite different from themselves. In another group, for whom a rigid upbringing had the effect of inculcating a tendency to panic when faced with the strange or unusual, prejudices may be easily aroused. Some of these persons may cling to their own ways as the only right or proper ones. They could easily drift toward treating with disdain children or parents who are of different races, religions, nationalities, or economic circumstances.

MIDDLE-CLASS BACKGROUNDS. Some teachers with middle-class backgrounds do a very good job of teaching working-class children. They have a broad and sympathetic understanding of children and of society, and they enjoy working with socially disadvantaged pupils if the school structure is reasonably stable.

Another teacher from a middle-class home may be dissatisfied and frustrated by a working-class group. For example, Louise Carson said of herself:

Considering my family background, my social and cultural surroundings throughout my life, and my formal education, I am definitely a middle-class person with typical middle-class values. My parents are college graduates. My father has been active in a prominent social club, and both parents have always been active in organizations such as Kiwanis, Girl Scouts, PTA, and the like. They have felt the responsibility of maintaining a stable, secure home, close family unity, and instilling the "right" values and an appreciation for the "finer things in life" in their children.

In spite of being rather sheltered from other classes of people, I am certain that I was influenced by my parents and teachers in being tolerant, fair, and feeling civic responsibility. These latter attitudes are probably the only factors which "saved" me at all when I graduated from college full of grand ideas about helping to develop little minds belonging to sweet, clean children who would understand the things I had to offer them; and when I found myself instead teaching children in a slum neighborhood. Disregarding the racial difference (although I must admit that even the first glance at my class of nearly fifty Negro children was a shock to me, since I had never before had so many Negro people near me at one time), I was stunned more by seeing so many shabbily dressed and dirty children. . . .

The impressions of my very first day of teaching are still vivid. I saw a girl from the eighth grade who was several months pregnant. At first I thought she was just a very young mother bringing her child to school, but I found out that she was a thirteen-year-old pupil. (When she appeared in this obvious condition she was immediately withdrawn from school.) In discussing this with the older teachers at lunch, I learned that during the previous semester the upper ungraded class had had a baby shower for one of the girls who had been forced to leave for the same reason. The teacher explained that she allowed the class to do this to "help soothe their feelings, since they thought it was very unfair that the girl couldn't finish the semester just because she was having a baby." I was shocked at this teacher, too, and I felt more confused than ever.

My other experiences that first day of school included listening to a dialect that was unfamiliar and almost uncomprehensible to me and to language that was shocking (most terms I had never heard before), and watching one seven-year-old boy emerge from the dressing room without any clothes on. When I went back with him to see that he dressed, I found that his underwear was filthy and ragged. It was held together with a large rusty safety pin that the boy claimed had been sticking him.

I tried—I really tried my best. I remembered how I had to be tolerant, and how these were just children who didn't know any better. I remembered how I wanted to be a teacher, and how I wanted to succeed on my first assignment. But I simply couldn't take it. I applied for a transfer after a few weeks, deciding that I had to get into a different school or withdraw from teaching altogether. I did stick it out for the rest of that year, but I never could overcome my feelings. It seems to me, in retrospect, that I spent all my time breaking up fist-fights and "butting" sessions, trying to retrieve stolen objects, and pretending not to hear the remarks that made me blush. . . .

I've been in a middle-class school since then, and I'm happy with teaching now. But I still feel guilty and somehow ashamed of myself. I wish I could have been different. But at the same time, a person had to be honest with herself, and has to be comfortable in what she's doing, or she can't do anything at all. . . .

It is, of course, not only middle-class teachers dealing with lower-class children who can provide us with varying examples of how social origin and personality interact in influencing teaching behavior. Some teachers have difficulty in working with children whose families are of higher social levels than their own. Thus, while many teachers from lower-status families prefer to teach middle-class children, others do not. Sometimes a middle-class teacher may find it difficult to adjust to an upper-class group of children.

Working-class Background

Among teachers coming from lower-status families, we must also expect to see differing patterns. One, for example, tortured by inner feelings of inferiority, may regard his origin as a thing of shame to be lived down. Another, having a powerful identification with his father and older siblings, may so conduct himself as to retain and exemplify his family's social rank, and in so doing ally himself with pupils and parents of similar origin. A third, imbued with strong achievement drives, may seek to deny his origin by accepting middle-class standards and by being unusually strict, if not actually punitive, against the children and parents from whose ranks he sees himself as having risen by dint of self-denial. These illustrations, of course, do not by any means exhaust the possibilities. Jim Mallory is an example of a teacher who has moved a long way up the social ladder, and whose flexible personality has made him unusually successful:

Jim Mallory was born in 1917 in the state of Washington. His family's income was derived mainly from fruit picking, and each member was responsible for some aspect of the family endeavor. It was often Jim's lot to do the cooking, family wash, mending, and the making of clothes for the entire family. Since the Mallorys lived in a tent much of the time, it was also his job to erect the tent at the fruit picking locations and to "keep house" in any and all aspects.

Since fruit picking was seasonal work and the father not too steady a provider, responsibility for food and money often fell on the shoulders of the children. At one time Jim spent five hours each evening setting pins in a bowling alley at a nearby army base. If he told the soldiers he was hungry they would bring him food from their mess hall. This food plus the money earned from pin setting was for a time the sole family subsistence.

When Jim was sixteen he joined the army, but was given a medical discharge a year later. He stayed with his family for about two weeks subsequent to his discharge, and then stowed away on a fruit truck and went to Texas. There he enrolled in a junior college. After two years, he entered a large university in a pre-law curriculum. World War II interrupted his college work, but he received his bachelor's degree shortly after the war. He then went into graduate work in psychology, where he specialized in counselling and guidance. He became an avid student of "nondirective" counselling and "student-centered" teaching, finding this general approach in keeping with his implicit world-view. He is nonauthoritarian and he holds sacred the value of the individual and opposes institutionalization of human life. He is never so delighted as when he is discussing the conflicting values of American culture, especially those of the middle-class in general and of school administrators in particular.

Jim's values are apparent in his attitudes toward his own children. They are allowed to solve their own personal and social problems, and the limits on their behavior are kept to the absolute minimum. This attitude is not always approved by his neighbors and colleagues, but it poses no special problems in Jim's eyes. . . .

Jim has been a successful teacher in high school and is now one of the most popular and admired teachers on a college faculty. His unique teaching methods in the classroom, and his sympathy and permissiveness in the counselling situation—his ability to give the student a sense of worth—this combination is one that appeals strongly to almost all his students. . . .

Attitudes of Big City Teachers

The attitudes of teachers toward their jobs are positive, on the whole, although the foregoing examples indicate that there are some negative attitudes. It can be safely assumed that suburban teachers are somewhat more content than central city teachers with their present situations.

A general indication of the attitudes of teachers toward their job in a central city is given in Table 7.6, which reports data from a survey of Chicago teachers. The teachers were asked, "What is your attitude, in general, about your present position?" They could indicate their attitudes by checking on a five-point scale as follows: very favorable, favorable, neutral, unfavorable, very unfavorable. Their answers were heavily "favorable" and "very favorable" with 72 percent of elementary school teachers and 71 percent of high school teachers giving these two responses.

However, there are some reliable differences between subgroups of teachers, as can be seen in Table 7.6. The older and more experienced teachers give more favorable answers than the younger and less experienced. Also, women are more favorable than men in their answers to this question.

The type of school area has the closest relation to teachers' attitudes toward their present positions. Elementary school teachers in upper- and middle-class areas are 65 percent very favorable toward their present position, while those in lower-class or slum area schools are only 17 percent very favorable, with 22 percent unfavorable or very unfavorable. There is a similar difference, though not so striking, among high school teachers.

Preparation of Metropolitan Teachers

Most young teachers will work for a time in an inner-city school. Some will master the job, and get real satisfaction from doing difficult work

Table 7.6   Teachers' Attitude Toward Present Position Related to Experience, Sex, and Type of School Area: Chicago, 1964 (percentages, unless otherwise stated)

YEARS OF TEACHING EXPERIENCE	ELEMENTARY SCHOOLS						HIGH SCHOOLS					
	VF	F	N	U	VU	Number	VF	F	N	U	VU	Number
1–2	20	42	19	14	5	806	19	50	16	12	3	428
3–15	25	43	16	12	4	2,768	21	48	16	12	3	1,254
16+	46	36	9	6	2	1,592	36	41	14	7	2	693
Total group	31	41	14	11	4	5,166	25	46	16	11	3	2,375
TYPE OF SCHOOL AREA												
Upper- and middle-class	65	25	6	4	0	264	35	46	11	5	3	242
Mixed middle- and working-class	41	41	11	5	2	1,537	29	47	13	8	3	1,187
Stable working-class	38	39	13	7	3	912	19	47	18	13	2	391
Lower-class and slum	17	43	18	16	6	2,409	14	45	21	16	4	505
Total group	31	41	14	11	4	5,122	25	46	16	11	3	2,343
SEX												
Male	9	14	19	20	21	720	41	47	53	49	65	1,123
Female	91	86	81	80	79	4,430	60	53	47	51	35	1,250
NUMBER	1,576	2,083	731	541	185	5,150	581	1,087	363	246	66	2,373

Note: VF = very favorable; F = favorable; N = neutral; U = unfavorable; VU = very unfavorable.

Source: Robert J. Havighurst, The Public Schools of Chicago, p. 344.

well. Some will hate the job, and will transfer to an easier school as soon as possible. Some will find a well-run inner-city school and deliberately stay there, knowing that they are doing an important thing by teaching disadvantaged children effectively. Others will move to another type of school, but will remember that they served creditably for a time, even thought they eventually made a change.

The inner-city school teacher needs special preparation, and is getting it in an increasing number of colleges. In addition to the usual training program, the prospective teacher studies urban sociology and observes and then assists in a number of community agencies, such as community centers, playgrounds, and summer camps. Eventually the prospective teacher does practice teaching in an inner-city school.

Such programs are increasing, but still a good many young teachers have to learn on the job. One of the most difficult things for new teachers (and many older ones as well) to learn is that the inner-city community has a style of life which the school teacher must understand, and respect to some degree. This is illustrated by the incident described below, which has been written up by a teacher-training group at Hunter College of the University of the City of New York. This is a real incident, though the names of the people have been changed. (Fuchs, 1966.)

The Samuel Slater School, in New York City, was located in an area where Negroes and Puerto Ricans lived. The principal, Mr. Fields, had worked in this school for a number of years. He prided himself on his understanding of the community and its children.

At the beginning of the year Mr. Fields sent a letter to the fifteen new, inexperienced teachers who had been assigned to his school. He knew that most of the new teachers were from middle-class communities and had not been exposed to the kind of community in which they would be working. He thought he would help them to get over the "culture shock" which he knew they would feel.

In his letter he referred to the following facts: The children came mostly from families that were disadvantaged financially, academically, and socially; many of the children had no father at home; the language used at home was the speech of illiterate parents or it was Spanish; thus many of the children would not be "ready" to learn the school subjects, nor would they understand the care of textbooks and notebooks.

On the other hand, these children could learn. They had as much innate ability as other children. The teacher's responsibility was to train the children in: listening, reading, speaking, and arithmetic; and also cleanliness, punctuality, care of school property, keeping neat note-books, and desire for academic achievement.

Mr. Fields sent a copy of this letter to the President of the Parent Teachers Association, because he wanted the parents to know that the new teachers were receiving this kind of assistance.

The board of the PTA was angry about this letter, which they thought cast reflections on them as parents. They sent a committee to ask the principal for an apology. Mr. Fields was surprised, annoyed, and refused to apologize for what he intended as an effort to improve his school.

The parents then began to circulate a petition calling for the resignation of Mr. Fields. They quoted a number of phrases from his letter to the new teachers and asked: Do these statements accurately describe you and your family?

This actual incident can help us to understand the complex matter of differences between the school staff and the parents and children of a socially disadvantaged section of the big city. It is an oversimplification to say that the problem is due to differences in values. The parents who objected to Mr. Fields' letter did so not because they had different values from Mr. Fields and his staff. They did so because they *share* values with Mr. Fields, and are angry because he is critical of their performance as parents. But it is also over-simple to say that the parents and Mr. Fields have the same values. There are some value differences, and these need to be understood by the teacher.

Two Critical Roles of the Inner-City Teacher

One of the first things the teacher must learn is that there are two basic functions for a classroom teacher. They are: *Keeping Order* and *Teaching*. The first one, keeping order, is generally easy in a high-status or a conventional type of school, but it may be very difficult in an inner-city school. Some teachers end a day with the feeling that they have used up most of their time and energy just in keeping order, and they have not had time for much real teaching.

The problem of the teacher in this situation is illustrated in a number of recent books describing actual incidents in schools. For instance, Greene and Ryan (1965, p. 170-71) describe an incident in which the teacher put a problem on the blackboard—a long one—

and turned around to find five children in a heap on the floor, stabbing with their fingers at the others' eyes. A little girl nearby had her coat over her head, to shut it out. It was all completely silent.

Then there was a fight in the corridor between a third-grade girl and a fifth-grade boy. He beat her head against the wall. Children gathered round in a scared circle. A boy said, "Let her alone. She gotta learn to defend herself."

In another city, an eighth-grade teacher said, "The emotional problems that these kids have are beyond the scope of the schools. For example, I sent in problem reports on about 10 pupils in my room, and I can't get them out of the room. They use profanity; they're antagonistic. Each moment I have to spend just sitting on them. To tell you the truth, they get to the seventh and eighth grade and the teachers just can't handle them. It's not that we don't understand the reasons for their behavior. Sure, we understand the reasons for their behavior. Even though we have all the understanding in the world, the behavior in the classroom hinders the teacher and this is the most important part."

Teachers' Organizations

One of the major differences between central city and suburban teachers lies in the nature of their professional organizations. Suburban teachers generally belong to the National Education Association and its state affiliates, and so do most of the teachers of the smaller SMSAs. However, in the large central cities, the American Federation of Teachers has major strength.

By 1966 the number of teachers in American public elementary and secondary schools was over 1,800,000. Of this total, over 90 percent were members of state teachers' associations affiliated with the NEA; and over 50 percent held membership directly in the national organization.

In recent years, teachers' organizations have become more energetic. The *New York Times* in January, 1964, noted: "A resurgence of militancy among the nation's public school teachers marked the year of 1963. There was mounting evidence that teachers are no longer content to rule only the classroom to which they are assigned. They want a hand in the assignment and a voice in the policy that controls their professional lives. They are not asking to run the schools, but they want their views heard and heeded."

An Office of Education bulletin published in 1964, in commenting that this new militancy continued to mount during the spring of 1964, said:

New terms have evolved for the educator's vocabulary—strikes, sanctions, mediation, professional negotiation, collective bargaining, appeal, and arbitration.

The growing importance of the teacher organization as a vigorous, articulate, and forceful element in the improvement of working conditions for teachers is well recognized. Today's teachers are interested and increasingly active, through their organizations, in such matters as civil rights, academic freedom, manpower needs, and international affairs. Quite recently they have become vitally concerned about their rights and responsibilities in participating in the development of the policies and regulations which determine the conditions under which they work. (Steffensen, 1964, p. 2.)

The Representative Assembly of the NEA passed in 1962 two resolutions that read in part:

The National Education Association insists on the right of professional associations, through democratically selected representatives using professional channels, to participate with boards of education in the determination of policies of common concern, including salary and other conditions of professional service. . . .

The National Education Association believes that, as a means for preventing unethical or arbitrary policies or practices that have a deleterious effect on the welfare of the schools, professional sanctions should be invoked. These sanctions would provide for appropriate disciplinary action by the organized profession. (NEA Handbook, 1962–63, p. 64.)

These resolutions have provided the basis for the development of procedures for implementing the goals of the profession, procedures which are known as *professional negotiations* and *professional sanctions*.

Professional negotiations are a form of collective bargaining, although many educators disavow the latter term. Negotiations are carried on according to formalized procedures between the local teachers' association and the school board about matters of joint concern. (National Education Association, 1962–63, p. 10.) There are provisions for mediation through professional educational channels, should the association and the board fail to reach agreement. Teachers' salaries and other aspects of economic welfare have, of course, long been topics for negotiation. New developments, however, are the insistence that teachers, by right of their professional status, should have a say in determining matters which have hitherto been regarded as resting solely within the province of the school boards and administrative staff, matters such as qualifications for employment, class size, and special services.

In the summer of 1962 the first known professional negotiation agreement based upon the NEA resolution was adopted, and by spring, 1965, nearly 400 other school systems had followed suit. About half of these agreements provided for the resolution of deadlocks through mediation as recommended by the NEA. (NEA *Journal*, 1962, Vol. 51, No. 8, pp. 28–30; 1965, Vol. 54, No. 5, pp. 30–31.)

Professional sanctions are viewed by NEA-affiliated organizations as the ultimate weapon for correcting unsatisfactory conditions. They are applied, generally speaking, somewhat as follows:

A local association, unable to persuade the school board to correct what it feels are unsatisfactory conditions for professional service, requests the state education association to investigate the situation. If the state association's investigating committee agrees with the local association, it will make recommendations to the school board and allow it a reasonable length of time to meet them. If the board does not comply, the state association will publicize the matter, refuse the school district the use of its placement service, and sanction certain procedures by the local association to enforce compliance. Such steps might include the refusal to renew contracts or the withholding of certain services by the teachers. The state association might even rule that it would be professionally unethical for teachers to accept positions in that district.

The NEA has been successful in securing better salaries and better educational conditions in Oklahoma and Utah, for example; but in the larger central cities the American Federation of Teachers (the Teachers' Union) has competed with the NEA for the allegiance of the classroom teachers. The AFT had a membership of 61,000 in 1961 and probably has about 75,000 members in 1966.

Like the NEA-affiliated teachers' organizations, teachers' unions have negotiated on topics beyond the traditional ones of salaries and fringe benefits. Thus, for example, in 1962 the New York City teachers' union established a committee to develop a plan for making recommendations on school and class size, teacher specialists, integration, staff and community relationships, and teaching materials and techniques. This committee has worked with the administration on these matters.

Unions have been somewhat more militant than the NEA. For instance, in 1963 the AFT rescinded its no-strike policy and recognized "the right of locals to strike under certain circumstances." (Steffensen, 1964, p. 67.) There followed a threatened strike of New York teachers in 1963 and of Chicago teachers in 1965.

Teachers in the large central cities have tended to organize and act collectively more than teachers in suburbs and smaller cities because the large size of the central city school system tends to isolate them from the administration. In the smaller systems, the superintendent or the principal tends to deal directly with classroom teachers, and they feel that they have a voice in the making of decisions. In the larger systems a teachers' organization becomes useful as a spokesman for individual teachers who otherwise do not have a voice in operating the schools.

Negro and Other Minority Group Teachers

The various nationality groups that came to the United States during the nineteenth and twentieth centuries have entered the teaching profession as a natural part of the process of joining the American culture and of moving up on the socio-economic scale. Thus the Irish, Germans and Swedes became teachers in large numbers before 1900, and people with names suggesting these nationalities and the Anglo-Saxon make up the bulk of the teaching profession in the smaller school systems today. Then Jews, Poles and Italians came into the school systems and now have important roles, especially in the large central cities. Since World War II there has been a substantial flow of Japanese into teaching positions in western and mid-western cities, and teachers of Japanese ancestry abound in Hawaii. Puerto Ricans are now coming into the profession in noticeable numbers.

The Negro group is different from the other ethnic groups in the teaching profession because there was a segregated school system in the South and some border states for decades before 1954, and therefore there was a substantial group of Negro teachers in Negro schools. The largest group of Negro teachers is still to be found in the South teaching in *de facto* segregated Negro schools.

In 1960, five percent of college teachers and nine percent of the country's elementary and secondary school teachers were nonwhite, almost all of them Negroes. Of Negro school teachers, 76 percent were in the South. Table 7.7 shows the distribution of white and nonwhite teachers by age in 1960. White and nonwhite men are distributed by age in almost identical ways, but there is a substantial difference between white and nonwhite women teachers. There is a much higher proportion of nonwhite women teachers under 35 years of age than there is of white women. This probably indicates that young Negro women are finding opportunities in the schools, and especially in the big city schools.

Table 7.7   *Teachers in Elementary and Secondary Schools: Percentage Distribution by Sex, Color and Age, 1960*

WHITE TEACHERS	AGE			
	14–34	*35–44*	*45+*	*Number*
Men	47	25	28	441,000
Women	30	20	50	1,097,000
Total	35	21	44	1,538,000
Number	537,000	324,000	677,000	
NONWHITE TEACHERS				
Men	47	27	26	35,000
Women	43	26	31	109,000
Total	44	26	30	144,000
Number	63,000	38,000	43,000	

Source: *U.S. Census of Population: 1960.* Final Report PC(2)–7D.

Nonwhite teachers are much more likely to be residents of central cities of SMSAs than are white teachers, as is shown in Table 7.8. If we infer that most teachers teach in the cities where they live, this table shows that nonwhite teachers are more likely to teach in central cities than in suburbs and other smaller urban places. Negroes are relatively highly represented on the teaching staff in border cities such as Kansas City, St. Youis, Louisville, Cincinnati, Washington and Baltimore. For instance, in 1965, 28 percent of the public school teachers of Kansas City were Negroes, compared with about 18 percent of Negroes in the city population. This is a result of two factors: the existence before 1954 of segregated schools with segregated faculties, and a policy of employment since 1954 without respect to race.

Table 7.8   *Teachers' Place of Residence, by Color, 1960 (Teachers in Elementary and Secondary Schools: Percentage Distribution)*

RESIDENT IN:	WHITE	NONWHITE
Central cities of SMSAs	27	47
Urban fringe and other urban places	44	32
Rural areas	29	21
Number	1,540,000	144,000

Source: *U.S. Census of Population: 1960.* Final Report PC(2)–7D.

The more northern central cities have growing proportions of Negro teachers. Detroit had 23 percent in 1962. In Detroit the proportion of Negro teachers is very nearly the same as the proportion of Negroes in the total population. Chicago had 32 percent Negro teachers in 1966, and 25 percent Negroes in the total population.

The assignment of Negro teachers is largely to schools with a predominance of Negro pupils, but this practice is slowly changing. For example, Philadelphia in 1965 worked out an arrangement between the Teachers' Union and the school administration whereby 40 white teachers went into schools that were mainly Negro in pupil and staff composition, while 40 Negro teachers transferred to schools that were mainly white in pupil and staff composition.

Detroit in 1965 announced a "balanced staff" policy for the assignment and transfer of teachers. This policy proposes that it is educationally sound and desirable for children in all schools to come into contact with teachers who are young and old, male and female, white and Negro, etc. A balanced staff enables children to meet and work with teachers who represent the pluralistic pattern of the larger community. The Detroit school administration worked out with the teachers' organizations a plan for the assignment of new teachers and the transfer of teachers after three years of experience, which would work toward the goal of a balanced staff. At the same time, it was announced that teaching experiences in various types of schools was a prerequisite for promotion to the principalship.

The balanced staff policy assumes that there is no general advantage or disadvantage to a child's having a teacher of his own skin color. It assumes that the personality and the training of the teacher count more than anything else in determining what kind of class a teacher should teach. Some Negro teachers are especially good for work with Negro children, and some are not good for this, because of their own attitudes toward race. It is the same with teachers of various social class backgrounds—some should teach children of working-class backgrounds and some would do better with children of middle-class families, depending on their own personalities and their feelings about social class. The following two examples show the kinds of difference that exist, and indicate that no broad generalization can be made about the best placement of Negro teachers.

William Jones came from a Negro family which was well regarded in the community. His father was a post office clerk; his mother had been a maid for a fashionable white family. Their home life conformed to general middle-class standards. They were proud of themselves and belonged to a church and fraternal organizations. Their social life was confined largely to Negro friends. The family plans included college education for the three children. Choice of occupation was carefully discussed in terms of employment possibilities. Bill wanted to be an engineer, but the idea was vetoed on the grounds there were no jobs for Negro engineers. Teaching was his second choice. At college he joined a Negro fraternity and attended social events with this group.

After graduation he became a science teacher in a school in an almost solidly Negro district. Since the pattern set by his father and mother seemed good to him, he followed their example. In his own quiet way he did a good job of teaching. He was regarded by students and fellow-teachers as a steady influence. He enjoyed his life and hoped that students would sense the advantages of the path he had chosen. His own rewards took the form of a nice home, a good family of his own, and acknowledged position. He served on several boards and committees, was the spark plug in raising funds for Negro colleges in the South.

Not all of his friends approved of Mr. Jones. Those who were more concerned about such issues as FEPC called him an "Uncle Tom." This made him angry because he was race conscious and belonged to groups like the Urban League. He condemned the "hot heads" who were "always shooting their mouths off." He was even more contemptuous of the Negroes who were docile or servile towards whites. He felt that the existence of solidly Negro areas was a good thing for him; if these did not exist he doubted if he could have found so good a teaching job. He liked the Negro community because of his good position in it. Mostly, though, he wanted to be left alone to live his life in what had become a family tradition. (Stiles, 1957, pp. 51–52.)

Quite another kind of teacher is Alice Washington. Alice Washington grew up under the care of her grandmother, a Negro woman who did "day work" for middle-class white families. Alice's mother gave birth to Alice when she was 18 years old and unmarried. She gave the baby to her mother to bring up, and worked in a factory until she got married at 20. The marriage did not last, and she was left with another baby. She married another man, who left her after two more children were born, and she then applied for Aid for Dependent Children and lived on this money with her three children and two others that were born later. Alice never lived with her mother, but she often saw her on Sundays. She remembers that her grandmother warned her not to play with her half-brothers and sisters, and kept her away from her mother, telling her that her mother was "not fit to bring up children." The grandmother spent evenings with her, reading to her, and always took her to church on Sunday.

When Alice was old enough to attend school she found it a wonderful place. She learned to read promptly, and was the darling of her teachers. After school she often went to a neighborhood center where she was one of a group of ten girls who spent afternoons with a club leader they liked very much. This leader kept in touch with Alice and encouraged her to finish high school and to go to the local teachers' college. She was never so proud of herself as when she got her diploma, and looked down at her grandmother, sitting in the audience and smiling.

Alice teaches in a common-man type of school. The children are all Negroes, and they come to school fairly regularly and behave themselves while they are in her class. She runs her room strictly, and punishes her pupils for the least infraction of rules. She gives out homework to her fifth grade pupils and insists on their doing this work. She often tells her children that they are lucky to have such a good school, and they must work hard to show their appreciation. She will not tolerate lying, or copying. About a fourth of her pupils come from homes where there is no father present. She is especially strict with these children, and will not tolerate anything but the most earnest work from them. To those who do well she devotes much time, and she spends time after school getting them cared for properly in church groups and settlement houses. But those who do not do well in school find her a merciless punisher and a relentless taskmaster. When she meets physical resistance and active hostility from such a pupil, she becomes so anxious that sometimes she gets sick. Her principal has learned to help her with one or two such children each year, by removing them to the class of another teacher who can tolerate this kind of behavior better.

The Career of the Metropolitan Teacher

The career of the school teacher is now undergoing a considerable alteration, as would be inferred from the fact that the population structure of the country has changed so much during the past few decades, and also the social backgrounds of teachers have changed.

The Traditional Career Line

The traditional career for a school teacher began by teaching in a rural school, with one or two years of post high-school preparation; after a few years the teacher went back to college and completed a four-year course; then he or she went to work in the schools of a small city. Often the line of progress was from grade school to high school, as well as from small town to larger town. Peterson (1956) studied the careers of women school teachers in the Kansas City school system. In the early 1950's the Kansas City system had been stable in numbers for a decade, as had other cities, as a result of the low birth-rates of the 1930's. Kansas City and other central cities adopted a policy of employing only experienced teachers. Thus the teachers were likely to be over 30 years old. In 1953, 78 percent of the Kansas City women high school teachers were over 40 years of age.

Unmarried rural-reared teachers typically began teaching in a country school near their home at the age of seventeen or eighteen; moved to a small town school after about two years of experience and some additional education in summer school; secured a B.S. in education at about the age of 24; made two additional moves to large schools in larger towns; entered the Kansas City system at about the age of 31; moved twice within the Kansas City system; secured their current placement within the city system at the age of 35; and, in the course of continued summer school education, received an M.A. degree at about the age of 38.

The unmarried teachers from small towns followed much the same path. However, they tended to be somewhat older when they began teaching, because they often did some other kind of work in their home towns before going to school. Since many of the rural girls looked upon country school teaching as a way of earning money for further education, there is some similarity between country girls and town girls in this respect. There were, among unmarried teachers from the smaller towns, several who, like rural girls, began teaching in a country school when out of high school, saving their money for further education.

The early career phases of unmarried urban-reared teachers are noticeably different from the others. As a rule, urban-born teachers completed their degrees before beginning to teach, taught in small town schools for a much shorter period, and entered the urban system when younger. They were not, however, much younger than teachers from small towns and farms in moving to present positions within the city system, perhaps because "settling" within the city system is more closely affiliated with age.

An alternative career line existed in a few large cities, mainly in the East. Here the teachers were more likely to come from working-class and lower-middle-class families living in the central city. They went from the local high school to a municipal teachers' college or university, and then commenced teaching in the city schools. After a two- or three-year probationary period they secured tenure, and began looking for a school that was conveniently located near the area in which they would like to live. They would transfer once or twice until they found a school where they liked the principal, the pupils, and the neighborhood. A sub-group, of course, worked for promotion to an administrative position.

The Contemporary Career Line

Since 1950 a new career line has developed for teachers in a metropolitan area. The majority of them come from the central city and attend a local teachers' college. Upon securing a bachelor's degree and a teaching certificate, they start teaching in the central city system. The central city has actively recruited new teachers since about 1955, when the post war birth rate increase swelled school enrollment. Many teachers secure a Master's degree through part-time study. Then those who want to be administrators start preparing for examinations and getting a variety of teaching experience. The others look for the kind of school assignment that will be best for them. The beginning teacher runs the risk of being assigned initially to an unsatisfactory school, since schools that have many vacancies and no teachers requesting transfer to them are those in which something is "wrong"—otherwise the condition would not prevail. Schools in the lower socio-economic areas tend to be such "transfer vacuums." Havighurst (1964) found that 11 percent of the elementary-school teachers in Chicago's slum schools had only one year of teaching experience, while only 16 percent had more than 16 years' teaching experience. In contrast, in upper-middle-class schools only two percent of the teachers had been teaching only a year, while 58 percent had more than 16 years' experience. A few teachers found teaching in the slums a rewarding and challenging experience, but most had, through the transfer system, moved on to "better" schools.

There are, of course, a variety of reasons why teachers request transfers. Havighurst found only 16 percent of elementary and 12 percent of high school teachers wishing to transfer because of dissatisfaction with pupils or with the local community. The most frequent reason given was personal convenience—distance from home, for example. A teacher may also transfer for reasons of professional advancement, for example, to gain experience in another type of school, or a better position, or a teacher may be dissatisfied with his principal, or with certain aspects of his assignment that he feels mitigate against professional service. Nevertheless, more teachers request transfers from slum schools than from other schools in Chicago.

This career line leads increasingly often to a suburban school system. Since the suburbs have been growing rapidly, they cannot secure many teachers who were born in suburbs. They recruit from the central city or from the towns and cities outside the metropolitan area.

Thus there has developed a metropolitan teacher career line which remains entirely within a metropolitan area. More and more teachers are following their entire professional lines within a particular metropolitan area, teaching in a wide variety of schools.

This type of career is socially desirable if it does two things: (1) provides most teachers with opportunity to grow in experience and skill and salary in a set of situations where their particular personality fits in well; (2) distributes teachers among the schools so that the teachers who are best suited to each of the several types of schools are able to find places in such schools.

Exercises

1. If you have friends or colleagues who are Negro teachers, describe their attitudes toward teaching socially disadvantaged children. Can you relate differences among these people to differences in their personalities?

2. If you are teaching in a suburban school system, get career information from 10 or 12 of your colleagues who have been teaching 10 years or more. What has been a typical career line for them?

Suggestions for Further Reading

1. For a keen analytical and critical treatment of the American school teaching profession, read Myron Lieberman, *Education as a Profession*.

2. For questionnaire studies of school teachers see *The American Public School Teacher*, 1960–61, published by the Research Division of the National Education Association, and Chapter 16 and Appendix A of *The Public Schools of Chicago*, by Robert J. Havighurst.

3. Recent books describing teachers' reactions to inner-city schools are *Up the Down Staircase*, by Bel Kaufman, and *The School Children*, by Greene and Ryan.

8 ❦ School Systems and Other Social

Systems in the Metropolitan Area

The purpose of the human enterprise as a social venture is to make life more satisfying for all of those who live brief lives on the face of this ancient earth. This chapter asks and seeks to answer the question: how should the schools be related to other social systems in our urban industrial society so as to maximize human satisfaction and happiness?

To answer this question we need to look at education in a social setting; and for this we need to choose a social setting of a certain magnitude. Should it be the whole nation, for example? That would be useful, but too broad and distant a view for the kinds of interests we have developed in this book. Should it be the state? That would be better, but the metropolitan area is best from our point of view. It would not be useful to go down to the city or the municipality as the unit, for we have seen that this cannot give us a cross-section of American life with its economic, social and political problems to which education must be applied.

Having selected the metropolitan area as the unit of population and area upon which we will focus, we single out the major social changes which are now taking place, and which affect education and are affected by it. Education should be developed to take account of these social changes and to give a degree of rational control and direction over them.

The principal social changes are:

1. The labor force is increasingly composed of people with technical and professional training at a post high school level. Industrial production workers are not a growing component of the working force, and may decrease in relative numbers as have agricultural workers.

2. Services rather than production of goods are the principal elements of growth in the economy.
3. The basic problem of the American economy is no longer production of goods but the widespread and equitable distribution and consumption of goods and services.
4. The redistribution of population and of jobs between central cities and suburbs is making the metropolitan area into the rational unit for economic and political organization.
5. Government is increasingly involved in the financing and location of housing, in the provision of social security, health services and other forms of support for the material standard of living of a large segment of the population.
6. The metropolitan area is becoming a unit for a program of cultural development through the expansion of theater, concert music, graphic arts, adult education programs, libraries and educational television, with government subsidy.
7. A set of economic and political problems is arising out of the concentration of population in metropolitan areas—problems of water pollution, air pollution, urban sprawl and blight, transit, and economic and racial segregation.

Goals of Metropolitan Development

The Great Society, as conceived by American leaders, is to be achieved through working toward the following goals in the metropolitan area.

1. A high material standard of living.
2. Assistance to the disadvantaged through education and through specific forms of material aid.
3. Equality of opportunity for high quality education.
4. Freedom of choice in residence, occupation, politics, and religion.
5. Growing appreciation of expressive culture, with support for creative work in the arts.
6. Widespread participation by the common people in the making of social and political decisions about the metropolitan area.

For the achievement of these goals, educational systems must cooperate with other social systems. The various *social systems* carry on the business of a society. Where there is social change, there is change in these social systems. When there is rapid social change, as there is today, the various social systems change rapidly and they change in their relations with each other.

The educational system should change and develop its functions in relation to other social systems—this is the basic proposition of this chapter.

Social System Defined

The sociologist, as a scientist studying society, has invented several concepts as tools for his understanding of social structure and organization. One of the most useful of these concepts is that of a *social system*.

A social system is a system of the actions of individuals, the principal units of which are roles and constellations of roles. (Parsons and Shils, p. 197.) A social system has one or more *functions*, or things it does usefully (purposes it serves). It performs these functions through its roles or constellations of roles. A *role* is a set of behaviors that is appropriate to a particular status in a society.

An educational system is a set of roles and role constellations devised to teach children and adults some things they are not likely to learn efficiently in the family or at work. For another example, a police system is a set of roles and role constellations designed to protect order and enforce the law. Thus a social system is a systematic organization of the efforts of people to achieve some purpose of a society.

It is possible and useful to study a social system as a set of roles and role constellations, without looking closely at the individuals who fill the roles. This will be done at first, in this chapter. Later, the focus will be directed on the personalities and individual characteristics of people who fill key roles in the educational system.

Educational and Other Social Systems in the Metropolitan Area

In order to study relations between educational and other social systems there is need for a list of the social systems which operate in a metropolitan area, and this list should be organized into categories. In the list which follows, the social systems are divided into two large groups, *Critical* and *Supporting* systems.

The distinction between a critical system and a supporting system is a loose one. A supporting system is one which performs its functions in a routine, efficient manner, and is not changing its functions. This is the case with the water department of an ordinary city. However, if the water supply runs low, due to drought, population growth, or other circumstances, the water department quickly becomes a critical system. Also, if the water department is asked to take on a new function, such as that of preventing dental caries among the population through fluoridation of the water supply, this change of function may be complex enough, and controversial enough, to make the water department into a critical system.

The critical systems at any time are those faced with new demands or new functions that arise because the situation has changed in which the system operates. In the following list, those systems which have been designated as critical are ones concerned with pressing problems or ones whose functions are changing due to social change.

CRITICAL SOCIAL SYSTEMS AND THEIR SUB-SYSTEMS

Educational System
    Public school districts
    Roman Catholic schools organized in a diocesan district
    Other church-supported schools organized into districts
    Private, independent schools
    Universities and colleges
    County Superintendents' office or offices
    School boards' association
    Teachers' organizations
    Council of Parents and Teachers
    Adult Education Council
    Civic organizations interested in schools
Government System
    City government
    County government
    Special districts
    Court system
Welfare Agency System
    Welfare Council
    Community Chest
    Bureau of Public Assistance
    Employment Service
    Catholic Charities
    Jewish Charities
    Settlement Houses and Neighborhood Centers

Youth-serving organizations
    YMCA, YWCA, CYO, Scouts, Boys Clubs
Family service organizations
Economic System
    Banks
    Department Stores
    Industrial Corporations
    Chamber of Commerce
    AFL–CIO Council
    Better Business Bureau
    Retail and Wholesale Business Units
    Employment services
    Real Estate Board
Culture Agency System
    Public Library Districts
    Museums
    TV stations
    Radio stations
    Park districts
    Recreation agencies
    Booksellers
Transportation System
    Rapid Transit
    Airport
    Railway Terminal
    Department of streets
    Expressway system
    Automobile service stations
Church System
    Church Federation
    Roman Catholic Diocese
    Area or city-wide organizations
      of specific religious denominations
    Intra-church systems
Civic Organization System
    Civil Rights organizations
    Civil Liberties organizations
    Foreign policy organizations
    League of Women Voters
    John Birch Society
    Urban League
    Association for Mental Health
    Citizens Schools Organizations

SUPPORTING SYSTEMS AND THEIR SUB-SYSTEMS

Health Maintenance
    Board of Health
    Medical Societies
    Hospitals
    Nursing Homes
    Health Care Associations
Communication
    Newspapers
    TV and Radio
    Telephone system
Public Service
    Fire department
    Police department
    Water department
    Sewage disposal
    Commission on Human Relations
    Weather Bureau
Political Organizations
    Democratic organization
    Republican organization
    Independent Voters organization
Sociability Systems
    Country clubs
    "Service" clubs
    Social clubs
    Lodges and other fraternal organizations
Military System
    National Guard
    Civil Defense

Inter-system Cooperation

Certain social systems can operate most effectively as a rule when they operate alone. The water supply system is an example. It performs a technical and mechanical function, one which is clearly necessary and is clearly defined. It is seldom called upon to cooperate with other systems. Recently the water system has been asked to cooperate with the health maintenance system to supply fluoride in drinking water as a protection against tooth decay. Generally this new function has been taken on with little or no strain, but it involves an expansion of the functions of the water system which in some communities has caused conflict.

Other social systems must cooperate to a considerable degree because their functions are very similar and generally very complex. The educational system is an example of one that must cooperate with other systems.

For example, the school and the library systems have overlapping functions, which are worked out differently in various situations. The story of school and library cooperation in the City of Chicago is a good example. Much of the early part of the story is told by John A. Vieg (1939, pp. 57–67) who studied the schools of metropolitan Chicago in the 1930's.

In 1910 there were no school libraries in Chicago. At that time the Chicago Public Library provided a large number of fifty-book collections on long-term loan to classrooms in the schools. During 1916–17 the Library set up libraries in six high schools and maintained them for a short time, then closed them. A formal cooperative agreement was made in 1923 by which the Chicago Public Library provided books, magazines, supplies; selected librarians and supervised them; and the Chicago School Board paid the salaries of the librarians. This agreement continued until 1937, when 38 high schools and two junior college branches had libraries under this plan. There were no elementary school libraries during this period, but the classroom loan collections were continued. Although the cooperative agreement ran over a period of more than a decade, there was some dissatisfaction. For example, the 1935 annual report of the Chicago Public Library says that the services of the librarians were not fully appreciated by the schools. After 1937, the Board of Education assumed the cost of books and magazines and later took over the selection and supervision of librarians. A complete library system was established in the Chicago Schools during subsequent years, including almost all of the elementary schools. Thus the school libraries became integral parts of the school system, though the long-term loan collections from the Public Library continued in the elementary schools on a declining basis, with 32,000 books out on loan in 1962.

In this case the new function (school libraries) was introduced into the school system through inter-system cooperation, and then the cooperation was gradually discontinued as it became less useful.

7. How to take part in professional or business associations.
8. How to take a leading part in charitable and civic associations.

Upward mobile people learn these things in a number of ways. The most important thing for most persons who move from lower to middle class is to get a high-school education, then a college or university education. The mobile person watches and imitates friends and acquaintances who belong to a higher social class. He reads, travels, and observes the ways other people act in new situations. The mobile person learns also from a wife or husband who has higher social status.

Upward mobile people usually have a strong desire to rise on the social scale, they are quick learners, and they work hard to learn what is necessary for mobility. Thus, intelligence as well as initiative is required of a mobile individual.

The importance of social mobility in a democratic society can hardly be overestimated. The essence of democracy is equality of opportunity, not equality of people. And the kind of opportunity that most people want in a modern society is opportunity to get a better job, to make more money, to live in a better house than one's father. There are other kinds of opportunities, valued by many people— opportunity to speak one's mind freely on political matters, opportunity to enjoy good music and art, opportunity to enjoy leisure time. These are not closely related to social mobility, but they are not inimical to it.

The school system of a big city *must* maintain educational opportunity as the avenue to upward social mobility.

Causes of Social Mobility

The United States has enjoyed a condition of net upward social mobility throughout its history. That is, more people have moved up the social scale than have moved down, in any particular period of time. Some societies have less net upward mobility. England is an example. The degree of net upward (or downward mobility) depends on certain societal factors:

1. Technological change as it affects the distribution of occupations. The proportion of professional and managerial (middle class) occupations has increased and the proportion of people in unskilled work (lower-working class) has decreased in most if not all modern industrial societies. This makes for upward mobility.

2. Differential fertility of the various social classes. In the past, the upper and middle classes have had a lower birth rate than the lower classes. This has created a kind of social vacuum, in which lower-class youth are drawn up to fill middle-class posts left vacant by the lower-middle-class birth rate.

3. In-migration of groups whose social structure is different from that of the country into which they move. In the United States there has been until recently a large immigration of unskilled workers, which has tended to push native working-class people up the social ladder to positions the in-migrants could not fill.

4. Rapid population growth or decrease. The rapid population growth of the United States has kept the economy expanding at such a rate as to create many new middle-class positions which are then filled by lower-class people moving up.

Individual Mobility

Whether or not there is a net upward social mobility in a country or society, there is a great deal of balanced upward and downward individual mobility in a democratic country with an open class structure. In England it appears that there has been at least 30 percent upward mobility balanced by approximately the same amount of downward mobility. The causes of individual upward or downward mobility are the following:

1. TALENT, ESPECIALLY INTELLECTUAL TALENT. A bright boy or girl of working-class or lower-middle-class origin is very likely to move up the social scale in the United States. What this person needs is educational opportunity. An example of individual upward mobility is seen in the case of *Lawrence*.

Lawrence. His family is a typical lower-middle-class family. The father has a modest white-collar job, and has been able over the years to pay for a bungalow in a quiet neighborhood of unpretentious homes, and to keep it up quite well with a neat lawn and flower beds.

Lawrence was always an outstanding student in elementary and senior high school. He was not an athlete or a social leader, though he was well thought of by his fellow students. He has always been slender and good-looking in a quiet way. As a young man he is now a tall, neatly dressed individual who would be acceptable but not noticeable in any social group.

After graduating with high honors from the state university, where he had a scholarship that paid something like half of his living expenses, Lawrence went immediately to an Ivy League university on an all-expense fellowship for graduates who expect to enter college teaching. There he earned his Master's degree in comparative literature and is continuing toward a Doctor's degree. He says he wants to teach in a private university rather than a state university because he thinks it will give him more academic freedom.

At the state university he commenced in commerce but shifted to literature after the first year, after talking with his English instructor, and then during the summer with his employer in the store where he worked. His boss told him, "Lawrence, you are too good a student to be a salesman."

The interviewer mentioned that Lawrence had been one of the top students in high school and asked whether he really had to work hard for his high marks. "You bet I had to work," said Lawrence. "It gets me when people say they got good grades without working. I knew maybe one or two people who could do that but I did not have that much ability."

Lawrence appreciated the friendships he made in college. "College gives you a different outlook on life; and it is amazing the things a person doesn't know before going, and not necessarily in your own subject field. I think I appreciate many things I did not appreciate before." He was not a member of a social fraternity but he did belong to a language club and for a while belonged to a political club.

He is an independent person. During his freshman year at the state university he worked on the school paper, but he quit after having a disagreement with the editor, "because I didn't want to make it my whole campus life."

"I like to walk and at the university I do some running just for exercise. I used to play tennis but I gave that up since I didn't feel too competent at it. I read as much as possible except in the summer." Lawrence is not married and has no plans for marriage in the immediate future. He may go overseas to do some research for his Doctor's degree.

As he has gone ahead into graduate work, he finds it more interesting than undergraduate work which was too often "just busy work. In graduate work you are able to get right at the material you want to study."

2. SOCIAL EFFECTIVENESS.   A boy or girl with at least average intellectual ability is likely to move up the social scale if he or she is socially effective—gets along well with people and is something of a social leader. This kind of person is valuable in business or industry and is frequently found in such professions as social work. Also, this kind of person is likely to get administrative positions in the field of education. This kind of person is not so closely dependent on educational opportunity, but in the United States generally needs at least a high

school education and frequently a college education simply to become eligible for promotions due to his social effectiveness. An example of this kind of mobility is Paul.

Paul.   Paul was an average student in high school. He liked physical activities and played on the high school basketball team. He had many friends and his sociability gave him a high degree of social effectiveness. He is of stocky build, usually dresses in a sport shirt and slacks, and wears his hair cut short. He is a very talkative, outgoing individual, and is a happy person. He does not use precise English but his personality makes an impression. He is not a leader but when he is with people he is well liked; he is "one of the boys." The interviewer made several phone calls before contacting him because he was out with his friends, but the interviewer found this to be the most enjoyable interview he made. Paul's family is upper-working class.

The interviewer mentioned that Paul had made a good average record in high school. "I took mostly the courses I could get by on. I did have quite a bit of mathematics, three or four years, and I had biology. I took chemistry but I dropped that because I thought I would have to work too hard in it. I guess I had a pretty good time in high school."

While in high school Paul had a number of basketball scholarship offers. He attended a state university for his freshman year, but he failed to maintain an adequate grade average and dropped out at the end of the school year. The following year he worked on a state highway survey team. The next year he returned to a second college and has continued there on a board and tuition basketball scholarship. He will return to college this year as a senior.

The interviewer asked how hard he has studied in college. "Not very hard. I am not saying I am doing too well either. I guess that is because I don't apply myself. I didn't study hard in high school either. Of course everyone told me to; they told me to then and they have told me since but for some reason I don't have good study habits. I wouldn't say that I don't enjoy studying. It is just a matter of forming habits early. I might enjoy studying if I could just sit down and do it. It is not as bad as it used to be. I see people ahead of me now who graduated in my high school class. Some of them were teaching here this last year. That kinda hurts and makes me think a little more of the educational values. I am not swayed quite as easily as I used to be when the boys want to go out. It used to be 'Let's go get a coke,' and of course, now it's 'Let's go get a beer,' and I went often enough, and I still do but not as much. I think everybody is swayed to some extent."

When asked about his major study in college, Paul replied, "I am majoring in Business. I was going to get an accounting major, you know accounting is an open field, but football practice interfered with some of of the school system have changed the patterns of behavior which were defined in an earlier day as appropriate for the various roles. The teacher's role is different if she teaches socially disadvantaged children from what she learned it to be when it was fitted to docile children who are ready learners. The principal of an inner-city school has a different role from that of a principal of a school in a middle-income area. The administrator who has overall charge of the program needs a different set of skills and attitudes than the administrator of a stable system which performs the traditional functions of the common school.

At the present time in a changing metropolitan area, there are three roles that need to be worked out intelligently in relation to each other and in relation to the social situation. They are: superintendent, board of education member, and member of civic organization.

The Superintendent's Role

Traditionally, the superintendent's role has consisted of the following kinds of behavior:

1. He meets with the Board of Education and discusses matters of policy with them, generally as a mentor to them, though he is careful to yield to them in the making of decisions after he has helped them to understand the various alternatives of policy and their consequences in action.
2. He selects and organizes his assistant administrators and divides the work of administration among them.
3. He draws up the annual budget and presents it clearly to the public and to the Board.
4. He represents and speaks for the school system in relations with the public—explaining the policies of the system, hearing suggestions and complaints, and persuading the public that the system is performing its functions well or is working wisely on the problems it is meeting.
5. He represents the Board of Education in negotiations with teachers and non-professional personnel on their salaries and working conditions.

In the contemporary situation in most big cities, the role of the superintendent has three other major patterns of behavior:

6. He understands the society in which he works—its social systems and subsystems—and he strives to work out agreement with the other systems on allocation of functions and on cooperation.

7. He plans for development of the school system, encouraging innovation and the evaluation of innovation.
8. He analyzes the tensions in the community that affect the schools, and works effectively to reduce these tensions by assisting diverse groups to communicate with one another and to achieve a peaceful modus vivendi.

The Board Member's Role

The Board of Education does the following things, if it performs its functions effectively:

1. Represents the public interest and concerns about the school system in a balanced and temperate way.
2. Determines and formulates general policy with respect to the curriculum and methods of teaching, organization of the system into subdistricts, placing and building of schools, employment and working conditions of personnel, discipline of students, etc.
3. Conducts an independent and continuing scrutiny of the performance of the school system.
4. Determines the financial needs of the school system and works with appropriate government agencies to secure the money needed.

In the big city the roles of board member and superintendent must be separated, but they overlap and they overlap necessarily. Therefore every combination of school board and superintendent works out its own arrangements. These arrangements may be recorded in a temporary set of "ground rules." They may be guided to some extent by state law. They are often affected by statements of principles such as the one adopted by the Illinois Association of School Boards and the Illinois Association of School Administrators in 1955, entitled, *Statement of Principles and Procedures for Effective Cooperation Between a Board of Education and its Chief Administrator.*

The members of the school board are generally sensitive to the feelings and the moods of the public or of certain sections of the public to which they are especially tuned. They are likely to seek ways of meeting the desires of the public through adjusting the school program here and there and through compromise. Here they may find themselves dealing with a superintendent of flexible personality who works with them to make adaptations of policy. On the other hand, they may find themselves at odds with a superintendent who holds rigidly to time-hallowed precedents and principles.

When there is disagreement on matters of policy between the board and the superintendent, one of several things may happen.

a. The board may "give in" to the superintendent, on the ground that he has superior knowledge and experience.

b. The superintendent may yield to the board, and undertake to execute the policy determined by the board with all his energy and wisdom. At the same time he may warn the board that he believes the policy is unwise, and invite them to reconsider from time to time.

c. The superintendent may sabotage the board's policy by allowing or encouraging his subordinates to act on the policy stupidly or to ignore essential elements of it.

d. The superintendent may abdicate some of his executive responsibility to board members, asking or permitting them to draw up directives for putting policy into practice. He may then follow these directives to the best of his ability, or he may try to avoid following them.

Interaction of the Two Roles

There is a considerable amount of tension and conflict between the roles of superintendent and school board member in many big cities during the current decade. Several superintendents have resigned during such conflicts, and a number of school board members have been subjected to public criticism. An example of conflict which led to the resignation of the Superintendent occurred in Cleveland.

In February, 1964, the Superintendent of Schools gave sudden notice that he would resign at the close of the school year. He declined to discuss the matter in public, saying "I will not engage in public debate. The most important thing is the welfare of the Cleveland school children." His predecessor had resigned rather suddenly in 1961.

The Cleveland Education Association, a teachers' organization affiliated with the National Education Association, called on the NEA through its Commission on Professional Rights and Responsibilities, to investigate the situation, and charged that members of the School Board were "trying to administer the school system instead of merely setting policy." The National Education Association (1964) made an investigation and published the results under the title, "Cleveland, Ohio: When a Board of Education Fails to Fulfill its Proper Responsibilities."

We shall make no attempt to pass judgment on the Cleveland Board or the Superintendent, and we note that the report of the NEA Commission has not been balanced by a counter-statement that is more friendly to the School Board. It is clear, however, that the community and the School Board were split over issues of *de facto* segregation in the schools, and the Superintendent was charged by the President of the Board with inadequate and indecisive administration of policy with respect to racial integration.

At least partly as a result of the investigation, an administrative change has been made which places the Superintendent in full charge of the school administration. Prior to this time there had been three coequal administrative heads: the superintendent of schools who was head of the department of instruction; the clerk-treasurer, head of the finance department; and the business manager who was in charge of the operation of school buildings, the choice of sites for new schools, and the purchase of supplies and equipment. All three men were selected by the Board of Education and were responsible to the Board.

According to most experts in school administration, this form of government leads to role conflicts, and the Commission recommended that the triple-administration be abolished, with the new superintendent of schools the chief administrative officer for the school system.

Types of Superintendents

When an important role such as that of the superintendent is being considered, the man's own personality is of the utmost importance in determining the effectiveness with which the role is filled. And when cooperation among educational systems and between educational systems and other social systems is being studied, the personal characteristics of the principal actors in the directing roles need to be studied also.

As an illustration of the significance of the personality which fills the role, consider the following five hypothetical profiles of five superintendents in a metropolitan area. If a given metropolitan area had these five men in the roles of superintendent, its chances of cooperation among social systems would be different from what they would be if five other men filled these roles.

A. CENTRAL CITY SUPERINTENDENT. Mr. A has had a wide variety of experience, including classroom teaching, school principalship, superintendency in a small city, superintendency in a high-income suburb, and his present position, where he has been for about ten years.

Superintendent A has been much interested in the programs for gifted children. He developed such programs in the high-status suburb where he was before his present job and he has established a similar program in several of his high-status schools.

Well thought of among school superintendents, Mr. A does not spend much time with non-school people. He has put together a smoothly operating central office administration, and his Assistant Superintendents feel that he stands behind them and will back them up when they exercise initiative.

In his relations with the teachers' organization, he has generally gotten along well. Salary raises have come twice during his term of office. He consults with groups of teachers before taking any step that might mean a change in their work. Recently, he spent a great deal of time talking over the new compensatory education program for inner-city schools with groups of teachers, exploring their feelings about after-school classes, reduced class size, use of teacher aides, etc.

On the problems of racial segregation in the schools, Mr. A has been a sympathetic listener. He has given special responsibility to an Assistant Superintendent for working with Civil Rights organizations, and has recommended an open enrollment policy to the School Board, together with a limited amount of busing of Negro children from overcrowded schools to schools with a predominance of white children.

Mr. A has little contact with the other superintendents in the metropolitan area. He regards the problems of his system as quite different from those of the suburban systems. He works closely with the youth bureau of the city government and with the city commission on human relations. These agencies feel that they can count on his co-operation.

With another five years to go before he reaches retirement age, Mr. A's one concern is with two of his newer Board members, who persist in pressing him to take a bolder initiative on some school matters that are related to social urban renewal. He is essentially a "four-walls" superintendent, and he feels that the schools should follow social change, not make it. With his mild and likeable personality, he has the respect of the new members of the Board, and the full support of the older ones, who feel that he has "kept the schools out of trouble." Thus he is in tune with conservative forces that prefer little or no change, but he has not seriously alienated those who want change.

Those who would prefer a more aggressive "urban-community

school" program are now gathering their forces to influence the choice of his successor. Some of them are quite anxious about what they term the "lost time" from which they think the city will suffer, as the schools delay positive action; others feel that the community will make progress with a new superintendent all the more rapidly because they have had a peaceful period under Mr. A, and they will be able to make the changes that other school systems have tried out and found successful without the conflict that other cities are having.

B. HIGH-STATUS SUBURBAN SUPERINTENDENT.   Mr. B is a relatively young man, just turned 40, who took his present job after a successful superintendency in a county seat of 30,000. He has a Ph.D. from a state university graduate school of education. He has written a number of joint articles on administrative problems that show a concern for efficiency, for good school facilities, and for the development of a first-class teaching staff.

With one of the highest per pupil expenditures in the state, and with a stable school population in his district, he aims to give his community the best there is in education. He says so repeatedly, and his Board members are solidly behind him.

Superintendent B has selected his school principals carefully for their ability to use the best of the new school methods effectively and to organize the teaching staff for this purpose.

Mr. B attends meetings of the Metropolitan Area Superintendents' Study Council and was president for one term. He treats this largely as a social group. Whenever there are proposals for some cooperative project he asks for time to study it, and then goes along with it if he is sure it will not involve his district in taking on any responsibility beyond the bounds of the district. He has several times made it known that he does not favor cooperative activities which would in any way cost his district money.

Occasionally Mr. B allows himself to think of what may come next in his career. The only superintendency that would be a promotion is a big-city job, and he wonders whether it is worth the trouble it would be to him. Though ambitious, he congratulates himself when he reads in the papers about the conflicts and controversies that swirl around some of the big-city superintendents. Alternatively, he might go on the faculty of a state college, teaching in the field of educational administration. This prospect interests him, because he enjoys scholarly work; but he would have to take a 50 percent reduction in salary if he made such a change.

C. SUPERINTENDENT IN AN EMPLOYING SUBURB. Mr. C has been super-intendent of schools in this suburban town of 20,000 for three years. The population is almost a cross-section of America, including a work-ing-class Negro district on the edge of town and a number of middle-class Negro families. He came to this job directly after he obtained a Ph.D. from the state university and he then was 36 years old, having been a classroom teacher and a high school principal in the central city of this metropolitan area.

Superintendent C has given this rather nondescript town a "shot in the arm," with a number of young teachers whom he has hand-picked from the central city school system and brought with him, even though they took a $500 cut in salary at first when they moved. This year he succeeded in getting the town to vote the highest tax levy for schools in its history, and he has used some of the money to increase salaries.

Next year he will be president of the Metropolitan Area Superin-tendents' Study Council. He plans to start a cooperative special education program with two neighboring school districts, and has been chairman of the area-wide Educational Television Council which will receive state funds to inaugurate ETV as soon as the central city UHF trans-mitter is installed. His school district's plan for the use of federal funds for compensatory education of the socially disadvantaged was the first one to be submitted to the State Department of Public Instruction.

Since his is a relatively small district, he handles these details him-self, with several of his younger teachers helping him on committees. One evening a week he attends a research seminar at Central City University on Metropolitan Problems in Education. Some of his col-leagues have urged him to run for the County Superintendency, an elective office with the potential for initiating area-wide cooperative programs.

Meanwhile the two new members of the Central City Board of Education, and the Dean of the Central City University School of Education are hoping that he will stay where he is for the next five years and then be ready for the superintendency in Central City.

D. A WORKING-CLASS DORMITORY SUBURB. Superintendent D has been in this working-class suburb for six years as superintendent and high school principal. He is 50 years old. The school district has a school en-rollment of 2,000 pupils. The tax base is rather low. There is no indus-try in the district, and the homes are generally very modest, indeed. Only the recent rise in state aid has given him enough money to raise his per-pupil expenditure almost to the state average. Until 1953 this suburb was a small village with a two-room school that sent its high school pupils to a high school several miles away.

Mr. D would like to see greater cooperation among the school districts of the area, and above all some further consolidation of districts into an intermediate school district that would have a better tax base. He says that he would gladly give up his superintendency and go back to his job as high school principal if such a consolidation were achieved.

He has encouraged the principals of the two elementary schools in the district to develop their PTAs, and is building as much local understanding and support of the school system as he can. On his school board there is nobody with a college degree. The board members trust him with policy decisions, as long as he does not commit them to anything very expensive.

Mr. D supports Superintendent C in his plans for area cooperation for the development of school services.

E. AN INDUSTRIAL SUBURB.   Superintendent E has been for 15 years superintendent in this industrial suburb, which has a school population of 4,000. The one factory employs people from the town and from the surrounding area. For three decades this has been a low-tax town. People are accustomed to a low tax rate, and the factory management has used its influence to keep taxes down. The Board of Education has generally had two or three middle-level officers of the factory on it. The top-level management live in a high-status suburb several miles away.

At 60 years of age, Mr. E is tired and weary. He has refused to become involved in the conflict that is going on over the use of urban renewal funds. One small area of his district is almost solidly Negro, and has a small elementary school. Now there is a civil rights organization promoting urban renewal through the clearing of some of the hovels inhabited by Negroes and the building of several dispersed public housing units that would distribute Negro families widely over the community.

There is conflict on the school board. The one Negro member has been joined by a young lawyer to urge Mr. E to propose a tax increase and to work for a new high-school building and a junior college under the new state junior college program.

The compensatory education program of pre-school classes is being conducted at the YWCA, in a Negro church and a Catholic church, with Mr. E's passive support, though the active work is being done by a group of young women with the aid of a social worker from the county welfare department and a nun in the parochial school.

Mr. E has not met the new factory manager, a young man who has been instructed by the president of his corporation to cooperate actively in community improvement, as part of a campaign to improve morale among the workers. The factory management wants better schools and is prepared to pay higher taxes. The new manager is now engaged in studying the "power structure" of the community, and in relating the company's plans for expansion to the work of the Metropolitan Area Planning Commission, of which he is a member.

As soon as the factory manager gets his "feet on the ground" he will seek out Mr. E and he will talk with members of the school board. It does not seem likely that much will happen in the school system until Mr. E leaves.

Possibilities Among the Superintendents

These five hypothetical school superintendents illustrate the problem of getting cooperation over a metropolitan area. Only two of the five favor a program of active cooperation. Such cooperation as comes must be voluntary. A good many people must become convinced that cooperation among school systems is desirable before it will come about. However, social forces are pushing in that direction, and leadership has a way of appearing where it is needed.

The Role of Civic Organization Member

Closely related to the roles of board member and of superintendent is the role of member of a civic organization with an interest in the schools. The reason for this is that the citizens are deeply concerned with the changing functions of the school system in a period of rapid social change, and they generally wish to deal actively with matters of educational policy, rather than to sit back and wait for the school board and the school administration to solve problems which they regard as *their* problems.

The civic organization, for the purposes of this discussion, consists of any organization of citizens with an explicit interest in the school system. Some organizations are city or area-wide. Some represent a segment of the population, such as businessmen, or religious leaders. Some organizations come from local communities. The Parent-Teacher Association may be considered as a civic organization, though its special interest in the schools and its relationship to local schools give it special importance.

The role of a member of a civic organization consists of the following kinds of behavior.

1. Study the school system and attempt to understand its functions and its capabilities.
2. Formulate the educational needs of the particular group or section of the community which the organization represents—of the entire community if the organization represents the entire area.
3. Participate in communication with other organizations and attempt to arrive at a consensus.
4. Support the Board of Education in its plans for financial support of the schools.

During a period of social change and its consequent social conflict, the tendency is for civic organizations to come into existence as pressure groups for one particular sub-group interest. Thus the past five years has seen the rise of scores of pressure groups in every big city, which express their own needs as they see them, and take no responsibility for recognizing the needs and the attitudes of other groups in the city.

This is natural, and to some degree desirable, but it carries with it no method of making decisions. The pressure group separates itself off from the decision-making function, and feels no responsibility for a decision that balances the interests and the needs of the whole community. It assumes that some body, such as the board of education, makes the decisions. It strives to present its case persuasively to the decision-making body, and naturally goes to extremes to push its own case.

The small number of community-wide civic organizations have a special responsibility to promote communication among the more narrowly-based groups and to help them take a more responsible part in decision-making. Probably a big city should have regional Education Councils to serve this purpose, bringing the various local civic associations and parent-teacher organizations into a regional group that has some common interests and problems which are different from those of other regions of the big city.

If a city consists of warring factions with respect to school policy and program, it is unlikely that the superintendent and the board of education can work together in full harmony. The board members will be differentially sensitive to the various pressure groups. The superintendent may ally himself more or less consciously with certain factions in the city.

To bring about some harmony in the city with respect to the schools, a city-wide organization of leaders of the moderate groups may assist the board of education to get decisions made which produce the maximum good for the maximum number.

Conclusions on Intra-system Functioning

For the next decade there is bound to be tension and conflict in the metropolitan area over school policies and practices, because social change will require new practices which must be worked out by people who have differing interests and attitudes.

The board of education and the superintendent must adapt their roles to each other and to the changing situations. The cities which have the most success are those in which the board of education has worked out a relationship with the superintendent that allows the superintendent a maximum of freedom to administer and execute policies on which the board and the superintendent are fully agreed.

The superintendent is the key actor in the situation. He needs to understand the whole complex of social systems and subsystems, and he needs to work out his own role as one who promotes communication and cooperation among the systems. This is difficult for the modern superintendent whose training has disposed him toward working for efficiency within his own subsystem of teachers, pupils and administrators, and to guard jealously the isolation of these subsystems from the other systems and subsystems in the metropolitan area.

Civic organizations will learn to combine the function of special pleading for a special interest with that of seeking to communicate with other groups. They will learn to support a school system in which they have basic faith, even though they may be discontent with some specific programs.

The delicate art of operating a school system in a period of basic social change will contain action which:

Maintains communication and sharing in decisions with other cooperating systems.
Accepts new functions which are demanded by the social situation.

Maintains flexibility within the system for new roles to emerge and for people to learn the new roles.

Exercises

1. Make an analysis of your own school system as a social system. What are the new functions which are straining this system and forcing it to develop in new ways? What roles are best and what roles are least well filled?

2. Study and report on the performance of two persons in important roles in a school system. How do their performances relate to the nature of the roles they fill? How do their personalities cause them to fill their roles in unique ways?

3. Study the relations between the school system and some other social system in your metropolitan area where there is or has been cooperation. What has happened in this connection?

4. How do the public and private educational systems in your area cooperate? What are some of the problems?

5. Make an analysis of the public school systems in your metropolitan area. To what extent and in what ways do they cooperate? Has there been any consolidation of school systems? Is there now any talk of consolidation of school systems?

6. Study the relations between civic organizations and the superintendent and the board of education in your community. How well do you think the various roles are being filled?

Suggestions for Further Reading

1. For a study of the problems of a big city school board in working out its functions in relation to those of the superintendent, read the book by Joseph Pois entitled *The School Board Crisis: A Chicago Case Study*.

2. For a summary of examples of cooperation among systems in metropolitan areas, read Chapter 13, "The Cooperative Approach," in Bollens and Schmandt, *The Metropolis*.

3. For an analysis of the relations between personality factors and role structure in an educational system, read Jacob W. Getzels, "Conflict and Role Behavior in the Educational Setting."

✼ Appendix

Table A.1 *Central Cities' Proportion of Manufacturing Production Workers in Metropolitan Areas, 1899–1954*

	1899	1929	1954
Baltimore	91.8	85.5	62.9
Buffalo	74.7	59.8	43.1
Chicago	88.0	73.6	65.2
Detroit	83.6	75.2	53.5
Los Angeles	83.4	66.6	42.3
New York City, Jersey City, Newark	69.9	69.8	63.0
Philadelphia	78.4	65.7	56.0
Pittsburgh	53.1	27.1	22.6
St. Louis	80.6	69.9	63.9
San Francisco, Oakland	81.2	68.2	50.4

Source: Raymond Vernon, *The Changing Economic Function of the Central City.* New York: Committee for Economic Development, 1959, pp. 74–75.

Table A.2   *School Age Population of Chicago and Suburban Area:*
1950–1980 (Percentages of total age-group populations as
shown in right-hand column)

| YEAR | CITY OF CHICAGO | | SUBURBAN RING | | GRAND TOTAL |
	White	*Nonwhite*	*White*	*Nonwhite*	
1950					
5–14 years	55	11	33	1.0	697,000
15–19 years	58	10	31	1.0	300,000
1960					
5–14 years	36	15	47	1.5	1,133,000
5–19 years	42	13	44	1.4	405,000
1965					
5–14 years	32	17	49	2.0	1,250,000
15–19 years	34	16	48	1.9	523,000
1970					
5–14 years	26	21	51	2.4*	1,466,000
15–19 years	28	18	52	2.2*	637,000
1980					
5–14 years	22	22	52	4.4*	1,581,000
15–19 years	22	22	52	3.9*	751,000

* Estimates by the author.

Source: U.S. Census, and *Population Projections for the Chicago Standard Metro-*
politan Statistical Area and City of Chicago, Population Research and
Training Center, Universiy of Chicago, 1964.

Table A.3   *Proportion of Adults over 25 Years of Age Who Have Com-*
pleted Four or More Years of College. In SMSAs by Region:
1960

REGION	SMSA	CENTRAL CITY	OUTSIDE CENTRAL CITY
United States	8.8%	8.0%	9.8%
North and East	8.3	6.9	9.8
South	9.1	9.0	9.3
West	10.4	10.5	10.2

Source: U.S. Census Bureau: *U.S. Census of Population: 1960. Selected Area Re-*
ports. Standard Metropolitan Statistical Areas. Final Report PC(3)–1D.

Table A.4 *Proportion of Population in SMSAs that is Nonwhite: 1900–1960*

YEAR	PERCENT LIVING IN SMSAs	PERCENT LIVING IN CENTRAL CITY	PERCENT LIVING OUTSIDE CENTRAL CITY
1900	7.8	6.8	9.4
1910	7.3	6.9	8.1
1920	7.2	7.3	7.0
1930	8.1	9.0	6.4
1940	8.6	10.1	6.0
1950	10.0	13.1	5.7
1960	11.7	17.8	5.2

Source: U.S. Bureau of the Census. *U.S. Census of Population: 1960. Selected Area Reports. Standard Metropolitan Statistical Areas.* Final Report, PC(3)–1D.

Table A.5 *City-Suburban Income, Educational, and Occupational Differentials in SMSAs, 1960, by Age of Area*

CENSUS YEAR IN WHICH CENTRAL CITY FIRST REACHED 50,000	MEDIAN FAMILY INCOME		PERCENT WHO COMPLETED HIGH SCHOOL		PERCENT EMPLOYED IN WHITE-COLLAR OCCUPATIONS	
	City Higher	Suburban Fringe Higher	City Higher	Suburban Fringe Higher	City Higher	Suburban Fringe Higher
1800–1860	0	14	0	14	0	14
1870–1880	0	17	0	17	0	17
1890–1900	5	31	9	27	15	21
1910–1920	12	36	12	36	22	26
1930–1940	9	23	14	18	22	10
1950–1960	26	27	28	25	40	13

Source: Adapted from Leo F. Schnore (1963).

Table A.6 *Families Headed by a Woman, Color Differences*

YEAR	PERCENT OF TOTAL FAMILIES WHICH ARE HEADED BY A WOMAN	
	White	*Nonwhite*
1949	8.8	18.8
1950	8.4	19.1
1955	9.0	20.7
1960	8.7	22.4
1961	8.9	21.6
1962	8.6	23.2

Source: U.S. Bureau of the Census. *Current Population Reports.* Series P–20.

Table A.7 *Percent of Children Under 18 Not Living with Both Parents, by Color: 1960.*

AREA	CHILDREN UNDER 18 NOT LIVING WITH BOTH PARENTS	
	White	*Nonwhite*
United States	10.0	33.7
Urban	10.3	35.1
Rural Nonfarm	10.1	32.7
Rural Farm	6.6	26.5

Source: *U.S. Census of Population: 1960. Social and Economic Characteristics.* Table 79, p. 210.

Table A.8 *Census Reports on Ratio of Males to Females, by Color, July 1, 1963.*

AGE	MALES REPORTED PER 100 FEMALES	
	White	*Nonwhite*
Under 5	104.4	100.4
5–9 years	103.9	100.0
10–14	104.0	100.0
15–19	103.2	99.5
20–24	101.2	95.1
25–29	100.1	89.1
30–34	99.2	86.6
35–39	97.5	86.8
40–44	96.2	89.9
45–49	96.5	90.6

Source: U.S. Bureau of the Census: *Current Population Reports* Series P–25. No. 276, Table 1 (includes Armed Forces abroad).

Table A.9   *Comparison of Numbers of Children of Women Aged 35 to 44 Who Married Men of Two Different Social Classes, 1960.*

	CHILDREN PER WOMAN*	
	White	*Nonwhite*
Wives married at age 14–21 to husbands who are laborers and did not go to high school	3.8	4.7
Wives married at age 22 or over to husbands who are professional or technical workers and have completed 1 year or more of college	2.4	1.9

* Wives married only once, with husbands present.

Source: U.S. Bureau of the Census. 1960. PC(2)3A, Tables 39 and 40, pp. 199–238. *Women by Number of Children Ever Born.*

Table A.10   *Educational History of the School Class That Entered Philadelphia Schools in the First Grade in 1949.*

GROUP	PERCENTAGES	
	Graduated from High School	*Dropped Out*
All pupils	70	30
All girls	76	24
All boys	66	34
All whites	79	21
All Negroes	56	44
White girls	83	17
White boys	75	25
Negro girls	65	35
Negro boys	48	52
IQ GROUPS		
Top Quartile	91	9
II "	79	21
III "	72	28
IV "	35	65

Source: Adapted from Tables 4 and 6, William R. Odell, *Educational Survey Report*, Board of Education, Philadelphia, 1965.

Table A.11   *Intelligence Quotients of Negro and White Pupils in Phil-adelphia Public Schools*

IQ QUARTILE	PERCENTAGE OF PUPILS IN THE VARIOUS QUARTILES			
	White: N = 1065		Negro: N = 418	
	Boys	Girls	Boys	Girls
High I 112 plus	35	39	9	8
High II 103–111	24	31	14	24
III 91–103	26	20	20	27
Low VI less than 90	15	10	56	42

Sample of children who entered the first grade in the fall of 1949.

Source: William R. Odell, *Educational Survey Report*, Board of Public Education, Philadelphia, 1965. Table 1, p. 35.

ℜ Bibliography

ABRAMS, CHARLES (1965), *The City Is the Frontier.* New York: Harper & Row. (p. 128)

ADVISORY COMMISSION ON INTERGOVERNMENTAL RELATIONS (1964), *1965 State Legislative Program.* Washington, D.C. (p. 154)

AMERICAN INSTITUTE OF PLANNERS (1962), *The Role of Metropolitan Planning.* Chicago. (Quoted from Bollens and Schmandt, p. 304.) (pp. 144–145)

BERNSTEIN, BASIL (1960), "Language and Social Class," *British Journal of Sociology,* 11, 271–276. (p. 165)

———— (1964), "Elaborated and Restricted Codes: Their Social Origins and Some Consequences," *American Anthropologist,* 66, No. 6, Part 2, 55–69, Special Publication. December. (p. 165)

BLOOM, BENJAMIN S. (1964), *Stability and Change in Human Characteristics.* New York: John Wiley & Sons, Inc. (pp. 165, 194)

BLOOM, BENJAMIN S., ALLISON DAVIS, and ROBERT HESS (1965), *Compensatory Education for Cultural Deprivation.* New York: Holt, Rinehart, and Winston, Inc. (p. 194)

BOLLENS, JOHN C., and HENRY J. SCHMANDT (1965), *The Metropolis: Its People, Politics, and Economic Life.* New York: Harper & Row. (pp. 33, 50, 154, 242)

BUEHRING, LEO E. (1958), "New Pattern: Community Schools," *The Nation's Schools.* January. (p. 121)

CAMPBELL, ROALD F. (1965), "School-Community Collaboration in Our Cities," *White House Conference on Education: Consultants Papers,* pp. 144–151. Washington, D.C.: Superintendent of Documents. (p. 131)

CHICAGO COMMITTEE ON URBAN PROGRESS (1965), *A Pattern for Greater Chicago; Sub-Committee Reports.* (pp. 132, 139)

CLARK, KENNETH (1965), *Dark Ghetto: Dilemmas of Social Power.* New York: Harper & Row. (p. 194)

249

COLEMAN, RICHARD P. (1959), "Social Structure and Social Mobility in Kansas City." Unpublished research memorandum, Committee on Human Development, University of Chicago. (pp. 14, 16)

COMMITTEE FOR ECONOMIC DEVELOPMENT (1960), Guiding Metropolitan Growth, p. 13. New York. (pp. 134, 142)

CONANT, JAMES B. (1959), The American High School Today. New York: McGraw-Hill Book Company. (pp. 115, 124)

———— (1961), Slums and Suburbs. New York: McGraw-Hill Book Company. (p. 124)

———— (1964), Shaping Educational Policy. New York: McGraw-Hill Book Company. (p. 124)

DAVIS, KINGSLEY (1955), "The Origin and Growth of Urbanization in the World," American Journal of Sociology, 60, 433–434. (p. 28)

DETROIT AREA STUDY (1960), "Family Income in Greater Detroit: 1951–1959." Ann Arbor, Michigan: Survey Research Center, University of Michigan. (p. 40)

DEUTSCH, MARTIN (1965), "The Role of Social Class in Language Development and Cognition," American Journal of Orthopsychiatry, 35, 78–88. (p. 165)

DEWEY, RICHARD (1948), "Peripheral Expansion in Milwaukee County," American Journal of Sociology, 54, 118–125. (p. 66)

DOBRINER, WILLIAM, ed. (1958), The Suburban Community. New York: G. P. Putnam's Sons. (pp. 39, 70, 84)

DOLL, RUSSELL (1965), "Categories of Elementary Schools in a Big City." Research Paper, Department of Education, University of Chicago. (p. 92)

Fortune, Editors of (1957), The Exploding Metropolis. Garden City, N.Y.: Doubleday Anchor Books. (p. 84)

FRAZIER, E. FRANKLIN (1939), The Negro Family in the United States. Chicago: University of Chicago Press. (p. 160)

FUCHS, ESTELLE (1966), Pickets at the Gates. New York: Free Press of Glencoe, Inc. (p. 206)

GETZELS, JACOB W. (1963), "Conflict and Role Behavior in the Educational Setting," pp. 309–318 in Readings in the Social Psychology of Education, W. W. Charters, Jr. and N. L. Gage, eds. Boston: Allyn and Bacon. (p. 242)

GIBBS, JACK (1961), "The Growth of Individual Metropolitan Areas: A Global View," Annals of the Association of American Geographers, p. 381. (p. 50)

GIST, NOEL P., and SYLVIA FLEIS FAVA (1964), Urban Society. 5th Edition. New York: Thomas Y. Crowell Company. (p. 51)

GOTTMANN, JEAN (1961), Megalopolis: The Urbanized Northeastern Seaboard of the United States. New York: The Twentieth Century Fund. (pp. 48, 84)

GRAUBARD, STEPHEN R. (1966), "The Negro-American, I, II." *Daedalus,* Fall, 1965, and Winter, 1966. (p. 194)

GREAT CITIES' PROGRAMS FOR SCHOOL IMPROVEMENT (1964), *Promising Practices from the Projects for the Culturally Deprived.* Chicago: Research Council of the Great Cities' Program for School Improvement. (p. 124)

GREENE, MARY FRANCES, and ORLETTA RYAN (1965), *The Schoolchildren: Growing Up in the Slums.* New York: Pantheon–Random House. (pp. 207, 219)

HANDLIN, OSCAR (1959), *The Newcomers.* Cambridge, Mass.: Harvard University Press. (p. 34)

HAVIGHURST, ROBERT J. (1964), *The Public Schools of Chicago: A Survey Report.* Chicago: Board of Education. (pp. 58, 92, 194, 218, 219)

HAVIGHURST, ROBERT J., PAUL H. BOWMAN, GORDON F. LIDDLE, CHARLES V. MATTHEWS, and JAMES V. PIERCE (1962), *Growing Up in River City.* New York: John Wiley & Sons. (p. 25)

HAVIGHURST, ROBERT J., and BERNICE L. NEUGARTEN (1966), *Society and Education.* 3d Edition. Boston: Allyn and Bacon. (p. 25)

HAWLEY, AMOS H. (1950), *Human Ecology.* New York: Ronald Press. (p. 50)

HIGHLANDER FOLK SCHOOL (1956), Recorded from a Planning Conference at the School, Monteagle, Tennessee. March 3–4. (p. 173)

HILL, MOZELL C., and BEVODE C. McCALL (1950), "Social Stratification in Georgia Town," *American Sociological Review,* 15, 721–729. (p. 15)

HILLSON, HENRY T. (1963), *The Demonstration Guidance Project.* New York: George Washington High School, Board of Education of New York City. (p. 79)

HOOVER, EDGAR M., and RAYMOND VERNON (1959), *Anatomy of a Metropolis.* Cambridge, Mass.: Harvard University Press. (p. 144)

HOUSING AND HOME FINANCE AGENCY (1963), *National Survey of Metropolitan Planning.* Washington, D.C.: Government Printing Office. (p. 144)

HOYT, HOMER (1962), *World Urbanization.* Technical Bulletin No. 43. Washington, D.C.: Urban Land Institute. (pp. 27, 50)

JACOBS, JANE (1961), *The Death and Life of Great American Cities.* New York: Random House. (pp. 84, 127)

JOHNSON, LYNDON B. (1965, I), *Problems and Future of the Central City and Its Suburbs.* Message to Congress, March 2. 89th Congress, First Session, U.S. House of Representatives, Document No. 99. (p. 49)

———— (1965, II), *Commencement Address to Howard University Graduates.* June 4. Washington, D.C.: The White House. (pp. 163–164, 172)

KALLENBACH, WARREN, and HAROLD HODGES, eds. (1963), *Education and*

Society. A Book of Readings. Columbus, Ohio: Charles E. Merrill Books, Inc. (p. 25)

KAUFMAN, BEL (1964), *Up the Down Stair Case.* New York: Avon Book Div. (p. 219)

LIEBERMAN, MYRON (1956), *Education as a Profession.* Englewood Cliffs, N.J.: Prentice-Hall, Inc. (p. 219)

LONG, NORTON (1962), *Education in Urban Society.* Ch. 5. Edited by Chandler, Stiles, and Kitsuse. New York: Dodd, Mead & Co. (pp. 147–148)

LYNCH, KEVIN (1961), "The Pattern of the Metropolis," pp. 79–98 in *The Future Metropolis. Daedalus.* Journal of the American Academy of Arts and Sciences. (p. 154)

MADGE, JOHN (1962), "The New Towns Program in Britain," *Journal of the American Institute of Planners.* 28, 208–219. (p. 146)

MARRIS, PETER (1962), "The Social Implications of Urban Redevelopment," *Journal of the American Institute of Planners.* 28, 180–186. (p. 127)

MARTIN, ROSCOE E. (1962), *Government and the Suburban School.* Syracuse, New York: Syracuse University Press. (p. 154)

MARTINDALE, DON, and GERTRUD NEUWIRTH (1958), editors and translators of *The City* by Max Weber. New York: Free Press of Glencoe, Inc. (pp. 44, 45)

MASSACHUSETTS, COMMONWEALTH (1965), "An Act Providing for the Elimination of Racial Imbalance in the Public Schools," Approved August 18, 1965. (pp. 184–185)

MORRISON, J. CAYCE (1958), *The Puerto Rican Study.* Brooklyn: Board of Education of the City of New York. (p. 55)

MUMFORD, LEWIS (1961), *The City in History.* New York: Harcourt, Brace and World, Inc. (pp. 26, 51)

NAM, CHARLES B., and MARY G. POWERS (1965), "Variations in Socioeconomic Structure by Race, Residence, and Life Cycle," *American Sociological Review,* 30, 97–103. (pp. 16, 17)

NATIONAL EDUCATION ASSOCIATION (1962–63), *NEA Handbook, 1962–63.* Washington, D.C.: National Education Association. (p. 209)

——— (1963), *The American Public School Teacher, 1960–61.* Research Monograph 1963-M2. Washington, D.C. (pp. 199, 219)

——— (1964), National Commission on Professional Rights and Responsibilities, *Cleveland, Ohio. When a Board of Education Fails to Fulfill Its Proper Responsibilities.* Washington, D.C.: National Education Association. (p. 233)

——— (1965), *Research Bulletin.* "De Facto Segregation." 43, 35–37, May. (See also, *The Pupil's Day in Court.* Research Division of the NEA. Washington, D. C. 1965.) (p. 182)

NEW YORK CITY BOARD OF EDUCATION (1954), Minutes of the Board Meeting for December 23, 1954 (pp. 170–171)

———— (1959), *Sixtieth Annual Report of the Superintendent of Schools, School Year 1957–58. Statistical Section*. Brooklyn: Board of Education of the City of New York. (p. 55)

ODELL, WILLIAM R. (1965), *Educational Survey Report on the Philadelphia Schools*. Philadelphia: Board of Education. (pp. 163, 194)

ORLAND, HAROLD (1952), *Stevenage: A Sociological Study of a New Town*. pp. 97–101. London: Routledge and Kegan Paul. (p. 143)

PACE (1963), *Report by the Committee on a Plan for Action by Citizens in Education*. The PACE Association. (pp. 122–123)

PARK, ROBERT E. (1952), *Human Communities: The City and Human Ecology*. New York: Free Press of Glencoe, Inc. (pp. 36, 50)

PARSONS, TALCOTT, and EDWARD A. SHILS, eds. (1952), *Toward a General Theory of Action*. Cambridge, Mass.: Harvard University Press. (p. 222)

PASSOW, A. HARRY (1963), *Education in Depressed Areas*. New York: Bureau of Publications, Teachers College, Columbia University. (p. 124)

PETERSON, WARREN A. (1956), "Career Phases and Inter-Age Relationships: The Female High School Teacher in Kansas City." Unpublished Ph.D. dissertation, Department of Sociology, University of Chicago. (p. 216)

PETTIGREW, THOMAS F. (1964), *Profile of the Negro-American*. Princeton, N.J.: D. Van Nostrand Company. (p. 194)

PHI DELTA KAPPA (1963), "Educating the Culturally Deprived in the Great Cities," *Phi Delta Kappan*. Vol. 45, November. (p. 124)

POIS, JOSEPH (1964), *The School Board Crisis: A Chicago Case Study*. Chicago: Aldine Publishing Company. (p. 242)

RIESSMAN, FRANK (1962), *The Culturally Deprived Child*. New York: Harper & Row. (pp. 187, 194)

ROCKEFELLER BROTHERS FUND (1965), *The Performing Arts: Problems and Prospects*. New York: McGraw-Hill Book Company. (p. 124)

SCHMID, CALVIN F., and CHARLES E. NOBLE (1965), "Socioeconomic Differentials among Non-white Races," *American Sociological Review*, 30, 909–922. (p. 157)

SCHNORE, LEO F. (1963), "The Socio-economic Status of Cities and Suburbs," *American Sociological Review*, 28, 76–85. (p. 66)

SEARS, ROEBUCK AND COMPANY (1962), *ABCs of Community Planning*. pp. 4–5. Chicago. (p. 141)

SEXTON, PATRICIA (1961), *Education and Income*. New York: The Viking Press. (p. 59)

SHELDON, ELEANOR BERNERT, and RAYMOND A. GLAZIER (1965), *Pupils*

and Schools in New York City: A Fact Book. New York: Russell Sage
Foundation. (p. 197)

SILBERMAN, CHARLES E. (1964), Crisis in Black and White. New York:
Random House. (p. 194)

SPECTORSKY, AUGUSTE C. (1955), The Exurbanites. Philadelphia: J. B.
Lippincott Co. (p. 84)

STEFFENSEN, JAMES P. (1964), Teachers Negotiate with Their School
Boards. Bulletin 1964, No. 40. U.S. Office of Education. Washington,
D.C. (pp. 209, 211)

STILES, LINDLEY J, ed. (1957), The Teacher's Role in American Society.
New York: Harper & Row. (p. 214)

STRAYER, GEORGE D. (1932), Report of the Survey of the Schools of Chicago, Illinois. New York: Bureau of Publications, Teachers College,
Columbia University. (p. 227)

STRONG, JOSIAH (1898), The Twentieth Century City. New York: Baker
and Taylor. (p. 45)

TAEUBER, KARL M., and ALMA F. TAEUBER (1964), "Migration and City-
Suburb Differences," American Sociological Review, 29, 718–729.
(p. 70)

UNITED STATES COMMISSION ON CIVIL RIGHTS (1965), Civil Rights under
Federal Programs: An Analysis of Title VI. CCR Special Publication
No. 1. Washington, D.C.: U.S. Government Printing Office. (p. 175)

UNITED STATES DEPARTMENT OF LABOR (1965), The Negro Family: The
Case for National Action. Washington, D.C.: U.S. Government
Printing Office. (pp. 188–189, 194)

UNITED STATES OFFICE OF EDUCATION (1963), Programs for the Educationally Disadvantaged. Bulletin 1963. No. 17. Catalog No. FS 5.235:
35044. Washington, D.C.: U.S. Government Printing Office. (p.
124)

VERNON, RAYMOND (1959), The Changing Economic Function of the Central City. pp. 74–75. New York: Committee for Economic Development. (pp. 39, 40)

——— (1960), Metropolis 1985. Cambridge, Mass.: The Harvard University Press. (p. 84)

VIEG, JOHN A. (1939), The Government of Education in Metropolitan Chicago. Chicago: University of Chicago Press. (p. 226)

WARNER, W. LLOYD, MARCHIA MEEKER, and KENNETH EELLS (1960), Social Class in America. New York: Harper Torchbooks. (p. 25)

WARREN, ROLAND L., ed. (1966), Perspectives on the American Community. Chicago: Rand McNally & Co. (p. 50)

WEAVER, ROBERT C. (1964), "The City and Its Suburbs," New City, 2,
pp. 4–6, March. (p. 133)

WILSON, ALAN B. (1959), "Residential Segregation of Social Classes and Aspirations of High School Boys," *American Sociological Review*, 24, 836–845. (pp. 75, 88)

———— (1963), "Social Stratification and Academic Achievement," pp. 217–235 in A. Harry Passow, ed., *Education in Depressed Areas.* New York: Teachers College Bureau of Publications, Columbia University. (p. 76)

WILSON, JAMES Q. (1965), "Urban Renewal Does Not Always Renew," *Harvard Today*, pp. 2–8. January. (pp. 129–130)

❧ Index